AF539420

International Business Management

INTERNATIONAL BUSINESS MANAGEMENT

Edited by

J.M. Dewan
&
K.N. Sudarshan

DISCOVERY PUBLISHING HOUSE PVT. LTD.
NEW DELHI-110 002

First Published - 2011

Reprinted - 2023

ISBN: 978-81-7141-370-6

International Business Management

Published by:

DISCOVERY PUBLISHING HOUSE PVT. LTD.

4383/4B, Ansari Road, Darya Ganj

New Delhi-110 002 (India)

Phone: +91-11-23279245; 23253475; 43596065

E-mail: discoverybooksindia@gmail.com

discoverypublishinghouse@gmail.com

web: www.discoverypublishinggroup.com

Printed at:

Infinity Imaging Systems

Delhi

Preface

The management world is in transition. The causes of this transition are many, but the major one is the vast changes in knowledge and in the information that flows in and out of organizations. This changing information disrupts traditions, established processes, well-known procedures, and routine ways of doing things. New principles, concepts, techniques, ideas, expressions, processes, and procedures are emerging, moving us to a new plateau of professional practice. Trying to capture this changing knowledge and information is like trying to capture the atmosphere. How can you do it when the atmosphere is continually shifting and when you need the atmosphere to do the capturing? The best we can do is find a peak from which we can at least get a perspective on management as a whole, decide on the work and responsibilities of management, and gather in whatever practical management information we can. A team of experts in this series represent some of the best contemporary thinking and information available. They represent many major successful corporations, active consulting agencies, and well-known educational institutions, and all are experts on what is happening with the flow of knowledge and information in the management world. This is a lofty pinnacle from which to survey the management world.

Managers and supervisors clamor for current information and guidelines to help solve formidable problems in their work world—problems that range from "how to do it" to "how to resolve conflict when doing it." Many problems are generated from miscommunication and incompetence. As the management practice proceeds from the complex to the supercomplex, problem solving becomes a large-scale challenge requiring new knowledge and skills. Managers and supervisors cannot wait for research breakthroughs with real-world answers to solve these dilemmas. They must tackle them here and now with the useful information and proven practices immediately available. Whether making a decision, solving a problem setting up a procedure, designing a process, or resolving a behaviour conflict, a manager must rely heavily on information. To a great extent, management practitioners are information workers; that is, they generate, distribute, store, retrieve, and consume information. Competence in finding and using the right information at the needed time determines to a considerable extent competence in the management function, activity, or responsibility. The *DPH Management Series* attempts to fill this need for usable information in spite of the changing nature of its subject.

The *DPH Management Series* not a book to be read and later discarded. It is a reference book, a tool to be used by managerial personnel in the day-to-day work of an organization. Like a tool, it should never be more than a reach away when a new situation emerges that demands its use. This series aim to achieve a first-and practical and proven knowledge and information as a self-development opportunity for those who are moving into or upward in management. A complete spectrum of management subjects is immediately available for orientation, study, analysis, assimilation, and problem solving. Within one set of covers is the view of management as a totality. The management field is loaded with ideas that the organization of this handbook series unique logic. It follows both levels and areas of responsibilities of an organization.

The work of this handbook series is the collaborative effort of many outstanding people in the management field. The motivation for this work varied from individual to individual, but the central motivation that united us all was the excitement of capturing the management state-of-the-art and sharing it with colleagues in the dynamic profession of management.

This series should be of great help to managerial practitioners at any organizational level who are responsible for a function, department, or set of responsibilities. The handbook series will also give these practitioners insights into management roles and approaches in other areas as well. The subject matter encompasses top, middle, and lower management. Special emphasis was placed on managing people, time, space, budgets, and resources to give the handbook extra utility for middle and lower management. Students of management in university or educational institutions will find the series an invaluable resource for adding "real world" practices to their academic and theoretical foundations. MBA students will gain an invaluable overview of the total organization to complement their MBA degree. Administrators and public managers can become acquainted with practices employed by managers and supervisors in private organizations. These practices are not always directly applicable in public sector bodies, but with thought and modifications, these private practices can adapt to public organizations. Public and university librarians will find the handbook an indispensable reference for the multitude of questions on many topics from the general public, special groups, associations, and students.

Editors

Contents

1

The Nature of International Business

Differences

International business as a field of study and practice encompasses that public and private business activity affecting the persons or institutions of more than one national state, territory, or colony. The effect may be in terms of their economic well-being, political status, convictions, skills, or knowledge. The term "business" itself relates to organized human effort directed toward achieving some human satisfaction through the transfer of goods and services from one condition to another, or from one person or group to another, for a mutual profit stated in explicit terms on a *quid pro quo* basis; that is, the production and sale of goods by a government-owned entity for an internal financial profit is a business activity, but payment of social security benefits or foreign aid is not.

It follows that organizational problems of a large corporation operating internationally, as well as the operational problems of a local branch of an alien firm, both fall within the field, as likewise do the contractual relations between entities operating in different nations—from simple sale and purchase to licensing and management contracting—that is, they fall within the field of international business so long as these problems or activities relate to both domestic and foreign persons or institutions.

For example, a domestic business problem generated by reason of a feedback from an overseas activity is included. So likewise is an overseas organizational problem, the resolution of which is ultimately the responsibility of a domestically based management, or which affects that domestic management in some respect. Also, variables introduced from outside the international business field, such as government policy, but which affect business entities in more than one nation, lie within the compass of international business. Such externally generated variables may be considered environmental factors influencing the flow or structure of business relations an international, territorial, or colonial frontier.

As the web of international business relationships is woven ever more finely among nations, the distinction between domestic and international business becomes fuzzy. Indeed, in the final analysis domestic business is simply subsumed under international business, as some of our larger corporations are now doing in their organizational structure. In these firms, domestic operating companies merely constitute one regional or national group within an internationally oriented corporate structure. This relationship reflects a very different mentality from that present in a farm in which the "international division is on the same level as the domestic operating divisions, all being subordinated to a domestically oriented corporate headquarters.

Instantaneous communication, rapid transportation, the increasing complexity of industrial production, and the multiplication of goods and services combine to push irresistibly in the direction of making all business international in character. One day virtually all management decisions will have to be viewed internationally if optimum policies are to be maintained. A labor contract entered into in the U.S. will be communicated immediately to labor groups with which the company or its associates are dealing around the world. A draw-down on the company's credit line in the U.S. will become known immediately to all financial institutions worldwide, thereby affecting the credit lines of its associated foreign companies. Given the limited resources available to any one firm, a decision to try for deeper penetration in one national market must necessarily lead to a decision not to do so elsewhere. A promotion of Mr. Smith, a U.S. national, to a top executive position, may discourage Mr. Yamamoto, a Japanese national presently moving up in an associated Japanese firm. Thus, almost any decision is likely to have international implications. Only a few corporations have reached this point as yet, but the dynamics of international business push in this direction with compelling pressure. Therefore, it has become the view of the leading graduate schools of business management that *all* students should be exposed to the international dimensions of business.

International business differs from the purely domestic because it involves operating effectively within different national sovereignties; under widely disparate economic conditions; with peoples living within different value systems and institutions; as part of an industrial revolution set in the contemporary world, often over greater geographical distance; and in national markets varying greatly in population and area. Figure tracks some of the more important implications for management generated by these by six variables. To take an example: Different national sovereignties generate different legal, monetary, and political systems. Each legal system implies a unique set of relevant rights and obligations in relation to property, taxation, control of monopoly, business organization, and contract. These in turn require the firm to consider new organizational relationships, acquire new skills, and adopt new accounting and control procedures; new, that is, in the sense of being different from that acquired in a purely domestic setting.

Strategies

A wide range of considerations not relevant for domestic business become relevant variable in management decisions once the international dimension of business is seen as significant. Perhaps this distinction is best seen in the range of alternative strategies for building and maintaining an international business, for none of these alternative strategies lies within the range of vision of domestic management. Nor is there any reason why they should. For example, the strategies implied in cooperative export or participating debt, such as the *parties beneficiaries* in Brazil, are not present in a domestic setting within, for example, the U.S. Other strategies are not seen as relevant, for instance, the sale of equity or debt in a *local* operation or the asymmetry in parent-foreign subsidiary relationships implicit in the distinction as to the legal nature of the parent and associated firm arising out of the interposition of different political regimes representing differing interests.

The permutations and combinations of strategies we must consider are almost infinite because the alternatives fall into many different and nonexclusive categories, and even those within a single category are not necessarily mutually exclusive. Very few managements ever consider the full range of alternative strategies vis-a-vis a given foreign opportunity. Why this is so will become apparent as we go along.

The student will note that for purposes of analysis in this volume the field has been broken into nine sets of strategies: sales, supply, labor, management, ownership, financial, legal, control, and public affairs.

The problem for international management is essentially to relate these strategies to sets of relevant variables. What should management consider in selecting an optimum set of strategies? What makes the orderly analysis of these strategy sets difficult is the intricate feedback system arising out of the interdependence of these nine sets. One reaches a first approximation in regard to the first strategy set, moves on into the decision called for by a second strategy set, the results of which may call for revision of one's first decision. Constant adjustment is required.

Decision -making

A great many of these decisions are not in fact made consciously and explicitly by firms involved in international business. For example, choice of sales strategy is often simply an extension of a domestic strategy proven successful over the years. The question of whether it is the optimum strategy for achieving international corporate objectives is not really examined. Therefore, often in researching the strategies followed by U.S. firms one finally comes up against such a statement as "We do not have partners in our domestic operations, so why should we abroad?"

A reasonable business approach to the selection of strategies for the exploitation of overseas opportunities is posed by this query: Given (1) the domestic environment, (2) the socioeconomic environment of the host nation, (3) the structure of the international economic and political system—all three of which generate legal restraints—and (4) company resources, what is the most effective strategy for achieving corporate goals?

Considerable rigidly or noise—that is, inability to communicate accurately and to respond in an appropriate manner—is generated in this ideal system by at least four other variables: (1) past company experience, (2) existing company structure, (3) the quality of the communications system, and (4) personal likes and biases. These variables are, of course, closely interrelated. Company structure and personal likes and biases in part determine the quality of the communications system. And the quality of communications and personal likes and biases has the impact of altering the management's perception of external and internal environments.

Also, the four variables enumerated above, *in interaction with the other variables as perceived by management*, produce a set of perceived risks. The system very commonly generates a set of self-imposed restraints, most common of which are:

1. A time dimension in thinking—that is, those strategies are deemed to be optimum that most nearly achieve corporate objectives within a *given period of time*—one year, two years, five years. Profit, however and

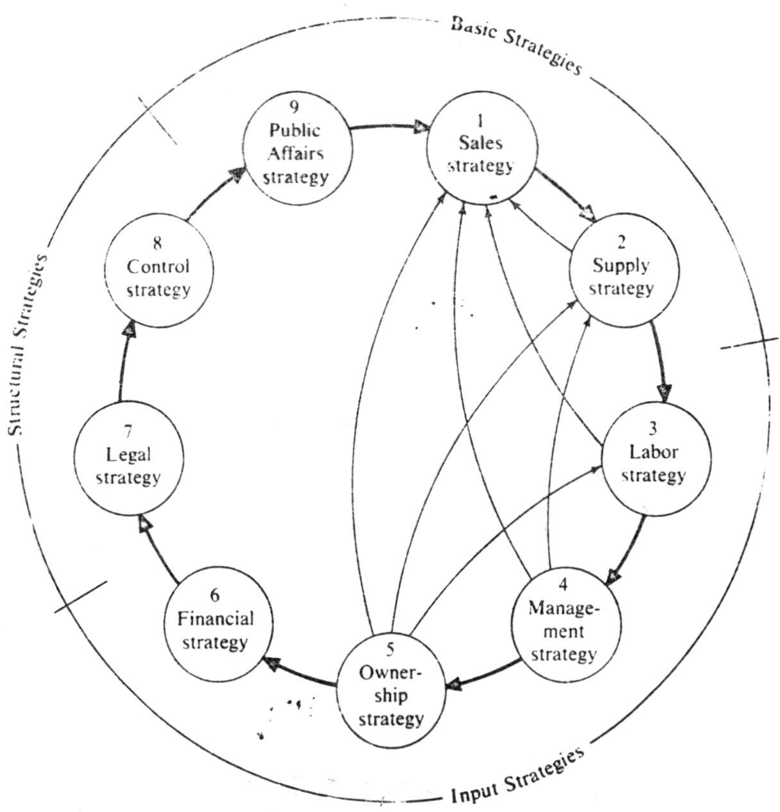

The Decision Circle

wherever determined, is maximized over that period. This dimension varies remarkably from company to company. It is probably safe to say that a longer time dimension is required for success in international business than in the purely domestic one because of the growth factor and associated restrictions on monetary movement.

Inputs

Outputs

Domestic Envrionment

Economic and Political Pressures

Host National Environment

Structure, Goals, Institutions

International Environment

Structure, Institutions

Legal Restraints

Quality of Communications

Chance

Personal Likes and Biases

Past Company Experience

Existing Company Structure

Management of a United States Firm

Company Resources

Corporate Objectives

Acceptable Strategies

Perceived Pressures

Perceived Risks

Self-imposed Restraints

Temporal
Product
Function
Geographical
Structural
Financial

Feedback Loop

The decision-making process

2. A limitation on the products to be sold and/or produced overseas.

3. A functional limitation.

4. A limitation on the geographical scope of operations. Such a limitation is often related to the development of export sales by the firm; that is, investment in productive facilities abroad tends to follow the development of export sales. But export sales may be

greater precisely for those products in which the home country has some distinct advantage and are, therefore, not necessarily a measure of the advantages of local manufacturer. In fact, imports may be a more conceiving indication of advantages accruing to overseas production.

5. Structural restraints.

6. Financial restraints. For a company to face a growth situation requiring situation requiring expansion precisely at the rate that can be financed out of earnings would be a rare coincidence. The point, of course, is that a firm operating under a policy of expanding only at the rate permitted by retained earnings is disciplined to reject investment opportunities once that growth rate is approached, hence, the apparent coincidence of rates.

It is within the parameters of these six self-imposed restraints, many of which may be entirely reasonable, that management defines corporate objectives, recognizes the alternative strategies, and perceives the relevant variables.

Perhaps of greatest impact is management's time horizon, whether determine implicitly or explicitly. It is of particular relevance in the international area because of the greater time lag between decision and implementation than in the typical domestic case and the greater range of long-run strategies, for example, the multinational option. If one or more of these factors do not rule to a time horizon longer than the current fiscal period, then management should probably not impose such a time restraint on its foreign market strategies. The point is that it is wasteful of time and effort, and therefore costly, to permit analysts to consider strategies that management will not accept, particularly in the international field, because of the greater time and cost involved in investigating and implementing many projects. Bear in mind that there is a significant difference between what management *can* and *is willing* to accept. This difference should be made explicit after careful study of company resources and the company's commitment to present markets.

A word about company structure as it relates to the selection of corporate objectives and acceptable strategies for accomplishing them is appropriate here. By "structure" is meant those organizational rigidities difficult to alter significantly in the short run, such elements as ownership, independence, divisional basis, size of company, contractual relationships or interdependence in respect to other firms. Indeed, if this last relationship is very important, management maybe prone to enter overseas markets only in concert, say, joint ventures, with the associated firms of the same nationality, thereby limiting its ownership strategy to minority participation with other domestic firms. This is the so-called paggy-back operation. Also, great size may limit consideration of overseas opportunities to international regional or multinational markets, thereby ruling out production for a single national market. Great size may also render product and process modification difficult, thereby eliminating market-oriented modifications of either. On the other hand, small size may limit overseas comments to one or two national markets, thereby ruling out geographical dispersion and resulting in increased risk.

By company resources, one refers to such variables as financial resources, personnel, technical knowledge, goodwill, intangibles, distribution system, political leverage. Management may perceive different trade-off values in its portfolio of resources. For example, a management may not be willing to trade its goodwill for external financing or for a stream of earnings. Past experience or company structure or personal likes and biases may rule out the use of this resource for such purposes, thereby possibly requiring wholly owned ventures as the vehicle for overseas expansion, if indeed it causes management to feel able to do more than select some form of exporting. In any event, the rate of expansion overseas is thus curtailed, and geographically limited involvement overseas can heighten risk.

A few words about corporate objectives are necessary, otherwise our concern about optimum strategy becomes meaningless. Optimum for what? First, let us all agree that the primary objective is to maximize profit, but to maximize profit where? for whom? over what length or period of time? Profit maximization if meaningless unless management first defines these parameters. If it does not, the system may be irrational in that management is not doing what it set out to do, to maximize profit. There are, of course, a number of perfectly valid reasons for limiting the international scope of the firm. One reason would be financial and personal inadequacies are not caused by some unnecessary self-imposed restraint but are genuine, externally imposed inadequacies. These self-imposed restraints may sometimes follow from management's fear of losing control by moving into unfamiliar areas or of the employment of new people unfamiliar expertise.

Profit-maximization for an international firm suggests long-run planning to achieve a geographically and functionally diversified international association of complementary enterprises. Long-run, profitable survival rests directly upon the selection of appropriate strategies under a given set of circumstances. This policy demands a high degree of flexibility in choice of strategy, which means elimination of as many rigidities in the system as possible, such rigidities as the casual extension of domestic policy, domination by the personal likes or biases of key personnel, management fear of the unfamiliar, or unchallenged projection of past experience into different places and times.

Decision-making

Empirical research would indicate that decisions by which a firm commits resouces to a foreign market differ from comparable domestic decisions in several important respects:

1. They are more expensive in that more variable are involved. It is more difficult to apply familiar measures; special legal and financial and area skills are required; the amount of time-consuming communication and travel is greater.
2. They are less likely to be stimulated by an internal company market survey and more likely to be the result of external pressure on the firm.
3. They are more likely to be the result of *selective* analysis of market opportunities, rather than universal and comparative analysis.
4. They are less subject to quantitative analysis because of the application of a subjectivity derived discount rate to anticipated earnings, a rate that may be someone's guess as to political risk.

The source of *initial pressure* on the firm on investigate a foreign market is very likely to be exogenous to the firm, more so than in the domestic situation. Second, company organization and policy may act as a check on this initial pressure, because the structure was designed with the needs on the domestic environment in mind, not those of the relevant foreign environment. Third, throughout the decision-making process personal interest on the part of key members of management is likely to play a larger role than in the domestic case precisely because of the greater number of imponderables in assessing a foreign-market opportunity. Once sufficient interest is generated in a firm in a given foreign market, an *evaluative process* begins that may be highly subjective, depending on the size of the firm, its past experience and the time available. The *decision to investigate* a foreign project is not to be taken lightly, for such a decision in itself may mean the investment of a substantial amount to the level at which the investigation is to be made and the nature of that investigation. How the *actual investigation* proceeds is likely to be strongly influenced by personal interest in the foreign case. And again, whether the investigation actually leads to an *investment decision* is likely to be conditioned strongly by the existence of personal interest at the appropriate level within the firm. Strong negative convictions may mean a negative decision simply by default. And, finally, the investment decision itself is in reality a two-fold decision: (1) where to invest, and (2) investment in what sort of facilities.

The organizational implications of this decision-making process are legion. It is sufficient to say here that among the organizational hallmarks of the successful international firm are·

1. Direct exposure of the firm to its foreign markets for market analysis, rather than dependence upon

intermediaries, whose interests may not coincide with those of the firm.

2. A centralized, globally oriented market research team that periodically looks at every likely market.
3. A central clearing house for overseas projects, whether generated by internal or external pressures, so as to assure that company assets, including personnel, are assigned to the highest priority markets and enterprises.
4. Employment of, or access to, individuals possessing the necessary international legal, financial, marketing, political, and economic skills to evaluate to overseas market opportunities and thereby reduce risk.
5. Intracompany credits to domestic operating divisions assisting in the penetration of overseas markets so as to make such participation attractive to division executives.
6. A specialized research and development group primarily concerned with the development and modification of products and processes vis-a-vis foreign markets.
7. An equal hearing at the level at which relevant decisions are made for spokesmen in favor of foreign projects, whether involving sales, purchasing, or manufacturing.
8. An understanding that successful international experience is a plus factor for promotion in respect to both technicians and management.

Appendix

The Stitcher Company

Historically, the Stitcher Company had gone into foreign projects as opportunities presented themselves. Decisions had been made on each project as it came up, management being guided by intuition rather than by formalized policies or objectives. The burden on top management became unwieldy, and it was decided to make a formal analysis of (1) what the company was then doing abroad and (2) lengths and weaknesses of the company in respect to overseas activities. The purpose of the study would be to define company policy in respect to what it should be doing.

To undertake this study, a committee was set up called the Overseas Policy and Planning Committee (OPPC). This group sent "task forces" into each country where the company was then operating and where it might consider operations in the near future. In each case, the initial question was: should the company be in the country? The studies of the task force groups were based on two premises: (1) that the company might consider going into any country in changing the nature of its investment in respect to either country or industry, or both. Furthermore, no time limit was stipulated during which investment was to be shifted. In other words, in making their studies and forming their recommendations, the task forces were given almost complete flexibility. The OPPC directed that detailed reports be made on 12 African, Asian, and Latin American countries in which Stitcher had interests or projects, plus "less penetrating analysis" of five others in which it had potential interests. The upshot was that on the basis of the task force country reports the OPPC reached certain conclusions as to the outlook for growth in each of these 17 countries relative to opportunities and risks. and in each, the growth industries were singled out for special study. Consideration was given to the company's position in each of the countries, and then related to those industries considered to be especially attractive from the point of view of growth potential. The study finally came down to a recommendation of investment by industry and by country. These recommendations became the criteria against which projects were to be measured. A section of the OPPC report detailed the criteria used in measuring the various "lines of endeavor" of possible interest to the company. It is reproduced in part below:

Summary of OPPC report. From the basic and secondary characteristics of the economics of the seventeen countries, we arrive at definite conclusions as to the criteria by which to determine the right lines of endeavor. If our criteria are correct, we have thus a clearly systematic approach to planning for overseas development in Asia, Africa, and Latin America.

Where then do they lead us? What are the guideposts for selecting lines of endeavor?

Primary specifications

1. As we have already mentioned, as a basic fundamental, ventures should be considered only if they *cut broadly through the urbanization and industrialization* trends in the economy. These are the deep and sweeping internal movements that will carry all else before them.

2. Investment policy must contribute to overcoming one of the great dangers in all the economies in which we would have serious interest, namely, the stringency of

foreign exchange, meaning that lines of endeavor selected should either be *foreign exchange* earners or help meet the exchange problem by substituting local production for imports.

3. There should be low *vulnerability to currency depreciation* with profitability anticipation commensurately higher as the vulnerability increases as in the case with investments involving higher proportions of working capital.

Secondary specifications

4. The lines of endeavor selected must have the characteristic of filling highly strategic "gap" *opportunities*. It must be in an industry in which consumption is very low compared with what it should be in an industry in which consumption is very low compared with what is should be considering the state of the country. It must at the same time have a long range growth potential higher than the rate of growth of economy generally and of personal incomes.

5. These must be long term *growth potential* at a rate greater than the "growth curve" of the economy.

6. "Unique opportunities" that fit into the strategic gaps are especially desirable—those that give an advantage in a market, especially smaller ones. Investments not having this characteristic in small markets would almost certainly be questionable.

7. There must be an *adequate* existing or clearly foreseeable local *market*, a gap opportunity or extraordinary growth, or these should be already an expanding world market.

8. Availability of *local raw materials* is a primary requisite in view of the foreign exchange problems. If imported materials are used they must be a small fraction of the final value of the ultimately finished product. Can-sealing compounds are a good example.

9. *Foreign entrepreneurship* should be a necessity; i.e., the line of endeavor must still be beyond the possibilities of local nationals now.

10. In the absence of a local capital market it must be *capable of financing its own growth* through retained earnings, particularly when further investment from abroad is not attractive or costly.

11. Finally, there is the desirability of *low political exposure*. For instances, the investment should not occupy a strategic position in respect to resources that have high emotional, appeal in underdeveloped countries.

We have not mentioned minimum profitability or rate of return here. This is a factor in determining investment policy that can only be considered in relation to the company as a whole and its parts. It cannot be set in accordance with country economic characteristics except that it should be obvious that if the lines of endeavor are selected in accordance with the criteria set forth here, the investment policy requirements for long range profitability will be easier to meet. Whatever minimum base is set on company-wise consideration should, however, be adjusted upward in varying amounts, country-by-country, depending on local risk factors and the specific rationale and expectations for the individual business.

Ranking lines of endeavor

The criteria were applied to a wide list of possible industries, particularly those that our surveys in each country brought out as industries that are considered "attractive"; that is, industries that should grow rapidly during the next ten years because of population growth, increases in total and per capital incomes and, most of all, which should tend to move up faster than these indicators. Actually, the industries considered included almost every possible line of endeavor. We put them all through the successive screens of our criteria to come up finally with the following main "lines of endeavor" that we concluded were the "opportunity industries":

First we isolated three lines of endeavor that can be considered as having this "opportunity" character without reservation. These are first

1. Economic intermediates of manufacturing.
2. Economic intermediates of distribution.
3. Economic intermediates of construction.

We should explain what we mean by the term "economic intermediates," as it is a term we had to coin. We mean thereby products that in themselves might be considered "finished products" but whose primary use is in making possible manufacturing, distribution, or construction and that are destroyed, absorbed, or used up in the process. An example of the typical "economic intermediate of manufacturing" would be the hermetically sealed motors produced in Mexico. An example of "economic intermediates of distribution" are packaging materials. Without such materials distribution would be impossible. Yet they are absorbed and used up in the process. Typical examples of "economic intermediates of construction" would be wallboard, paint, structural steel forms, sheet glass, and piping.

The characteristic about economic intermediates that makes them particularly attractive is that their own values is a relatively small part of the total finished product into which they are integrated. A secondary characteristic is that there is a relatively low labor content in their making. They have high capital intensity and they can be produced ordinarily in a fairly continuous flow process. The management requirements are similar in manufacturing where scheduling or raw materials, factor flow, and the overhead to total cost relationships are magnitudinally close.

It a further characteristic that without the intermediate the final product, whether a building, mine, or a piece of communications equipment, is not capable of being produced. In other words, the "economic intermediates" occupy strategic positions in respect to their essential nature for whole process, while at the same time negligible in the total cost-structure of the process itself.

We next isolated four "lines of endeavor," which are much more doubtful or which can be considered "opportunity lines" for our company only with reservations and restrictions. These are:

1. Export industries producing primary commodities. We call these "mining" for short even though the production of pulp would belong in this strategy.

   This category, however, applies only to "minor" extractive industries. "Major" extractive industries such as those mining major materials or producing petroleum do not satisfy the "opportunity criteria" in important aspects.

2. A major "opportunity line" is the building up of a "*distribution* system". By this we mean the actual apparatus needed to distribute goods from the manufacturer to the consumer and any part thereof, warehousing, transporting, financing, and finally, selling, whether wholesale or retail.

   There is no doubt that the development of streamlined and economical distribution systems is one of the greatest needs of many of these countries. It is doubtful, however, whether such a system can be built without undesirable financial characteristics, though the belief that this is primarily a working-capital investment is perhaps no longer quite valid. There is need for further study here.

3. *Economic intermediates of agriculture*. As we have seen, there is need, and encouragement can be expected to be given to increased agricultural productivity in almost all the countries. This means farm mechanization, fertilizers, insecticides, etc. More rapid introduction of agricultural improvements of this nature is being assisted by developed country assistance and by the economic policies of the respective governments. We should not, therefore, leave out of our thinking an agricultural sector, in at least one aspect of which, fertilizers, the company has expertness. Food imports, as we have seen in the previous chapter, constitute a sizeable drain on the foreign exchange positions of a number of countries. Efforts to substitute local production can be expected to be given emphasis and official encouragement. In

relation to the results that can be attained, expenditures for agricultural intermediates represent a fairly small portion of the final product.

4. As a further area that might, with reservations, satisfy the "opportunity characteristics" we list *certain consumer goods, namely those that provide "necessities of status"* rather than "necessities of life" or even "cheap luxuries."

Consumer goods industries, providing necessities, for example, textiles, clearly do not have the growth potential needed in view of the risk many of these countries pose.

The situation of "cheap luxuries" consumer goods is much better in that their growth potential is certainly very high, perhaps the highest.

Such "necessities of status" as durable consumer goods, home appliances, and so on enjoy a growth potential probably as large as that of the "cheap luxuries," though they have greater risks in bad times. At the same time they may be vulnerable in that they depend very much more heavily on the availability of foreign exchange for imports.

2

Strategies and Structures of the International Business

This book is for the reader who expects to be involved, one way or the other, in the conduct of international business. If the reader is like most of those that have used this book in the past, he or she will already know something about the concepts and tools of finance, marketing, production, and organization, and something about the interaction between the strategy of the firm and the characteristics of its environment. But the odds are that the reader will feel most at home with these ideas as applied in a single national economy, not in a world made up of many economies.

The object of this book is to add the international dimension: to present the institutions, forces, and problems that are involved when business managers try to operate in many economies at once, and to sort out the threats and promises that develop when they try to link their operations across national boundaries. Because the viewpoint is that of the manager, it begins with the firm itself as it looks outward at the international economy.

Of course, the transactions that take place across the borders of any country affect every part of its economy, not just the transacting firms. The pervasive impact of changes in the international oil market over the past few years illustrates the point well enough. But some kinds of enterprises are much more caught up than others in the dangers and opportunities that arise from developments that lie outside the home economy.

The multinational enterprises

The "multinational enterprises" of the world are especially exposed in this respect. Included in this group are enterprises made up of a cluster of affiliated operate in such a way that the affiliated firms, although in different countries, nevertheless share the following characteristics:

1. They are linked by ties of common ownership.
2. They draw on a common pool of resources, such as money and credit, information and systems, trade names and patents.
3. They respond to some common strategy.

About one half of the industrial output of the noncommunist world today is produced by firms that have developed a multinational structure. These enterprises have some special problems that arise from their being multinational. But they also face the problems and opportunities of any importer or exporter, or any lender or borrower, who deals across national boundaries. Accordingly, from the viewpoint of the manager who is interested in the international economy, our focus on the multinational enterprise does not narrow the book's approach.

Although multinational enterprises have come to

account for a large part of the noncommunist world's total output, they still consist of a very distinctive group of firms. By and large, international business is the game of big enterprises. Practically all the 400 or 500 biggest enterprises in the world have substantial business interests in the form of operating units located outside their own country. Ford Motor Co., for instance, has half its employees outside the United States, Philips of the Netherlands three quarters of its employees outside the home country, Saint-Gobain over half outside France, and Matsushita Electric over half outside Japan. In the past few years, the largest firms of Brazil, Mexico, and other industrializing countries have begun to take on signs of a similar trend.

Firms that have developed a multinational structure not only tend to be large; they also tend to be engaged in certain kinds of business activities. The manufacturing industries as a group account for more of these enterprises than any other category. Oil and banking each run well behind manufacturing, according to almost any measure. The numerous other activities in which multinational enterprises are prominent include mining, agriculture, and public utilities.

Within the manufacturing sector, the multinational enterprise is especially strong in certain kinds of industries. In practically all countries, multinational enterprises have a dominant position in motor vehicles, chemical products, petroleum refining, drugs, electronic products, and food products. Firms from developing countries such as Brazil and India, however, have sometimes managed to create a multinational network in less complex industries, such as textiles and food preparations.

Why have so many enterprises developed a multinational network in the past few decades? Analysts who have puzzled over the trend have come up with a variety of explanations:

1. *The multinational enterprise as financial intermediary.* Some analysts credit the growth of multinational enterprises to their special ability to tap the world's capital markets. If General Foods needs capital to finance the growth of its British subsidiary, and if the U.S. capital market offers the best terms at the time, General Foods is in a better position to tap U.S. funds than a national British food company would be. Part of the advantage, some analysts would say, stems from an illusion on the part of those that are providing the capital. Investors may be quite aware that a British firm borrowing dollars faces the risk that over the years sterling may lose some value in relation to the dollar; but they are less likely to realize that the same risk applies to General Foods. That oversight gives General Foods a competitive edge over its British competitors.

2. *The multinational enterprise as geographical diversifier.* Because of tariffs or transport costs or other barriers to international trade, firms often find it difficult to sell products across national borders. Nonetheless, the firm that can sell such products simultaneously in many different markets enjoys and advantage over the firm that cannot. Those that sell in many different markets are likely to have more stable sales. Such stability will be valued by investors, thus lowering the cost of capital to the firm.

3. *The multinational enterprise as oligopolist.*

Enterprises often manage to acquire some advantage that no other firm can easily duplicate, such as a patent on important technology, a commanding trade name, or a unique organization. A firm that acquires such an advantage and has some way of passing that advantage on to its subsidiaries operating in a foreign market may have an edge over national competitors in that market. If that edge cannot be exploited by way of exports, the enterprise may develop a multinational structure instead.

4. *The multinational enterprise as an internal market.* Firms that acquire a unique advantage of the sort mentioned in paragraph 3 could conceivably exploit that special advantage by licensing others in foreign countries to use their special strengths. But some strengths, such as a powerful trademark or a strong patent, may not be salable to others for what they are actually worth to the firm itself. Where these are the facts, firms are likely to set up their own foreign subsidiaries, thus creating their own internal market for the special advantages they possess.

Plainly, the theories that are summarized in the four paragraphs above are not mutually exclusive nor necessarily contradictory. In some given case, all of these factors could be operating in unison. But the evidence of various large-scale studies and the actual experiences of businessmen in the field indicate strongly that in most cases the factors summarized in paragraphs 3 and 4 are likely to play a central role in a firm's decision to set up foreign subsidiaries. Our next step, then, is to take a closer look at the special advantages that firms seem bent on exploiting, and to see what strategies they generate.

Exploiting a technological lead

In any industry heavily engaged in innovation and development, there is a strong likelihood that the leading firms will have numerous contacts with foreign markets outside the home base. In some cases, as in the aeronautical industry, the contact with foreign markets will take the form of exports; for instance, Boeing, Lockheed, Aerospatiale, or McDonnell Douglas depend on exports to a much greater degree than most manufacturing firms. In the chemical, drug, scientific instruments, transportation equipment, and machinery industries, exports also are comparatively heavy. To facilitate their exports, firms commonly appoint agents or develop sales subsidiaries in the foreign markets.

The linkage between technological leadership and foreign markets can be seen not only for firms based in the United States but also for those based in Europe and Japan. And behind the linkage lies an obvious set of causes.

Since the beginning of modern industry over one hundred years ago, a good deal of the research and development undertaken by industrial firms has typically resulted in new products. The emphasis on new products has been especially typical of the research and development efforts of firms in the United States, which are responsible for about half of all the industrial research and development expenditures in the noncommunist world Some of these products, such as drip-dry shirts, simply perform a familiar job for the consumer better than the existing product. Others, such as computer-controlled machine tools, help the producer perform his tasks more efficiently. But many, such as penicillin and commercial aircraft, are not in serious competition with any existing products at the time of their introduction and can be regarded as satisfying wants that were never previously addressed.

Here already we can begin to see some of the reasons for expecting different patterns of behavior between firms based in, say, Germany and those based in Brazil.

The disposition of a country to develop new products is not a matter of pure chance. For substantial industrial innovations to take place in a country, a body of trained engineers and interested businessmen must exist. But that is to quite enough. Businessmen and engineers need an incentive to innovate: the hope of gain or the fear of loss must be strong enough to justify the effort. In some national environments, where the position of individual firms is rendered fairly secure by agreements with potential competitors or by government controls, the motivation to innovate may be quite low; in other environments it will be higher.

Even where the capacity and incentive to innovate are strong enough, innovators are likely to react differently in different national environments, developing those products that seem most wanted in the national environment in which they operate. To be sure, all countries welcome new products or processes that will cut costs. But in a country where, say, skilled labor is exceedingly scarce and dear while capital is abundant and cheap, businessmen and engineers are likely to concentrate on labor-saving devices. In countries where labor is the abundant resource and raw materials are scarce, the innovations that capture the interest of businessmen and engineers tend to be material-saving. Various studies show that in past years the innovations emanating from the United States have stressed labor-saving needs while Europe's innovations have been weighted more heavily toward material-saving objectives. Today, innovators in the United States, Europe, and Japan are all found concentrating on energy-saving innovations.

There are also characteristic differences in consumer products. Countries with very high per capita incomes offer opportunities for the sale of new products or services that have not been seen before. Countries with low per capita incomes, on the other hand, offer unique opportunities for the adaptation of existing products to lower-priced versions. European and Japanese innovations have commonly fit that pattern in the past, while countries like Brazil and India seem prepared to perform that role in the future.

There are other variables that influence the propensity and direction of industrial innovation in any economy. Countries in which the military buy large quantities of hardware from their producers generate one kind of market, and countries in which the government buys large quantities of medicines quite another. Big countries induce innovations that are associated with economies of scale; small countries may not. And so on.

Once a firm establishes a technological lead in some product, certain characteristic patterns are likely to ensue as the product grows more mature. These patterns, commonly referred to under the rubric of the "product cycle," will be referred to more than once in the chapters that follow.

In any event, the firm's first question is how best to

exploit the innovational lead. Sometimes, as in the case of the Boeing 757 or the Airbus A-300, exploitation in foreign markets can be achieved well enough through exports. A buyer of a Boeing 757 who is located in Melbourne does not think of the aircraft as less available or less attractive simply because it is designed and produced in Seattle. Besides, at the early stage of any product's development, the manager is not acutely concerned with questions of production cost. For various reasons, his attention at that stage is on other factors:

1. The lines separating the development stage, the pilot-plant stage, and the first commercial production stage for a new product are often not clean-cut. In these early stages the manager is likely to be most concerned with maintaining effective communication among the key development engineers, production men, controllers, salesmen, and prospective first users of the product. If the product proves successful, the manager is likely to discover suddenly that his first production unit is already in place, at the site where the development of the product was taking place. More than any other factor, this explains the U.S. automobile industry's early location in Detroit and the chemical industry's early location in New Jersey.

2. Even if the manager could take his choice of locations, he would have great difficulty in determining the least-cost points of production and distribution. Products that are in their infancy often come in a variety of experimental shapes, sizes, and materials; witness the radio market of the 1920s. Unsure of the exact inputs that the product eventually will require, unsure of the size of the market or the geographical distribution of demand, the manager is

disinclined to give much weight to cost-minimizing calculations that depend on factors such as these.

3. At the early stages, the pressure on the manager to consider cost explicitly and carefully is not likely to be great. In new products such as nylon, video tapes, and laser aiming devices, the number of competing producers is small, at least at first. Besides, the earliest customers as a rule are not very sensitive to small variations in price; at that stage, in economic jargon, the product is not very price elastic. The need of the seller to hold down product costs in order to increase sales comes later.

In time, however, the manager is forced to worry about costs again. This is the case for a number of reasons.

1. As the product matures, it begins to assume characteristics that permit easier comparisons from one producer to the next. Automobiles, for instance, took some time before they eventually settled down to a four-wheel vehicle with a steering wheel and a gasoline engine.
2. As the product matures, the original producer's special knowledge and special skills, whatever they may be, are shared with others at home and abroad. The threat of price competition becomes more tangible.
3. As the demand for the product grows, the later users are generally found placing much more weight on questions of price than the first users. In economic terms, the price elasticity of demand associated with the later users is higher than for the original users. Moreover, differences in price between brands—cross-

elasticities—generally matter more with these later users.

4. As total demand grows and as the volume of sales in some foreign markets increases, the possibility of producing from foreign plant locations grows. In these later stages, a formal analysis to determine least-cost production points is more likely to suggest the establishment of foreign production sites than in the earlier stages. The timing, of course, depends partly on (a) the importance of scale economies in production, and (b) transportation costs for the materials required by the plant and for the plant's output.

5. As the product matures, importing countries may begin to ask if there are ways of encouraging local production to take the place of imports. Import restrictions sometimes develop at this stage. Some are overt restrictions, such as tariffs and import licensing requirements; others are more subtle restrictions, such as "but-at-home" policies on the part of government agencies and other public buyers.

This is the point at which the firm must decide between licensing the production of its product to an independent firm located in the foreign market or exploiting its innovational lead through a foreign subsidiary of its own. In terms of the four groups of theories summarized earlier, this is the point at which the firm must determine if an efficient market exists for its technology. If so, it may decide to grant a license to an independent licensee. It may provide for a flow of unpatented technical information to the licensee; it may grant patent rights to the licensee covering specified countries; it may authorize the licensee to use the licensor's trade name in given markets; and it may make provision to supply some exotic line of machinery or industrial supplies. In return, the licensee will be obliged to make various payments to the licensor, typically on the order of three or four percent of its gross sales. The licensee may also be obliged to take on various commitments to the licensor, such as confining its sales to certain markets, buying its intermediate products from the licensor, and so on

But from the point of view of many innovating firms, the licensing of independent producers can have many drawbacks—drawbacks so important that the license fees do not represent adequate compensation. It is often very difficult, for instance, to communicate subtle and complex technologies successfully from one firm to the next, especially if the recipient is an independent firm operating in another culture; accordingly, heavy costs may be involved in effectively transmitting the necessary information. It is also difficult as a rule for licensors to be sure that licensees are maintaining adequate quality control in their production, a particularly worrisome point for the licensor when the licensee is using the licensor's trade name. Spurred by considerations of this sort, innovating firms have commonly preferred to exploit their special strengths in foreign markets through their own foreign subsidiaries.

Accordingly, for many products, multinational enterprises eventually begin to test the attractiveness of various overseas sites as production points

Figure1 indicates from the firm's viewpoint the comparative cost situation of

1. producing in the home market and exporting to the foreign market, *versus*

2. producing in a new facility set up in the foreign market for the purpose of serving that market.

The diagram assumes the marginal cost of production is rising in the home facility. It assumes further that in any new facility created in the foreign market, factory costs will fall throughout the range of production OB. On the assumptions in Figure I, whenever demand in the foreign market reaches OA units, the firm will find that the cost of the units produced at home when delivered to the foreign market will exceed the cost of units produced in a separate facility inside that market.

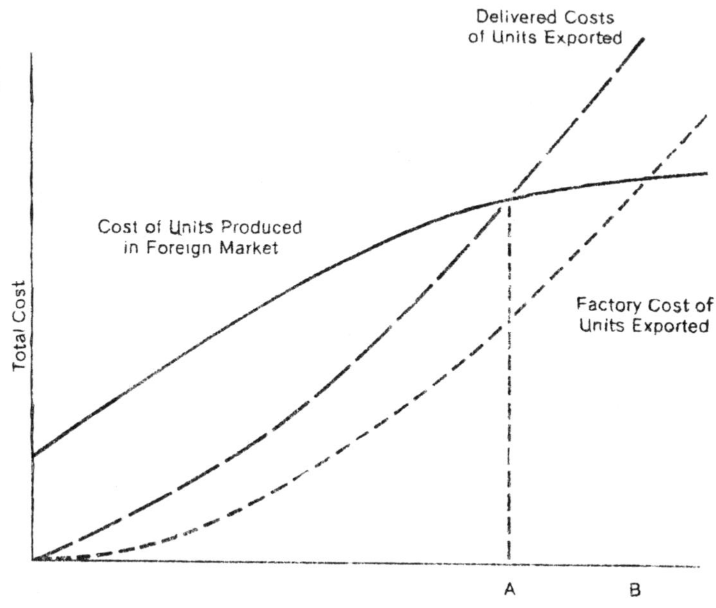

Fig. 1 Cost of product delivered to foreign market: exports and foreign production compared

To be sure, this method of formulating the issue is only the beginning of the analysis. The possibility has to be explored of separating some aspects of the stages of manufacturing from others, perhaps in order to place only the later stages in the foreign market. The possibility that the import duty may be raised, thereby raising the foreign delivered cost, must also be considered. As that contingency is introduced, appropriate account must also be taken of the possibility that the increase in price may lower internal demand or encourage new sources of domestic competition or both. But these aspects of the problem can usually be managed in a systematic way. It is this sort of calculation that has led many U.S. inovators eventually to set up production facilities in Western Europe and many West European and Japanese innovators eventually to set up production facilities in the United States.

The maturing of technologically advanced products, therefore, tends to press enterprises toward the establishment of overseas production units, a move necessary to protect or prolong a position that was originally based on a technological lead in those markets. With a decline in the importance of the technological lead, the relatively straightforward calculations of least cost begin to play their familiar role once again.

Exploiting a strong trade name

Another strategy that has led enterprises to create producing facilities in foreign countries is to exploit a strong trade name; this is an obvious example that falls in the third category of theories mentioned above. In the modern world of easy international movement and communication, trade names can sometimes gain strength in a foreign market without much conscious effort on the part of the firm that owns the name. Casual unplanned exports sometimes establish a position for a foreign brand. Military installations on foreign soil sometimes perform that sort of role. International tourists, movies, and television can also be the carriers.

As a rule, the strength of the foreign trade name is associated with the fact or the illusion of superior performance. Fact or illusion, the expectation of superior performance is often strengthened and fortified by copious promotional expenditures, as is commonly the case for name-branded pharmaceuticals and food preparations.

Sometimes, too, the strength of a brand name is associated not with superior performance but with predictable performance. When that is the case, the existence of a strong trade name may rest on some technological capability. For instance, delivering a packaged food product such as chocolates or biscuits in a reasonably standardized condition on a reasonably reliable basis can be a technically exacting job.

In any event, whether based on substance or illusion, some trade names command a premium in foreign markets. Whether the firms that control the names eventually will also produce in such markets is influenced in part by the technical considerations described in the preceding section.

On these criteria, the decision for some industries has been clear-cut. In packaged foods, soft drinks, and drugs, where trade names play a critical role, enterprises have often discovered that they could not adequately exploit their advantage by way of exports and have commonly established plants in their foreign markets. Once established in such markets, these producers have generally had to confront national competitors who were operating on roughly the same cost basis. Indeed, the foreigners have sometimes been handicapped by added costs, such as the costs of communication and control associated with the maintenance of a multinational organization. In such cases, the special strength of the trade name has usually been indispensable for the foreign firm to maintain a competitive position.

Nevertheless, although foreign trade names have been known to endure for long periods of time in such markets, their ability to command a price premium in a given type of product against the competing offers of national producers often erodes in time. As long as the product itself remains unchanged, the national producers learn either to match the performance of the foreign product or to overcome the illusion of a difference that was never there. When that happens, multinational enterprises find themselves obliged to share their foreign markets with national producers. In most instances, foreign-owned firms continue to sell their product, albeit to a smaller share of the market; in some cases, they find themselves obliged to abandon the market altogether to their national competitors.

Exploiting the advantages of scale

In sheer quantity terms, most of the output of multinational enterprises is in products whose sale depends on neither a strong technological lead nor a strong trade name. In oil, copper, aluminum, heavy chemicals, and many other products, differences in technology and differences in trade name strength play a quite secondary role in marketing.

The strategic need

The strength of the leaders in these industries lies primarily in the fact that large firms are in a position to be more efficient than small. Once again, therefore, the third category of theories is relevant. A new challenger, as a rule, has to find some way of assembling the funds, physical assets, and organization that are capable of producing, distributing, and controlling on a very large scale; otherwise, the newcomer usually runs the risk of being a high-cost competitor. If the capital markets of the world were highly efficient they might be expected to provide a newcomer firm with the needed capital at an appropriate cost, in spite of the scale of the funds required; similarly with the provision of ready-made functioning management teams.

But the market for large-scale capital and management teams is notoriously imperfect. In many industries, therefore, leaders can feel reasonably secure that new rivals will not be appearing overnight.

In fact, even after the capital, facilities, and human skills have been put together by a newcomer firm, it still faces the problem of financing a period of learning, a running-in period for the organization. In large, complex organizations, that period generally has to be reckoned in terms of years, not days or months, during which the efficiency of the organization is well below its potential.

An enterprise already established on a large scale has an obvious edgeover a newcomer. Its strength lies in the fact that its marginal costs are low, so that it has a certain measure of price flexibility for a portion of its output. Still, there are latent weaknesses in the firm's position. For one thing, with production facilities in place, the established firm has lost some degree of flexibility in both technology and location.

The ability of a firm to exploit the strategies associated with scale is enhanced if that firm is established in a number of countries. The next few pages are devoted to exploring the connection between strategies associated with scale and the existence of a multinational network.

Shut-out pricing

In oligopolistic markets, a standard reaction on the part of the established leaders to the appearance of a newcomer is the obvious one of drastically, albeit temporarily, reducing the going price. This is a reaction of especial importance in the kind of industry that is dominated by multinational enterprises.

Picture a well-defined market in which the leaders of an industry have settled down into an acceptable equilibrium. Each leader has a stable share of the market and no great uncertainties about the price. Now a newcomer appears in the market. The newcomer may have adequate resources, financial and technical, to make a serious bid for a share of the market. This possibility is based on the fact that the newcomer is already well established in other related lines or in the same line in other markets. Since entry into the market is not easy, profit rates are likely to be fairly high. The newcomer who is able to overcome the entry barriers may therefore be in a position to cut the price in a bid for a share of the market. Confronting the newcomer, the leaders may respond in various ways, but two possibilities are obvious:

1. The leaders may disregard the newcomer's bid and permit him to capture some share of the market, relying on the expectation that the newcomer's goal in

share-of-market terms is limited and that equilibrium will reassert itself once the goal has been achieved. In this case, the cost to the leaders of the newcomer's appearance is the quantity of sales lost *multiplied* by profit per unit.

2. An alternative strategy for the leaders is to reduce the price to a shut-out price, thereby retaining the previous volume of sales but accepting for the necessary period a lower profit margin on those sales. In that case, the cost to the leaders is the quantity of shut-out sales *multiplied by* the decline in profit per unit. Such a strategy, it is apparent, is particularly attractive to the leaders if they can continue to operate at their old profit margin in other countries while doing battle with a newcomer in a particular market. Accordingly, in applying such a strategy, firms that have developed a multinational network may enjoy a special advantage.

Vertical integration

The producers of standardised products that are manufactured under conditions of high fixed costs have an especially compelling need to stabilize the demand for their product. One method is to acquire captive customers. The existence of captive customers may not eliminate all the sources of variation in demand; but at least it eliminates the variation that is produced when customers switch between suppliers. In this case, the fourth category of theories applies.

Once the leading producers of such products begin to recognize the need for controlling their downstream users, a difficult strategic choice is offered to the users. Those that do not wish to be absorbed are confronted with a growing need to capture their own source of supply. For as vertical integration proceeds, the users that remain independent find themselves more and more obliged to buy their materials from vertically integrated firms with which they are in direct competition.

Under those conditions, the vertically integrated producer may decide to supply its captive downstream users in more generous quantities and on better terms than its independent customers, thereby imperiling the independents' existence. A realization of that risk has led to the pattern of expansion portrayed in Fig. 2.

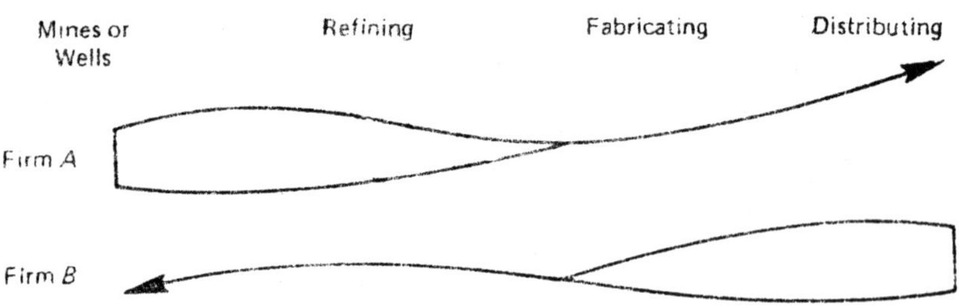

Fig. 2 Typical paths of expansion in industries producing standardised products with high fixed costs

The process of vertical integration often leads to the multinationalization of operations. As enterprises move upstream or downstream to complete their vertical structure, they often reach beyond the national economy in which the integrating process began. Either they need new sources of supply not to be had in their part of the world, or they need markets that do not readily exist at home. In either case, national enterprises commonly become multinational enterprises as they pursue the integration strategy.

Multiple markets and multiple sources

The dominance of multinational enterprises in the capital-intensive industries that produce standardized products is explained in part by the advantages of diversification, a factor already mentioned in the second category of theories presented earlier.

An enterprise that serves several different markets is less vulnerable to the random variation of demand that affects any national market, and less vulnerable to the interventions of national governments. If the market is shrinking for any reason in one nation, it may possible be increasing in another. An act of nationalization in one market can be offset by an expansion elsewhere. The strategy in this case is to try to develop facilities around the globe which enjoy the stability that goes with multiple markets.

The same principle applies, of course, with respect to sources of supply. Enterprises that rely on a number of sources are less vulnerable to stoppages than enterprises that rely upon a single source. Natural calamities, strikes, and the acts of national governments are less likely to affect the total flow.

Managers of multinational enterprises understand this principle well enough. In an extension of the principle, managers have often tried to stretch the geographical spread of their sources of supply by creating joint ventures abroad in partnership with other multinational enterprises in the same industry. By pursuing the joint venture route, multinational enterprises are able to spread a given amount of investment across a larger number of locations, thereby reducing the risks. In the aluminum industry, as a result, a considerable number of bauxite mines of the world located outside the United States are joint ventures between competing firms, often of different nationality. The same pattern is seen in large oil fields and large copper mines throughout the world.

Follow-the-leader

In an industry made up of a small number of firms that see each other as competitors, another common strategy that often leads to the multinationalization of the dominant enterprises is the follow-the-leader strategy. This is a strategy that does not fit easily into the four conventional categories listed earlier. Although the strategy may appear in an industry in which a few large leaders dominate, it is especially common in industries in which the leaders are selling identical products.

Picture the limiting case, that is, the case in which an industry consists of only two firms, both producing the same standardized product and both located in the same country area. Other firms are barred from entry because of the problem of sheer scale in the industry. Overt agreements between the two firms are illegal and none exists.

Now firm L. (the leader) learns of the existence of a new site in another country from which production and distribution would be less costly—a new rich copper ore deposit or a new oil field. Should it set up in the new location?

That, of course, depends in part on its anticipation of the way in which firm F (the follower) is likely to respond.

1. One possibility which firm L may consider is that firm F will not react at all, and that it will passively accept firm L's improvement of its profit margins. That

possibility, although hypothetically possible, would seem unlikely. The existence of major differences in profit margins would place firm F at the mercy of firm L, exposing firm F to the possibility that firm L might try to increase its share of the market at some later date. Moreover, the cash flow of firm L would exceed that of firm F, adding to firm L's aggressive strength. So firm L cannot ordinarily count on inaction from firm F.

2. Firm L must consider another possibility: firm F may follow firm L to the new location; there will be a period of uncertainty, during which each assesses the aggressive intentions of the other in the light of the new cost structures; and the new equilibrium established at the end of the period of uncertainty will generate a price level and profit margin no more favorable than the one that existed before the move. In that case, firm L will hesitate to move.

3. A third possibility is that firm F would follow firm L to the new location with favorable results for both. This can occur if both firms retain their old price structure; it would be better still if both—acting as a profit-maximizing monopolist would act—adjust their prices to a new level, a level that would increase their total sales and total profits. This outcome, seen through the eyes of firm L, would be a happy one.

In the real world of multinational enterprises, of course, industries are rarely made up of just two firms, and barriers to entry are rarely so high as to eliminate the worry on the part of the existing firms that newcomers may enter. Indeed, in oil, aluminum, copper, steel, and basic chemicals, the number of large enterprises in world markets has been increasing, not decreasing, in the quarter-century since World War II.

Managers, therefore, are generally obliged to worry about the possibility of newcomer firms. If such newcomers appear, however, the existing firms may resort to imitative behavior to protect their position. The existing firms, for instance, may locate an added productive facility where the newcomer has located. If the new location imparts special strengths to the new firm, imitation by the established firms will limit the new firm's ability to upset the existing equibrium in the market.

To be sure, the facts about production costs or other characteristics relating to some new location are never all that clear. Neither the new investing firm nor the established firms can avoid the possibility that estimates may be prone to major error. That increases risks in all directions: the new firm may have a bonanza or a disaster on its hands. Still, although both possibilities exist, a consistent practice of follow-the-leader may be the best available response.

For if the new location proves more advantageous than the best prior estimate might have suggested, the desirability of limitation is even stronger. If, on the other hand, the new firm's move proves to be ill-considered and to afford no advantage over existing facilities, the error may still not prove very costly. For if the oligopoly is small enough in number and imitative enough in behavior, the cost of the error may be absorbed by a general increase in the price.

Figure 3 illustrates in more detail some typical sequences and indicates more precisely why imitative behavior commends itself as a strategy. In both cases

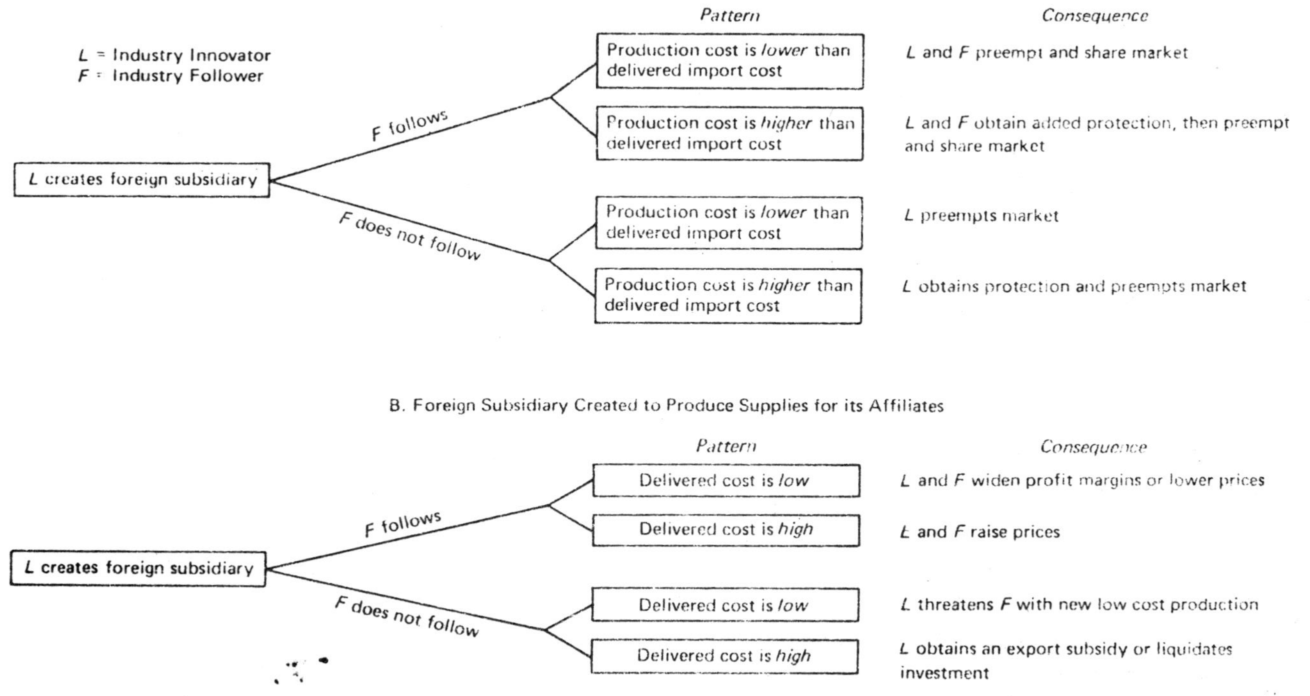

Fig. 3 Follow-the-leader investment strategy

shown, the failure of firms to follow the leader entails high risks, whereas the cost of following the leader is limited.

In the end, of course, this kind of strategy may break down. Too many firms may enter the industry. Imitation as a hedge against risk may prove impossible. In that case, a strategy based on the existence of barriers to entry must come to an end.

Exploiting a scanning capability

When the cost of production and distribution takes on major importance in the competitive situation in any industry, the relative efficiency of the multinational enterprise in scanning the world for low-cost sources of production may prove to be an asset of some significance.

Picture a product, for instance, in which the firm has lost most of its original technological lead; as far as new entrants are concerned, neither the product nor the related processes present formidable hurdles, whether in terms of money, skills, or organization. Although the product may be sold under a well-known brand name, the power of the name to command a premium is small and appears likely to weaken still further. Sheer scale factors offer no major hurdle for the newcomer and no major element of protection for the leaders. The established leaders in the industry have no intention of remaining forever is a business that is beginning to display the conditions of sharp price competition, but neither are they eager to abandon the business prematurely. The cash flow from the existing business is still large, even though the unit markup may be small and the future dubious.

In cases of this sort, the capacity of the multinational enterprise efficiently to search out new low-cost production sites comes into play. The word "efficiently" needs to be stressed. Any firm presumably can search out a new production site, if it is prepared to pay the price of the search. The problems for most firms starting form scratch in such a search, however, are several:

1. Firms located in an efficient production location may not be aware of the existence of a foreign market for the products that they can efficiently produce; if aware of the market, they may feel insecure about their ability to retain it for long.
2. Firms already established in the market as distributors may be unaware of the production possibilities elsewhere; if aware of the possibilities, they may be unsure of the reliability of suppliers.
3. Firms in either situation, to the extent that they require added information, will have to acquire such information at full cost.

The multinational enterprise generally has an advantage on all points; its earlier expansion has equipped it with an oligopolistic advantage that makes further expansion more likely. When the enterprise is vertically integrated, it supplies it sown market, as in the case of components for automobiles and for consumer electronics; accordingly, hesitations over the availability of market and the reliability of the suppliers can be held in bounds. Besides, the information that is required for comparing distant places as alternative points of production is more efficiently gathered and assessed by a multinational enterprise in the business than by an entity operating from one end of the prospective chain; at least that is a reasonable starting presumption. For the moment, therefore, the multinational enterprise operates at a distinct advantage.

The competitive power of an effective information-gathering network in international business is evident not only in the occasional big decisions to establish a new foreign source or invade a new foreign market but also in the day-to-day operations of some foreign business activities. These are activities that require the continuous passage of information over long distances.

Numerous studies have demonstrated two things regarding the communication of information:

1. Failures in effective communication between two widely separated parties are extremely high. The party at the source may be unaware of the information needs of the user; the user may be unaware of the capabilities of the source; the user may be inattentive to the messages actually sent; the message may be garbled or diverted, without the parties being aware.
2. Failures are less likely when both parties perceive themselves as members of a common group responding to a set of common goals.

The rapid growth of multinational banking networks over the past two decades is illustrative of the importance of an effective communication network that is contained within a single organization. Most of what multinational banks do for their customers in the international field can technically be done by a national bank operating through independent overseas correspondents. But multinational banks have managed to capture a high proportion of the international business once done by national banks, an achievement that rests in part on their internalizing of the communication function.

Another illustration of the strategic role played by the internal communication network is provided by the historical role of the Japanese trading company. Such trading companies have traditionally been involved in two distinct activities; in importing standardized bulk commodities and raw materials, such as coal and iron ore; and in exporting the manufactured products of relatively small Japanese manufacturers, especially products that sell in world markets on a straight price basis. In both connection, the trading companies collect information about sources and markets, schedule shipments, and finance transactions, relying for their competitive strength mainly upon their communication network.

The position of the trading firms in the movement of bulk commodities and raw materials has remained unimpaired over the years. Indeed, that position has vastly expanded, as the trading companies have used their networks to build up their sales and shipments between third countries not involving Japan.

The position of the trading companies in other products, however, has been less stable. In the 1960s the trading companies enjoyed a strong competitive edge in exporting such products as textiles, batteries, noodles, and stoves to the poor countries of Asia. Their early export lead, however, has gradually given way to local production. Because of their early foothold, the Japanese trading firms managed to obtain an equity interest in some of the national plants set up to produce such products, often organizing three-way partnerships with local distributors and with the Japanese firm that previously had provided the exported product. But in such partnerships, the trading firm no longer contributed any special strength on which the plants were heavily dependent. Accordingly, the position of the trading companies in such enterprises in the latter 1970s was increasingly precarious.The Japanese trading company illustrates the key role of the internal communication network in still another way. As the Japanese economy has advanced, its manufactured exports have changed markedly in character. Instead of textiles, toys, and noodles, Japan has exported much more complex branded and differentiated products such as Nikon cameras, Yamaha motorbikes, Datsun automobiles, and Technics hi-fi equipment. But the successful design, manufacture, and sale of such products have demanded international communications of a highly specialized and subtle nature. Accordingly, each producing firm has found it essential to internalize such communications within its own network. As a result, the trading companies have had a rather limited role in the export of such products. Meanwhile, many of these Japanese manufacturing firms have set up increasingly elaborate foreign networks in response to their needs, thus taking the first steps toward the structuring of a multinational enterprise.

Links with foreign affiliates

A choice of links

Multinational enterprises can implant their presence in foreign locations either by entering into some form of contract with an independent enterprise, by creating or acquiring a local enterprise, or by various hybrid combinations. Although the choices are infinite in variety, the reader can think of four "pure" types, always bearing in mind that reality itself is usually a good deal more complex. The four types, arranged in ascending degree of parental control, are as follows:

1. The *licensing agreement* or *technical assistance agreement* is an arrangement between the foreign licensor and an entity created under the local law of

the host country; the licensor provides a combination of management services, technical information, or patent rights, and receives payment in money.

2. The *foreign-local joint venture* is a corporate entity or partnership created under local law between the parent and local interests.
3. The *foreigners' joint venture* is a corporate entity or partnership involving a number of parents, all foreign to the area in which they operate.
4. The *wholly owned subsidiary* or *branch* is an entity created under the local law of the host country, but wholly owned and wholly managed by the parent.

The labels, of course, can sometimes be misleading. Although licensing agreements generally entail only a limited amount of control by the foreign licensor, there are cases of licensing agreements that tie the local enterprise had and foot, requiring it to buy its intermediate products from the foreign licensor, adhere to quality standards set by the licensor, and confine its marketing efforts to areas defined in the license; indeed, practically all licenses include some of these limitations. There are also cases of the opposite sort in which wholly owned subsidiaries are scarcely influenced by the foreign parent and operate on so long a leash that the local manager has many of the powers of an unrestrained local owner.

Generally speaking, the strategy that a firm has chosen predisposes it in its choice of links. These preferences develop because the different kinds of links generally have certain predictable costs and benefits, which vary according to the strategy that is pursued.

Cost and benefits

The formal methods of calculating the net benefits to the firm from any given commitment are well developed and can be found in any standard text that deals with capital budgeting. Underlying such methods is a comparison of a stream of future costs with a stream of future benefits. Each will be suitably discounted to its present value; each may be suitably adjusted for the risk and uncertainty associated with the projection.

There are always some knotty problems of quantification involved in making projections of future costs and benefits. Where the question is to choose between exporting to foreign markets and entering into one of the arrangements mentioned above, the problems are multiplied. Table 1 offers a few statements on comparative costs and benefits ordinarily associated with various local arrangements. The assumption implicit in the table is that a foreign-parent enterprise is linked to a local entity which is engaged mainly in manufacturing for the local market.

Costs and benefits from viewpoint of a foreign parent enterprise, ranked according to form of local link

	Licensing Arrangement	*Foreign Local Joint Venture*	*Foreigners' Joint Venture*	*Wholly Owned Subsidiary*
Costs				
1. Cost of capital commitment	1	2	3	4
2. Cost of management commitment	1	2	3	4
3. Restraint on strategic and operatior at				

flexibility of rest of multinational firm	4	3	2	1
Benefits				
1. Amount of payment to parent	?	?	?	?
2. Stability of payment to parent	4	?	?	?
3. Political security for parent	4	3	2	1
4. Contribution to parent's store of knowledge	1	2	3	4
5. Contribution to value of parent's trademark and trade name	1	2	3	4
6. Future availability if local outlet to parent	1	2	3	4

A glance at the table indicates that, when measured in costs and benefits, none of the arrangements emerges uniformly as the most desirable. Judgments on the relative merits of the different arrangements depend on two kinds of questions; both involve weighting.

1. Where one arrangement outranks another in some element of cost or benefit, what is the size of the difference?

2. Where an arrangement is ranked high in one element and low in another, is there some common measure that can be applied to the elements so that a single net judgment can be reached by the manager?

The answers to these questions are far from obvious, but a few points may be helpful.

First, one needs to understand perhaps a little more fully the purport of the rankings in Table 1. At best, they represent general tendencies rather than ironclad relationships. Some of the factors that lead to the rankings in the table are self-evident nonetheless. Take, for instance, the question of capital commitment and management commitment on the part of the foreign parent. When a license is all that ties the local enterprise to the foreigner, capital and management support from the parent are not ordinarily involved, except on a very restricted scale. Similarly, in terms of capital and management, joint ventures generally draw on the foreign parent to a lesser extent than the wholly owned subsidiary. The order of ranking for capital commitment and management commitment, therefore, is straightforward.

In terms of flexibility, on the other hand, the licensing agreement generally imposes a heavier cost on the foreigner than do most ownership arrangements. Whereas a foreign owner may be able to reshuffle its arrangements with a subsidiary as circumstances require, the right and obligations of an independent licensor and licensee presumably cannot be changed without an arm's-length renegotiation. In the licensing case, for instance, the foreigner may be irrevocably tied during the life of the license to using the licensee as its instrumentality for serving some given market. In arrangements in which the parent is linked to the local venture by ownership ties, the capacity to redefine the function of the local venture from time to time is likely to be greater.

Table 1 gauges not only costs but also benefits. A priori, there is nothing to be said as to relative amounts of payment to parents associated with the various alternatives; a licensing agreement that called for payments of, say, 3 or 4 percent of gross sales may yield just as much revenue to the licensor as an equity commitment. The return on a joint venture would presumably be less than that on a wholly owned subsidiary, at least in absolute amounts; but it could be more or less than the income from a licensing agreement. The question of stability of payment, however, is more determinate. The stability associated with the anticipated income flows would ordinarily be higher for the licensing arrangement, because such arrangements generally provide for payments that are fixed in amount or are a function of production volume, rather than for payments that are a function of profits.

The other rankings almost speak for themselves, although none is altogether beyond question. The table assumes that licensing arrangements involve less political risk than ownership arrangements. It assumes, too, that the existence of a wholly owned subsidiary allows the foreign firm to capture certain other advantages which are not so surely available through other types of links. The knowledge that foreign firms pick up about the local market, the spread of their trade names in the country, or the access they gain to local distribution systems can more certainly be put to work for other products of foreign firms if the link is a wholly owned subsidiary than if the arrangement entails a lesser degree of control.

Joint ventures and wholly owned subsidiaries

The cost-benefit calculations suggested by Table 1 are difficult to make. But the job is rendered a little easier by the fact that they very predictably according to certain explicit conditions. These conditions have been carefully studied in connection with the choice between joint ventures and wholly owned subsidiaries.

1. Some countries regard local ownership as an important national objective. Western European

governments and the United States, although nervous about the possibility of foreign ownership in some industries, are not acutely concerned over the question. Japan, on the other hand, is greatly preoccupied with the issue, strongly preferring licensing to ownership, and preferring joint ventures to wholly owned subsidiaries. Like Japan, the governments of India, Mexico, Nigeria, and Tunisia place heavy weight on this consideration. Accordingly, in some countries the manager may not have the full range of choices suggested by Table 1; or if he does, he may have to weigh the differences in political risk associated with the various alternatives against the differences in the other costs and benefits listed in the table.

2. Local partners in some countries are in a position to provide local capital and management more readily than in others. A foreign parent that is in a joint venture with a local partner located in Europe, Japan, or the United States may very well be getting a genuine contribution of capital, management, or information; in Haiti or Ecuador, the contribution would be more problematical

Although some of the factors that determine the manager's choice may be imposed on him by the circumstances in the country he confronts, the manager's choice is likely to be determined even more strongly by the kinds of resources that are already available to his firm and the kind of strategy that the firm is pursuing. A few key propositions have emerged from the studies made so far that offer some guides to an optimum strategy from the manager's point of view:

1. Long overseas experience on the part of a firm goes hand in hand with a preference for wholly owned subsidiaries over joint ventures. It may not be experience itself that causes this tilt, however. Instead, firms with overseas experience may also have readier access to the information, skills, and capital needed to launch a foreign subsidiary. Although local partners in a joint venture may provide information, skills, and capital, the implicit cost to the parent of acquiring these resources from a local partner may be relatively high. In the terms of Table 1, the rankings assigned to capital commitment might still be right; but the absolute size of the differences might be smaller for the more experienced firms, thereby tipping the calculation toward the choice of the wholly owned subsidiary.

2. Where an effective strategy demands that the firm should be able to exercise a high degree of control over its foreign affiliate, the presence of others participating in the direction of the affiliate will be counted as a negative factor, especially if the interests of the others threaten at times to be adverse to those of the parent. Although a licensee or a local partner is likely to share many common interests with the foreign parent, there are also issues over which their interests may conflict. Accordingly, where control is important, a wholly owned subsidiary will be preferred. Control is likely to be important if the firm's strategy, for instance, depends critically on its ability to control the quality of output, the production schedule, or the sales area of a foreign affiliate. In that case, the rankings in Table 1 will reflect absolute values that give heavy weight to these considerations,

thereby tipping the choice toward the wholly owned subsidiary.

Principles such as these suggest that, from the viewpoint of the multinational enterprise, the optimum ownership arrangement may vary from one foreign affiliate to the next. Moreover, from the viewpoint of the multinational enterprise, the optimum ownership arrangement for an affiliate with a given function in a given country may vary over time. When foreign affiliates are set up in protected markets, separated from world competition by high import and high export barriers, a subsidiary's operations often bear very few links to a global strategy. In such cases, joint ventures may not be confining. But as the barriers come down, the utility of the original joint-venture choice is often questioned. If the continuation of the joint venture would interfere with a coordinated global policy relating to the price or quality of a product, or to the choice of location for production, that fact will be counted as a cost to the system.

Of course, a joint venture may break down at some stage not because of its inappropriateness to the foreign parent but because of its inappropriateness to the local partners. Partners that originally thought themselves benefiting from access to a scarce technology or a valued trademark because of their link to a foreign firm may see the value of that link decline as local market conditions change. Developments such as these have commonly led to the end of joint ventures, as well as to the end of licensing arrangements.

Links and strategies

Certain kinds of strategy have been associated with certain kinds of foreign links. That relationship, already evident from some of the examples in the last few pages, can be sharpened a little by thinking back to the various strategies of the multinational enterprises.

The technological lead

According to various studies, firms that place heavy weight on research and development as a basis for their strategy typically adopt two quite different patterns in the creation of foreign links. Those with very narrow product lines lean in one direction; those with broad product lines in another. Firms with a narrow product line, such as IBM or SKF, lean strongly toward wholly owned subsidiaries; firms with a broad product line, such as Sperry Rand, make greater use of joint ventures or licensees. Although it is always a little reckless to jump to conclusions about the factors that lie behind different approaches of this sort, in this case the reason for the distinction seems fairly clear.

Technologically oriented firms with a narrow product line are generally committed to an effort to maintain their lead in a limited, well-defined market. Confined to that market, they have a high stake in maintaining quality standards, in holding their technological skills close to the chest, and in maintaining a tight control over the market strategy to be applied to their few products. The strategic decisions may be relatively few, but each is highly important and each affects the enterprise as a whole. Hence the emphasis on wholly owned subsidiaries.

Technologically oriented firms with a broad product line are generally playing a different game. They see themselves as comparatively efficient at developing technological leads. Because they know such leads are perishable, their strategy is to make the widest possible application of any technological lead that they may develop. Since such leads can be exploited over many products and in many markets, these firms rely upon others to provide the specific market information and the specialized distribution machinery needed to exploit such leads. Hence their willingness to enter into licensing arrangements or joint ventures; the expectation is that such arrangements will represent a more efficient way of acquiring information and achieving distribution than the development of the necessary capabilities internally via a system of wholly owned subsidiaries.

The strong trade name

The same distinction is seen in the use of trade names. In some cases, such as Ford, the trade name is applied to a very narrow range of products, and in others, such as 3M and FMC, to a much broader range. When the trade name is applied to a broad range of products, it is intended to convey only a general aura of reliability, not a narrow and explicit set of expectations about a particular product. Accordingly, firms with a broad product range have a lesser need for tight control of production and marketing. For such firms, therefore, the risks of weakened control associated with operating through joint ventures are more tolerable.

Yet the case of the trade-named product serves to remind the manager that there are more ways to maintain tight controls than through wholly owned subsidiaries. Coca-Cola, for example, is quite relaxed about taking local interests as partners in its foreign bottling plants, because Coca-Cola still controls the vital marketing functions, such as the trade name, the advertising program, the flavor, and the bottles. Exxon, BP, and Shell also are known to be tolerant of such partnerships at the distribution level. In cases such as these, the local joint venture still exists largely at the pleasure of the foreign parent, relying upon the parent for some critical input. When that is the case, managers of the multinational enterprise are in a position to choose their preferred form of foreign link without concerning themselves greatly over the threat of losing control, and can make their choice on the basis of the other considerations listed in Table 1.

The advantages of scale

In industries where firms rely on sheer scale as the barrier to the entry of rivals, as in oil or aluminium, the established firms are likely to give heavy weight to two goals in choosing among different types of foreign links:

1. Achieving stability in the operation of a large capital-intensive facility, including stability in the demand for output.
2. Encouraging an industry structure that will reduce the risk of an outbreak of price competition among the leaders of the industry.

One preference arising out of these considerations already has been noted: multinational enterprises commonly join together as partners to own and operate large capital-intensive facilities such as aluminum smelters, petrochemical complexes, large oil fields, and pipelines. Joint ownership tends to create a common cost structure for the leading firms, a common exposure to risk, and a common vehicle for adjusting supply to demand without upsetting the relative position of the individual firms in the industry.

Downstream from any jointly owned facility, however, each partner is likely to have its own fabricating and distribution network. The preferred patterns of ownership in the downstream facilities depend heavily on how stability of demand can best be assured. If the firm can count on the fact that a joint venture with a local interest will remain tied to the firm's source of supply, such joint ventures may be acceptable and even desired by the firm. If, on the other hand, such joint ventures entail a risk, as is sometimes the case, the firm's need for stability may push it in the direction of favoring wholly owned subsidiaries.

New developments in the 1970 raised the question of whether new types of links might soon appear between the owners of highly capital-intensive installations on the one hand and foreign fabricators or distributors of the product on the other. New state-owned plants were rapidly coming into being in the Middle East, North Africa, Mexico, Brazil, and Venezuela, designed for the fabrication and exportation of petroleum products, aluminum, steel, heavy chemicals, and other such products. Some were joint ventures with the established leaders in the industry, leaders that already owned and managed installations of the same type of other countries. In such cases, active management of the plant often rested in the hands of the established leader despite the existence of a state-owned partner.

In an increasing number of cases, however, the state partners were taking a hand in managing these installations or were grooming themselves for the job. State-owned enterprises in some countries, such as Iran, Algeria, and Venezuela, are in charge of the full range of management decisions, including the foreign marketing decisions. The question in these cases is what organizational link can be established with processing and distributing units in foreign countries that would satisfy the usual strategic needs of stability and cooperation in these industries.

1. One possibility is that the independent state-owned enterprises, lacking organic links to their markets and to the leaders of the industry, will fall into difficulties whenever petroleum and the other products are in easy supply. As suppliers of last resort, they may find their sales falling more rapidly than the sales of their vertically integrated competitors. Although severe price cutting may redress the balance, it would lead to an industry-wide round of reductions that wipe out profits and leave market shares unchanged.

2. Another possibility is that some of the state-owned enterprises will become multinational enterprises in these standardized products, complete with their own processing and distributing facilities in the countries where the output is marketed.

3. A third possibility, more amorphous and obscure, is that some new type of organic link will be forged between the large-scale, capital intensive units and their related downstream facilities in foreign markets, a link that will not involve actual common ownership yet will still allow for the application of unitary strategies that cover the whole vertical system. One special variant of such a strategy finds state-owned enterprises reaching out to other state-owned enterprises in long-term buy-and-sell arrangements that combine the search for stability with a touch of ideology and politics.

The hope in some countries that new institutional forms might be devised that would dispense with the need for relying on multinational enterprises has been encouraged a little by the fact that in the years after World War II the Japanese managed to develop a formidable aluminum smelting, copper refining, and steel industry in Japan without having extensive ownership of the foreign mines that provided the raw materials. In those cases, consortia of Japanese buyers were created, often under the guidance of the Japanese government. The institutional link between the Japanese buyers and the overseas mine owners generally consisted of two elements: (1) a long-term development loan from the Japanese to the foreigners, and (2) a long-term purchase and sale contract.

One feature of these Japanese arrangements, however, suggests that the Japanese case may not prove applicable to other newcomer countries. Practically all the final product of the Japanese fabricating firms until the middle 1970s was being marketed in Japan proper, and the Japanese market was being effectively protected from the competitive imports of other sources. As long as the leading Japanese firms moved together in the prices they paid for their raw materials, their long-term contracts with foreign sources created no intolerable competitive strains inside Japan; thus, for instance, cheaper sources of the raw material developed elsewhere could not greatly affect Japanese firms selling in the Japanese market. It was only as the Japanese market began to open up to foreign sellers that these long-term purchase arrangements began to show strong signs of strain. By the end of the 1970's, the verdict on their durability was not yet in.

Organisation and strategies

The challenge for the manager is to find the form of organization that is most consistent with his strategy. Organization in this sense includes both the structure inside the parent enterprise that is intended to guide and control the multinational network and the structure of the network itself which develops through the choice of foreign links. The problem of developing an appropriate organization is rendered all the more difficult by two considerations:

1. The strategy associated with any given product line is likely to change as the product itself changes and as the market evolves. The direction of these changes may be reasonably predictable; but they still leave the manager with the difficult problem not only of adapting the organization to its current strategic needs but also of allowing for future changes in those needs.
2. The organization appropriate to one product line in an enterprise may be quite different from the organization appropriate to another. The firm that produces both aircraft engines and electric refrigerators may have good reason to produce both; but the organizational requirements for the two lines will be quite different.

Considerations such as these lead at times to the creation of organizations that a appear incredibly complex to the outsider. But these complexities should not deter us from trying to find underlying patterns that contribute to an efficient structure for the multinational enterprise.

First principles

Organizations, it is evident, are created to link the behavior of individuals: to collect and pool information, skills, or capital; to engage in related actions toward the achievement of a set of goals; to monitor performance, initiate corrections, and define new goals.

In the multinational enterprise, three types of building

blocks are almost invariably involved in creating an organization to serve these purposes.

1. *Functions,* which are generally defined as production, finance, marketing, control, personnel, research, and government relations.
2. *Products or product groups,* which are generally grouped according to some key product or market characteristic, so that the items in any such group are more like each other with respect to the key characteristic than like those in any other group.
3. *Countries or areas,* which are generally grouped on the same principle of maximum homogeneity within a class.

In some cases, the strategy of the organization relies so heavily upon one of these three dimensions that the general structure of the organization is almost predetermined.

For instance, the multinational manufacturing organizations that were created by Japanese trading companies depended in their early stages upon two special strengths: a store of information about foreign markets, which the Japanese trading company had developed in the course of its exporting activities; and access to financial resources. As the trading company developed foreign subsidiaries that were engaged in manufacturing, the trading company itself remained intact at the center of the web, reflecting the importance that was attached to maintaining its original functions. Sitting intact at the center, the trading company could continue to perform the financing, search, and control functions. Figure 2-1 portrays the resulting pattern.

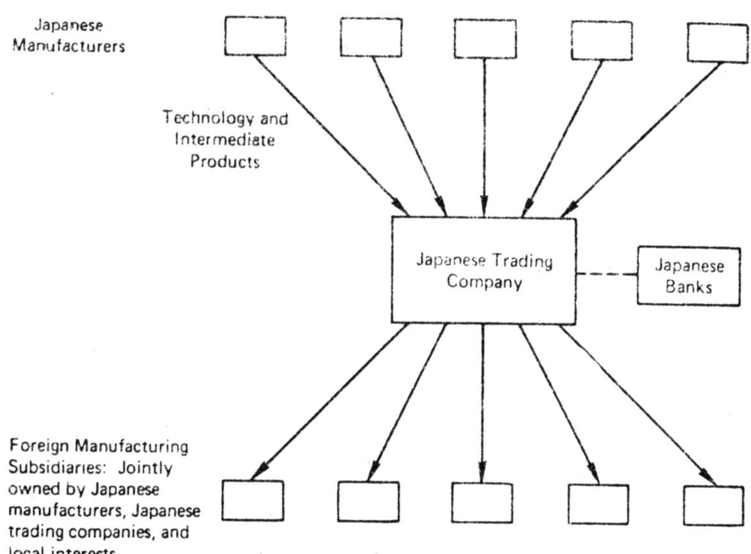

Fig. 4 Schema of a Japanese trading company's multinational structure

Another case of a relatively simple multinational organization is that commonly created by European-based parents, at least until the 1960s, which is structured on a mother-daughter pattern. In these organizations the links between parent and subsidiary were mainly forged at the very top of the organization, between the home president and the overseas president. If staff was involved in any respect in these linkages, the finance staff was more likely to be involved than any other. Outside of the area of finance and below the very top of the hierarchy, very little communication occurred.

The simplicity of these European-based organizations was generally a reflection of the simplicity of the multinational strategy that they pursued. Many of their overseas affiliates had been created under the impetus of some historical factor that had temporarily given the parent an edge. In some cases, the foreign subsidiary had come into existence in the colonial era at a time when the parent could be assured of a favored position in the market. The availability of a trusted manager, such as a family member, and of access to credit at especially favorable terms was sufficient to create a basis for a subsidiary. As long as competition in these distant markets was weak, there were very few stimuli to push the subsidiary and parent toward closer coordination in production, marketing, or research and development. Relations between parent and subsidiary, therefore, were mainly concentrated on two kinds of questions: (1) large strategic choices, involving major questions of expansion or liquidation, and (2) the maintenance of a flow of cash, normally from subsidiary to parent.

But these comparatively simple patterns were transitional forms. In most cases, the strategies of multinational enterprises demanded more complex structures.

A hypothetical approach

Some simple principles of organization are suggested by the Japanese trading organization and the European mother-daughter organization. Picture and enterprise that knows exactly what it wants to do and is only concerned with the appropriate organization for doing it. Assume also that the pattern of needed communication inside the Firm can be more or less foreseen. Think of each message in the pattern as stemming from a source inside the firm and going to a destination inside the firm. Each source and each destination is identified according to the function, product, and country to which it relates. The enterprise sees its activities as breaking down into, say, 6 functions, 8 products, and 10 geographical areas. They the number of points in the communication grid could be though of as 6 x 8 x 10 = 480.

For simplicity, assume further that every message in the organization originates from one of the 480 points and is directed to another of the 480 points. Some points in the communications grid could be expected to have a heavy flow of communication with another, such as plastics-marketing-France with drugs-marketing-France; some will communicate hardly at all, such as plastics-production-France with pesticides-finance-India. The fundamental challenge for the firm is to devise a structure in which the necessary communications can take place with the highest degree of efficiency.

Of course, this formulation of the organizational problem, like any abstract formulation, begs many questions. But it is not a bad starting point in a search for the appropriate organizational structure.

In addition to establishing the 480 points, the manager is also obliged to relate the points in some form of organizational grouping. The grouping will be established on the basis of a number of criteria. But one key criterion will be to handle the efficiency of communication.

Now look at Figure 5. Here we see the case of the firm that has decided to create a series of worldwide product divisions and to organize each product division on a geographical breakdown. Such an organization will mean

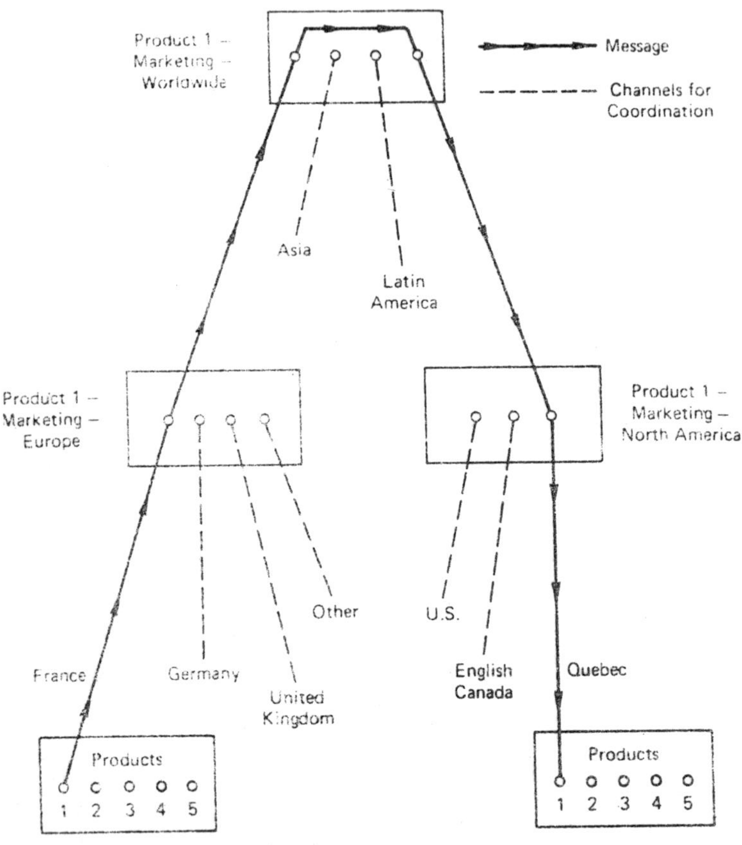

Fig. 5 Assumed path message in multinational enterprise, produt-1-marketing-France to product 1-marketing-Quebec

that when product I-marketing-France communicates with product I-marketing-Quebec, the message remains inside the product 1 division. If it moves in formal channels, it ascends first to Europe, then to Worldwide, whereupon it descends to North America and finally to Quebec. Is this an efficient way for the message to be communicated? To help the firm find the answer to this question, the student has to bear in mind a number of other considerations, which are familiar to specialists in organizational theory:

1. Junctures or nodes will have to be set up where control and coordination take place in the organization. Yet each such node entails a cost; so the efficiency with which communications flow between two points in the organization depends in part on the number of nodes through which the communication must pass from sender to receiver.

2. The cost of passing through a node is a function of the number of channels that the node controls; the larger the number of channels being controlled, the higher the cost of passage. In other words, where the span of control is very wide, the cost of passing through the node is very high.

3. When messages originate and terminate within the same group, they avoid the need to pass through a coordinating node. The length of the journey is thereby shortened. One way of reducing the number of coordinating nodes, therefore, is to enlarge the number of originating points that fall within a single group. This possibility has its disadvantages, however, which derive from the fact that the efficiency of communication within a single group is a function of the size of the group; the larger the group, the lower the efficiency.

These concepts allow one to formulate the organizational problem in the following way: How does one best organize the 6x8x10 = 480 communications points in groups and in coordinating nodes such that the formal channels for communication promise the highest degree of efficiency? Intuitively, one can frame a number of propositions. One of these is that the shape of the optimum organization is greatly influenced by the anticipated pattern of messages. If the common element of identity shared by senders and receivers in an organization is usually the product, then "product" will be used as the principal coordinating category. If the common element of identity is usually the area, "area" will be the principal coordinator.

Responsive to these general propositions, different segments of the organization may be set up in different ways. If the main divisional breakdown of the organization is by product, for instance, some product divisions may be organized quite differently from others. The main breakdown with the "plastics" division could conceivably be functional in nature, whereas the main breakdown in the "drugs" division might be geographical in nature. Everything will depend on the pattern of communications envisaged within each product division.

Typical patterns

So much for introductory principles. In practice, functioning organizations evolve over time by adjusting to visible strain. As strain develops, informal, out-of-channel contacts are generally used at first to deal with the new problem. When the formal adjustment is finally made, it is greatly influenced by the structure that preceded it and by the personalities that have to be accommodated within it.

Despite all the qualifications, however, there have been some visible regularities in the organizational change of multinational enterprises. To understand the nature of

A. Organization with Narrow Product Line

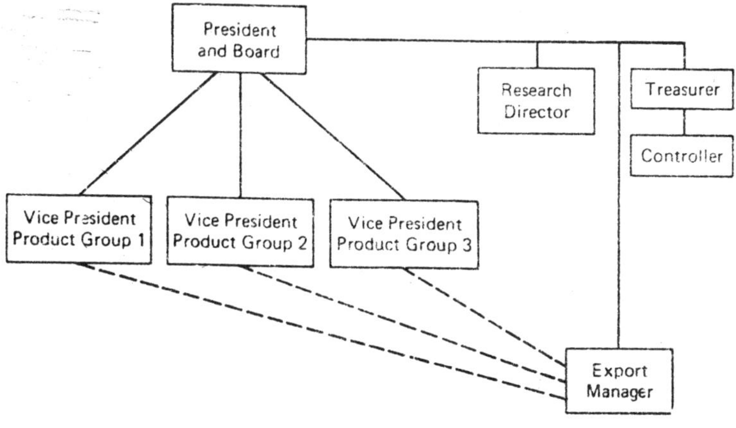

B. Organization with Wide Product Line

Fig. 6 Typical organisation of multinational enterprise before establishment of first overseas manufacturing subsidiary

these regularities and the forces underlying them, one can begin with Figure 6. The figure describes some of the features of two typical organizations before they have embarked on a program of overseas investment. At this stage, the organizations can be thought of as relatively "small" by the standards of multinational enterprises, confined to a few product lines or a few markets, and wrestling with a comparatively limited number of strategic decisions. In organizations of this sort, strategic decisions are typically made by the president, based on the contributions of the vice-presidents. Contact with foreign markets is achieved mainly through exports. An export manager, if he exists, is thought of as an adjunct to marketing, whose principal communication needs are with the marketing vice-president and others in the marketing group.

As the enterprise grows, the diversity of its problems increases. This is especially that case of growth occurs by adding to the number of product lines. At the same time, if the products are increasing, the chances are that the exports of the enterprise will be growing too, perhaps even faster than domestic sales. Out of the growing choice of products, several will have reached a stage of rapid growth in overseas demand. At first, the increased traffic may be handled by an export manager on the pattern suggested in Figure 6.

One key assumption about the communication patterns that lie behind the organization is fairly evident. Those concerned with production and marketing for areas outside the home market, it is assumed, will have more to communicate with one another than with their counterparts in the product groups. This key assumption has been widely made in the first stages of overseas expansion, especially by U.S.- based firms and other firms with large home markets. Typically, however, the production and marketing specialists in the international division find themselves obliged more and more to consult

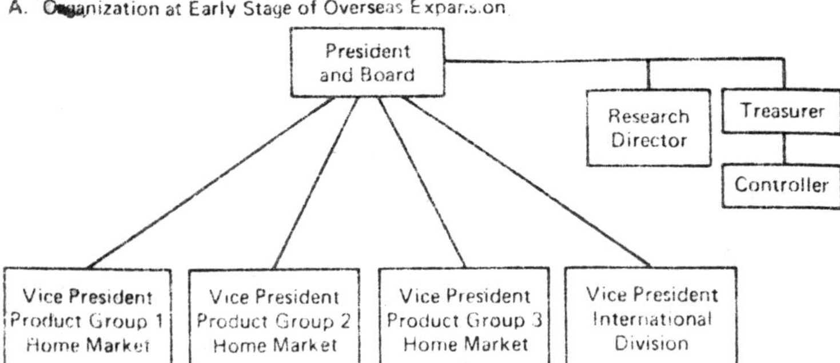

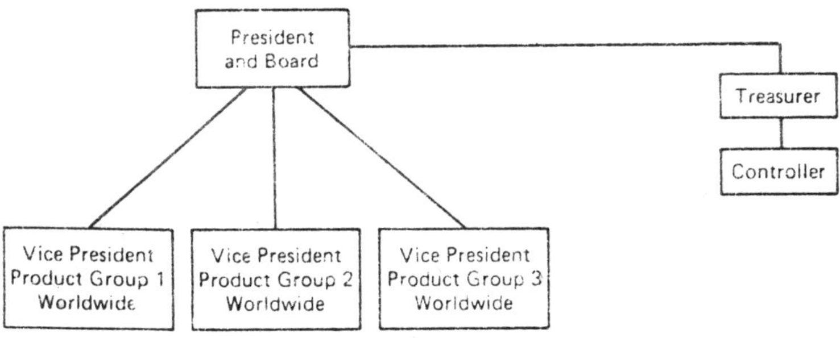

Fig. 7 Typical organisation of multinational enterprise with wide product line after establishment of overseas manufacturing subsidiaries

with their counterparts in the various home product divisions. Information must be exchanged; plans must be coordinated. Accordingly, two sources of strain begin to break the international division apart: (1) the strain of sheer size, creating a problem of declining efficiency in communications within the division, and (2) the strain of a heavy flow of communication with other divisions involving attenuated lines of communication between sender and receiver.

The outcome is to be seen in the short life and high

rate of mortality for international divisions in large, U.S. - based multinational enterprises, and by the similar strains that are beginning to appear in European-based enterprises and Japanese trading companies. As the international division disappears, the product group divisions are concurrently assigned worldwide responsibility for production and marketing. At this stage, too, they may be delegated responsibilities for some or all of their related research activities, which reflects the fact that the communications of the researchers need no longer be directed to two constituents, the international division and the appropriate home product division.

A special point has to be made, however, with regard to enterprises that expand overseas on the basis of comparatively narrow product lines. Enterprises with narrow product lines, such as IBM or Volkswagen, have tended to organize their operations on a highly integrated basis in any region of the world and to link the separate production and marketing facilities of the regions into fairly tight interdependent patterns. Within their regional markets, the pricing practices, trademark practices, quality-control standards, and production patterns of the enterprises are closely related. A plant in one country may be assigned to a specialized task, such as the manufacture of a limited range of components for assembly and sale in a number of contiguous countries. Enterprises of this sort have been relatively slow to adopt a product division organization. Among firms of this sort, for instance, there has been a preference for an organization based on functional divisions. Besides, once such firms have established an international division to handle their overseas business, they have tended to find such a division adequate for a relatively long period of time. Because the

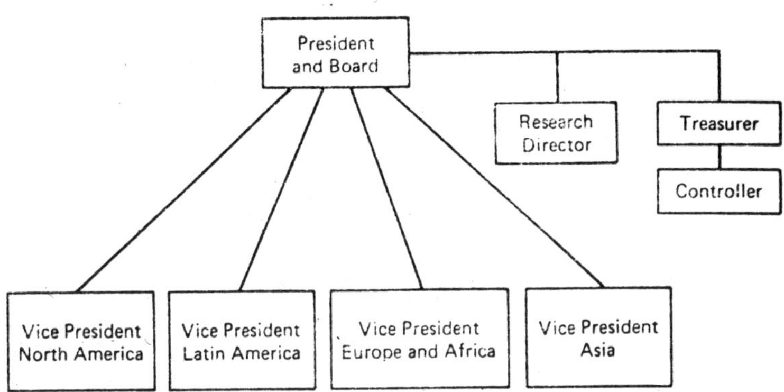

FIGURE 2—5 Typical organization of multinational enterprise with narrow product line at advanced stage of overseas expansion

Fig. 8 Typical organisation of multinational enterprise with narrow product line at advanced stage of overseas expansion

patterns of communication inside such organizations are heavily influenced by affinities of geography rather than by affinities of product, the organizational breakdown between the home market and elsewhere has not been wholly inefficient. Eventually, however, enterprises of this sort based in the United States have been found to break up their non-U.S. interests into regional divisions, to produce the sort of structure depicted in Figure 8.

The elusive balance

Whatever the choice of organizational structure, whether in the directions suggested by Figure 7 or those suggested by Figure 8, the process of coordination and communication seems repeatedly to flush up apparent shortcomings in the structure.

One shortcoming to which U.S.-based firms seem particularly vulnerable arises out of the premature movement of enterprises from the stage A to stage B in

Figure 7. Some studies suggest that, contrary to expectations, a reorganization of that kind sometimes reduces both the interest and the effectiveness of a firm in foreign markets. This result may be traceable to the fact that for most U.S.-based firms, the U.S. home market remains far and away the largest single market of the enterprise. The managers who are designated as worldwide product leader, therefore, often have neither the expertise nor the interest to exploit their opportunities abroad.

Even when an organization avoids that trap, it may fall into others, Organizations structured on product lines find their product groups operating at cross purposes in a given country or region, simply because of the inefficient lines of communication among product groups within each region. Those organized on a regional basis find that the inter regional coordination of product strategy leaves something to be desired.

Operating largely by trial and error, some enterprises have concluded that the most desirable pattern is one that allows for a mixed answer. In organizations of this sort, a few *functions* are coordinated across all products and regions, some *products* are coordinated across all regions; and other products are coordinated primarily by regions.

The financial function, for instance, has typically been a candidate for close coordination across different regions and different products, because money and credit come close to being a fungible resource for the firm; hence, those concerned with the financial function tend to communicate frequently, irrespective of their product and area association. Production, on the other hand, has generally been coordinated on a narrower geographical basis; the production of industrial products with large-scale economies and high transportability have commonly been coordinated regionally, while bulky consumer products have been controlled on a national basis. The personnel function has also been more decentralized to the various national market because wages, working conditions, and labor practices tend to vary by countries. Considerations of this sort have produced organizations of the type shown in Figure 9.

Diagrams such as Figure 9, of course, leave many questions of organization unanswered. One common problem, for example, is how to coordinate the firm's activities within some given geographical territory as the situation requires it. Situations of that sort arise, for instance, when a host government insists on viewing the firm's activities within its territory as a single unit for some regulatory purpose, such as taxation. To deal with that kind of situation, enterprises have sometimes created umbrella committees or umbrella companies which act to pull together the diverse interests of the enterprise in a given territory whenever such action is needed.

The organization shown in Figure 9 needs to deal with other problems as well. In various portions of the chart, for instance, primacy of one dimension of the organization over another is portrayed ambiguously. Within each global product division, for instance, do the managers with regional responsibility have primacy over those with functional responsibility, or does primacy run in the opposite direction? The answer to that question, in practice, can vary from one division to the next; and within any division, can vary according to the type of problem that is being addressed. The various practices in

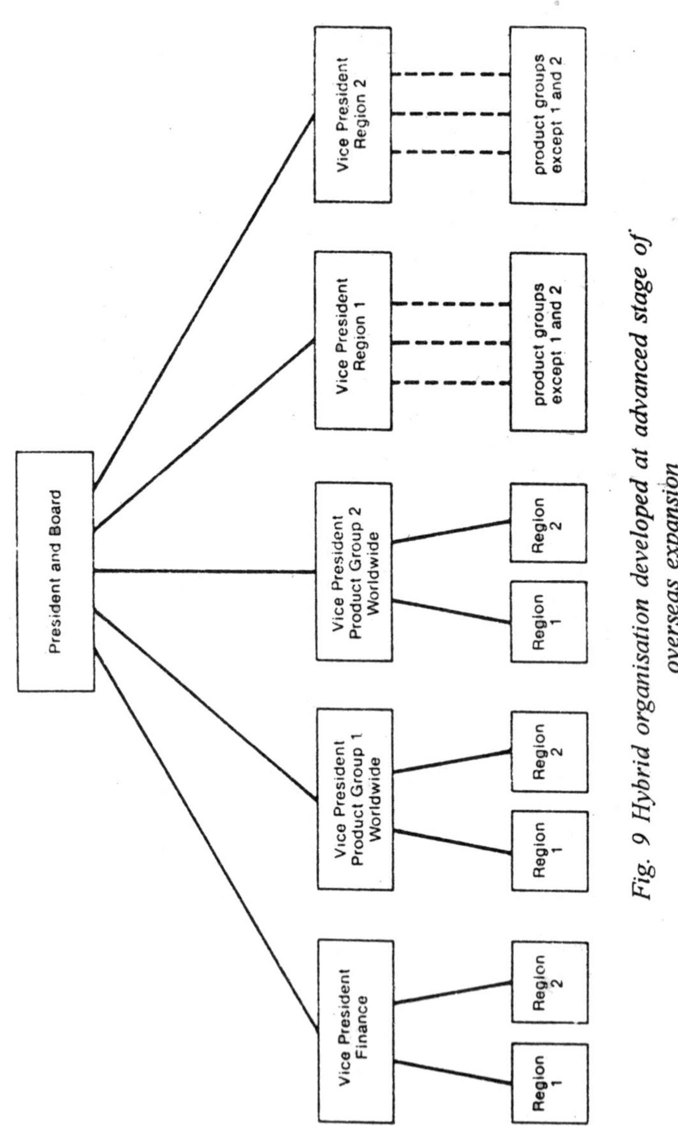

Fig. 9 Hybrid organisation developed at advanced stage of overseas expansion

the firm's operating procedures may be formally codified, or else they may be maintained informally.

The need for coordinating the firm's operations n more than one dimension has also produced on occasion as so-called matrix structure inside the firm's organization. This is a structure in which a given operating unit, say France-paint, reports simultaneously to two superiors—one concerned with all the firm's activities in France, the other concerned with all the firm's activities in paint. In such cases, where the different viewpoints of the two supervisors suggest different course of action for France-paint, it remains for the supervisors themselves to find ways of reconciling their differences.

3

The Competitive Global Business Environment

Evolution of the competitive global business environment

The competitive global environment of the 1990s began evolving after World War II and started to change rapidly in the late 1970s when global firms were organizing. International forces that contributed to the emergence of global firms and the present competitive business environment include:

1. The rise of Japan's and Germany's dominant economies, which supported many of the non-U.S. multinational corporations now responsible for ending American dominance in several world markets.

2. The entrance of newly industrialized countries such as Spain, Taiwan, and Korea, which produce and push low-cost, high-quality commercial products into markets faster that U.S. firms.

3. The convergence of consumer needs and preferences in what Kinichi Ohmae termed the "Triad," which includes the economies of Japan, Europe, and North America—a combined market of 640 million people

with purchasing power. The firms that penetrate and control these markets dominate their global competition. Since 50% of free-world trade is concentrated in the Traid, global films that can mass produce consumer products ahead of the competition will win marketshare.

4. The emergence of other new market economies and blocs in addition to the Triad, such as eastern Europe, the C.I.S., and Canada/United States/Mexico, are also dropping trade barriers, expanding the competitive playing field, and providing new opportunities, rules, and success criteria for competing.

Some of the major competitive success factors of global firms in this emerging global economy include(1) the capability to design, manufacture, and deliver higher quality, innovative products to world markets at lower costs; (2) the ability to deliver products that complete in service and price; (3) just-in-time manufacturing capability to transform innovative ideas into commodities backed up by service; and (4) the ability to be flexibly organized around customers and ;en-users in order to; close the gap between product idea and delivery. The key to global competitiveness is integrated companies that operate on the imperatives of continuous quality improvement, responsiveness, speed, and loose-knit and entrepreneurial structures that collaborate and link the firm to suppliers, competitors, venture capitals, and other resources to focus on targeted markets. These success factors are different from the assembly line, top-down control and manufacturing processes that U.S. firms used right after World War II to dominate markets.

Competitiveness and competition

In a survey of 4,000 *Harvard Business Review* readers in the 50 states, the District of Columbia, Puerto Rico, and 34 other countries, participants responded to the question, "Do you think there is a competitiveness problem?" Their responses showed that 92% believe U.S. competitiveness is deteriorating; 87% believe the problem predates the overvalued 1980s dollar; 95% believe that lowered competitiveness will harm the economic performance of the United States for the foreseeable future; and 89% think the problem is a threat to our standard of living and economic power.

Competitiveness is measured by the four indexes of the Council on Competitiveness: standard of living, productivity, trade, and investment. The annual growth rate from 1982 to 1991 is as follows: Japan 3%, France 2.2%, Germany 1.8%, Britain 1.5%, and the United States 1.1%. The United States has lagged in growth compared with Japan, West Germany, and other major countries. U.S. capital investment as a percentage of gross domestic product dipped below 18% in the mid-1970s and has remained lower than that of Germany and Japan and flat throughout most of the 1980s. Spending on nonmilitary R&D as a percentage of gross national product has also lagged behind Germany and Japan and has been flat since the 1980s.

The changing U.S. trade and budget deficits are partly responsible for our lack of global competitiveness since these deficits (1) raise interest rates, which in turn increase the costs of doing business; and, (2) pull investment dollars away form R&D and plant renovations. The cycle becomes vicious: U.S. companies must pay higher costs to operate because of poor domestic economic conditions, which, in turn, constrain U.S. firms from succeeding at global competition. This is, of course, an oversimplification of a complex problem. Other documented factors that critics argue contribute to this country's low competitive global standing include stodgy managerial habits and organizational structures, and unfocused work cultures; the fixation of American business on short-term profits; pluralistic and antagonistic U.S. systems of government, law, and unions that create a "divide and conquer" environment for American businesses that face united, powerful national industrial strategies of countries like Japan; aging industrial plants and equipment; uncompetitive school systems; and an equalitarian cultural system of values and ideologies that treat foreign competitors on an equal footing with U.S. businesses. These factors are discussed in the following section because they influence the values and practices that govern stakeholder relationships.Multinational Competition: Japan and the United States.

Successful multinational competition in world markets has demonstrated several important lessons: First, corporate competitiveness, as the Japanese have shown, is based on focused and coordinated, government-supported, long-term capitalized blueprint strategies Second, global competitors focus less on piecemeal, random market approaches and more on domination of targeted critical industries and technologies to capture mass markets. Third, there has been an emphasis on low-cost, high-quality products backed by a work force committed to continuous improvement. In this section we compare Japanese with American competitiveness. We focus the discussion on how corporate competitiveness relates to national culture, the government system, and human resources as part of two very different uses of capital. Some Japanese scholars argue that their system of capitalism is unique and different from that of the West.

Interest and debate continue to surround Japan's industrial strategies in winning markets and overtaking U.S. competitors. Since World War II, Japanese companies have leveled, and in some cases dominated, the current playing field in the following industries: consumer electronics, automobiles, semiconductors, machine tools, steel, textiles, and flat-screen computer panels. However, the United States presently maintains its competitive edge in university education, supercomputers, software engineering, artificial intelligence, computer-aided design and engineering, telecommunications, genetic engineering, laser and fiber optics, and high-performance materials. The question that has gained the attention of the media, the White House, Congress, U.S. corporate presidents, and business schools, is, "Why are the Japanese so successful?" Less attention has been given to the question, "At what and at whose costs?" We look at the success factors first.

The success factors behind "Japan, Inc.," as it has been called, are a mix among national cultural values and practices, business/government/political institutional relationships, corporate structures, human resource strategies and uses of capital, and human resource management. The nature and results of these combined relationships make up Japan's unique system of capitalization.

Cultural Characteristics Japan is a homogeneous culture. Maintaining purity of its race is a valued cultural priority. This entitles keeping foreign elements out. The principal values of the Japanese society include; *amaze*, *on*, *giri*, and *ninjo* begins early in human development and continues throughout adulthood. It is this feeling that underlies adults' emotional attachment to each other, the group, the corporation, and even state. *On* involves obligations hat the recipient is indebted to repay. *Giri* relates to moral obligations that are mutual within a collectivity. *Ninjo* refers to what people prefer to do as well as what they believe they must avoid doing because of status or group membership. Maintaining harmony in the family, the group, the work organization, and the state is the theme around which these values revolve.

The family, household, and group form the center of the Japanese social structure. Individualism and standing out from the group are not valued. Respect and veneration for authority and interpersonal relationships are also highly valued. All of the above values and characteristics are shared by the society and are reflected in all major Japanese institutions, including corporations. Teamwork, consensus decision making, and a holistic concern for employees are all based and supported in these cultural values.

The veneration of authority in vertical relationships is also a central part of the Japanese culture. This relationship begins at home and is found in informal and work groups. Authority and respect in such relationships is absolute. leaders are expected to show leadership characteristics, such as wisdom, vision, sympathy, and unselfishness. This tradition is based on the Confucian system of ethical conduct and was passed on in the ideologies and practices of the Samurai.

Sociopolitical context: The sociopolitical context of

Japanese institutions can be summarized as an interdependent network of shared values, strategies, and traditions. Economic power has historically been—and continues to be—shared by government and business. This relationship was further cemented after World War II when the government actively sought to rebuild and support business growth. Government, unlike in the United States, Coordinates business activities through long-term planning and industrial policy and manages businesses that are in trouble. also, top-level government officials are generally well educated and respected and exercise powerful decisions in business activities. One of the most powerful agencies of Japan's six "economic bureaucracies" is MITI, the Ministry of International Trade and Industry. This agency shares significant power with private enterprises. This is especially the case, since MITI, like the other ministries, provides financial assistance and guidance to corporations. It is working partnership.

Even though Japan's political system is a democracy, it is best characterized as semifeudal in nature. Because Japan never experienced a "people's revolution," the political system has few shared traditions with the public. Political parties compete for power and privileges, status, and positions within the ministries. Consequently, "Wheeling and dealing, bribery, coercion, collusion, threats and violence. In effect, the power and authority of the political system is ineffective in controlling business activity to protect the public. Scandals are discovered after the fact, and attempts are made to have business and political crises quickly resolved.

It should also be noted that Japan's social system focuses on the commercialization of knowledge. Japan's industries and companies are interweaved with government to the extent that business activities are rewarded, as these bring returns on investment to the society—more so than to any single individuals.

Industrial groups: *Keiretsu* Against this cultural and political background are embedded the powerful *keiretsu*, oligopolistic firms networked together in industrial cartels. To understand the success of the Japanese competitive enterprise is to understand the *keiretsu* and its strategies and use of capital . The *keiretsu* are the inheritors of the post-World War II zaibatsus, economic monopolies started by powerful families and broken up by the American occupation. *Zaibatsus* were holding companies with large stock ownership in core companies. Each *zaibatsu* was controlled by a family trust. The core companies included manufacturing enterprises, a bank, a trust company, an insurance firm, and several smaller companies. *Keiretsu* are organized around the former *zaibatsu*.

The six dominant *keiretsu* include Mitsubishi, Sumitomo, Mitsui, Fuji, Sanwa, and DKB. As of 1980, these six groups accounts for 18% sales, 14% corporate profits, and 6% employment in Japan. BY 1992, the *keiretsu* accounted for almost a quarter of Japan's total business assets and revenues. The *keiretsu* share stock ownership with the large firm holding equity, its suppliers, and the suppliers holding equity in the main company. They are interlocking partnerships and allies.

At the center of each *keiretsu* is a bank or cash-rich company that offers low-cost capital. Stocks are held mostly by other companies, therefore allowing managers to plan and operate on long-term market domination goals.

The largest manufacturer in the *keiretsu* dictates everything from prices to terms of delivery to the hundreds of suppliers that are bound to it. These cartels, then, have ready available capital from their member companies, from the bank in their group, and from government funds to target and exploit any market or technology on the globe.

Japanese capitalism: The *keiretsu* make up the industrial or business segment of Japan's unique system of communal capitalism, as depicted in Figure. This system is summarized as follows: (1) There are close alliances between government and business. These intimate relationships allow prices to be controlled, strategic industries to be targeted for growth, and the regulation of industry through fuzzy guidelines instead of rules, which also serve to keep outsiders out. If you do not understand the rules, you cannot play in the games, (2) The *keiretsu* control Japan's business interests. Cartels enable business groups to coordinate and focus capital from banks, the government, and other sources to obtain strategic global marketshare. (3) In the *keiretsu* system, the role of independent shareholder is, as stated above, weakened, since three quarters of Japanese companies' stocks are held by other firms. Consequently, Japanese managers concentrate on investing in long-term R&D projects and in competing for a long-term marketshare instead of meeting short-term quarterly profits. (4) The relationship between Japanese workers and their firms is also different in this capitalist system. Lifetime employment, consensual decision making, collective implementation of responsibilities, a slow evaluation and promotion system, informal and implicit control by peer groups and cultural norms, nonspecialized career paths, and a holistic concern for employees all mark different human resource practices than those found in the West. Taken together, these four components of the Japanese capitalistic system present a formidable force in competing against countries and companies that are less organized and that have less infrastructural support.

Capitalism Japanese-Style

	Government-Industry Ties
Benefits:	Protects failing industries, nurtures growth industries
Drawbacks:	Distorts market prices, hinders newcomers' entry
	Keiretsu
Benefits:	Relationships between companies allow high-risk sharing, access to capital and technology
Drawbacks:	Excluded companies have trouble competing
	Corporate Loyalty
Benefits:	High productivity and quality, stable work force and top management team
Drawbacks:	Excessive employee obedience and dependence limits time for socializing and leisure.
	Few Outside Shareholders
Benefits:	Managers don't need to focus on short-term results
Drawbacks:	Managers don't feel shareholder accountability

Ethical issues with Japanese management and capitalism
The Japanese management system has demonstrated superior performance in global markets. As with other countries, the management is embedded in the culture and in the capitalist system. At a closer view, this system does have problems. Workers lack individual freedom in the militaristic, rigid systems of control. Substandard wages, unsafe working conditions, and discrimination against women and temporary workers are also some of the more

prominent moral issues in the Japanese management system. Lack of incentives for creativity and innovation are also a result of the consensus-oriented, conformist work group structure.

Lifetimė employment is not a benefit shared equally by all; it is, in practice, more a function the prosperity of the industry and firm. Most employees retire at age 55; in firms that are more successful, 58 is the retirement age. Moreover, retirement benefits are minimal. Wnen forced into retirement, as is more often the case in larger firms, many retirees have financial difficulties.

Lifetime employment is believed to be given to 35% to 40% of the work force; that number is 40% to 60% in larger manufacturing firms and trading houses. Recession and other economic downturns are also affecting lifetime employment practices. Layoffs have occurred and are occurring in Japanese firms. It is also important o note that women are excluded from the lifetime employment benefit. Moreover, women often take more menial jobs than do men.

Long and exhausting working hours with little leisure or time off is another problem in the Japanese management system. Quality of work life has been a foreign concept to Japanese workers. Government agencies are studying how to maintain high performance while building more leisure attitudes and time into the work force.

Problems with Japanese capitalism: As recent stock market upheavals have shown, Japanese capitalism is not immune from the risky investments of the 1980s or from economic downturns. Institutional ownership of stock does not protect falling value of investments.

At a system level, problems have evolved with Japanese capitalism from an international perspective. Japan's $1 trillion current-account surplus has caused critics to question Japan's trade policies and practices. Japanese companies, for example, have been caught and fined for price fixing and dumping products in the computer and electronic consumer products industries in the United States.

Critics also claim that the *keiretsu* oligopolies do not go after marketshare only; they strategically target U.S. industries to dominate and ultimately put them out of business. Critics have accused Japan of practicing "predatory capitalism" in a military, warlike fashion. Japanese automobile and computer firms, for example, surrounded designated U.S. companies and deliberately seek to dominate and control these industries and firms by moving in the *keiretsu* manufacturing, finance, technology, and component suppliers with the aim of lowering prices until the competitors cannot compete on price or quality. The U.S. auto parts industry is one example. Although U.S. auto parts are world-class leaders in price and quality, the industry has failed in selling parts to Japanese automakers in Japan and in the United States. Why? One response follows:

> A number of academic studies have demonstrated that Japanese multinational companies don't act like other multinational companies when they go overseas. They are far less likely to buy local parts and equipment and to hire local people for high management positions than are European and American multinationals, and they are far more likely to give most of their business to other Japanese companies.

Former President Bush's now-memorable trip to Japan was an attempt to convince Japanese automakers in the United States to double their purchases from U.S. suppliers from $7 billion in 1990 to $15 billion by 1994. Some have argued that this agreement represents "managed trade" and argue that Japan's markets for critical technologies and products remain closed.

Some of the criticisms of Japan's industrial and trade practices may be unfounded. Defenders of Japanese capitalism and competitiveness claim that U.S. industries and companies are not accustomed to being second best or less successful than the Japanese. Holbrooke stated that, "accepting a more assertive and independent Japan will prove difficult for many American, who have come to regard Japan as a junior partner on most important foreign policy issues." It is also argued that American industries that are conservative and unwilling to change management practices are to blame for lack of competitiveness, not Japan. It is also pointed out that without Japanese investment and manufacturing operations in the United States, Americans would suffer even more, since competitors from other countries would pose similar threats to our standard of living and industrial weaknesses.

The debate countries over whether and to what extent Japan is competing fairly in international markets. Is Japan combining protectionist trade practices, price fixing, and predatory tactics with legitimate *keiretsu* strategies to dominate U.S. and other global prize industries such as auto, electronics, and semiconductors? Is Japan simply playing by the rules of the countries in which it does business and capitalizing on industry and corporate weaknesses and trade loopholes? The moral and industrial challenge for Japan will be its ability to maintain its productivity while competiting in other countries in ways that are politically and legally compatible with other capitalist systems.

American capitalism and management

The American capitalist and management systems differ significantly from those in Japan. In this section we summarize some of the major themes already alluded to in other parts of the book, namely, dominant characteristics of American national culture, government, and the corporate management system. Our aim is to compare U.S. uses of capitalism with Japanese uses and to discuss the problems of American capitalism in the global arena.

Cultural context: America is a country of countries. Gareau argued that historically and culturally there are nine nations in North America. As such, America is an ethnically diverse society in which distinctive traditions and customs coexist and share the following common values: individualism, self-reliance, self-dicipline, and Protestant-influenced work ethic, the value of private property, and the belief in fairness and individual rights. Some argue that the Protestant work ethic has undergone significant change. Preoccupation with self has developed into narcissism, and justice is being defined as fairness.

Individual rights and ownership of private property are at the center of the American value system. The Declaration of Independence focuses on rights as *inalienable*. Ownership of private property reinforces individualism in the social fabric. Americans also value family and collective group membership. Group membership, however, is based more on voluntarism than cultural norms. The distinction between American and Japanese values is apparent. Japan is essentially a collective, group-oriented culture, whereas American values center on self and individualism. These value differences are reflected in the way American businesses reward and recognize individual entrepreneurs and inventors. Knowledge as it is patented and protected legally is the private property of the individual, not of the society, as is the case with Japan. In Japan the individual is not considered the focal point of industrial innovation or success.

Sociopolitical and government context: The United States is a pluralistic political and government system. The Constitution grounds ultimate authority in the people and separates power among the executive, legislative, and judicial branches of government. Within this pluralistic system, government, business, and unions share power and solve problems through an adversarial relationship. Cooperation must continually be negotiated through advocacy, argument, and special interest and political action group lobbying.

Competition and fragmentation are built into the system, the very infrastructure of government and politics. Federal and state governments compete over the power of budgets, policies, and resources. For example, the national government lacks an industrial policy for the country, and the states develop their own and compete with each other for domestic–and foreign investment. Iowa has used a handsome tax incentives to convince Japanese auto manufactures to build and operate along Interstate 1-75. At the same time, Detroit automakers have unsuccessfully lobbied the president to adopt some form of a broad national industrial policy to limit Japanese auto imports and manufacturing in the United States. While Japan operates in global markets as a united front through combined government, unions, and *keiretsu* cooperation and strategies, the United States operates in a piecemeal, state-by-state, corporation-by-corporation manner. As one U.S. auto parts manufacturer commented onthe comparison of American and Japanese business practices, "Japan is blueprint; the United States is an event."

American capitalism: American capitalism is based on the ideology of "free-market enterprise." Large business corporations have in the past embodied and modeled the wealth and success of the American business enterprise and therefore have defined the rules of the capitalist system. Larger corporations obtain equity capital from private investors and capital markets. These institutions compete among themselves and with the government for funds. Unlike the Japanese example, U.S. banks are not permitted to buy stock in corporations; this helps to prevent conflicts of interest. Also unlike Japanese *keiretsu*, the government is more often than not the watchdog and regular of business growth and activity—not the strategic partner. The U.S. corporation, then, must depend on the attractiveness of its stock on the open market to survive and succeed.

Because most of the larger corporations sell shares to the public, the stock market defines the health of a firm. The trading price of a company's shares also determines the firm's ability to obtain capital and resources to grow and innovate. Corporations, then, walk a tightrope between their debt and equity in their capital structure. "A highly leveraged company is more risk prone and must pay a higher cost for funds unless its growth prospects are phenomenal and investors are willing to assume above-average risks".

Consequently, U.S. corporations are continuously monitored by the public and shareholders. The trading price of a company's stock, the quarterly earnings reports, its profit and loss statements, and the perception of a firm by financial markets all define American capital as a short-term, price-sensitive enterprise. For American managers, unlike their Japanese counterparts, this means that short-term planning, investing strategies are the rules and boundaries by which managers can operate. This system is currently being pressured by global competition and the changing nature of international markets to change.

American management practices: In practice, the American management system is not a single system. American entrepreneurs have not followed—and probably will not follow—any single set of rules for borrowing, inventing, investing, or doing business. However, there is a historical background of management systems and thought that, again, larger and more traditional corporations have embodied and followed.

Although entrepreneurial firms differ from larger, older ones, and although there are a variety of management system and changing styles in the United States, we can still make certain generalizations about American management practices, as these have been historically grounded in the dominant value system, as these have been historically grounded in the dominant value system, the sociocultural context, the business/ government relationship, and the America form of capitalism. These generations include an emphasis on (1) short-term time, profit, planning, and strategy horizons based on some of the cultural and sociosystem background factors explained above; (2) individual decision making, responsibility, performance, and rewards; (3) the manager having been understood, trained, and treated as a professional separate from any specific knowledge base; (4) outcomes over process, measured and monitored by short-term financial tools; (5) specialized and vertical career paths; and (6) individual career development. These characteristics are familiar, since they have been addressed in management literature and journals.

American management practices have also been greatly influenced by the school of *scientific management*, proposed by Frederick Taylor at the turn of the century. Taylor separated managers from workers and viewed managers as having a professional status; he articulated a logical for making and maintaining a division of labor and a chain of command; he laid the basis of building organizational structures to carry out separate tasks; and he defined work and management so that both could be measured and executed "scientifically," in a cost-benefit, compartmentalized, individualistic, and piecemeal way.

The legacy of scientific management left us with the stovepipe organization and isolated, specialized management functions. The artificial division of worker from manager, top-down decision making, and the eventual need for unions to advocate benefits for alienated and economically disadvantaged workers from management were also set in motion. Productivity was defined apart from the enterprise's mission and more on an individual piece-rate basis. Attention to process was lost. These are components of American management that are being ripped apart by global competition and the changing rules of knowledge technology as it replaces the linear assembly line.

Problems with American capitalism and management: The American capitalist system's short-term overemphasis on financially measured corporate growth and returns has not been successful when compared with the Japanese *keiretsu* system. Not only have the Japanese mastered process technology, total quality, continuous improvement, and just-in-time inventory and management techniques for getting product ideas to market in one-third less time than U.S. competitors, but they have a head start of several decades in doing so. Moreover, our adversarial system of pluralistic competition and governance is still intact. The relationship pluralistic competition and governance is still intact. The relationship along government, business, and unions is still politically divisive.

Among the most prominent problems with America's lagging competitiveness have been the blindspots—the inability of American managers to recognize the importance and prowess of international competition. The results of the 1989 Korn/Ferry—Columbia study, "Reinventing the CEO," stated,

> it is troubling that the executives of most U.S. corporations, perhaps by virtue of minimal international exposure, discount the importance of an international outlook. What is most disturbing is that they do not acknowledge this liability, and so risk selecting a successor with the same narrow vision.

The U.S. legal system may also be part of the problem of America's competitiveness. While antitrust and other regulatory laws effectively controlled monopolies in this country at the turn of the century, these same laws are impeding the ability of American firms to form *keiretsu* like coalitions to compete with the Japanese. Like professional managers, lawyers have mushroomed. The United States has 307.4 lawyers per 100,000 people, compared with Britain's 102.7, Germany's 82, and Japan's 12.1. In 1971, the United States had 355,242 lawyers compared with 750,000 in 1990 and a projected 1 million by 2000. In 1984, there were 14.1 million state court filings; by 1990, that number reached 18.4 million. Moreover,the legal costs U.S. companies pay could be spent in R&D and other competitive pursuits. For example, Dow Chemical spends more than $100 million a year on legal services and liability insurance. The question arises, How much law and how many lawyers are necessary in the United States to do what, for whom, at what and at whose costs? Presently, many companies are hiring dispute settlement professionals to lower legal costs.

Given these observations, it is important to note that the global competitive game is just beginning. The European Community market is just beginning to take off. U.S.-based multinationals are also competing with German, French, Italian, Swiss, and other European multinational competitors in the new global marketplace.

Because many larger corporations and traditional industries are losing competitiveness in the emerging global market, traditional and questionable U.S. management practices of governance and leadership have also come under scrutiny. The public is morally as well as economically eroding, the effectiveness of our school system is challenged, the role of government and politicians is questioned, out standard of living is deteriorating, and there is uncertainty about whether America will be a technology and manufacturing leader in the future or an assembler and distributor of other nations' innovative products. The effectiveness of our entire system of business, government, education, research and development, and production has been challenged. Immoral conduct and practices in government, business, education, and other American institutions are likely to be less tolerated by the public in such a deteriorating economic and competitive environment.

Steps to regaining competitiveness

Not all U.S. companies are stodgy and uncompetitive. Some of the more entrepreneurial flagship American firms include Sun Microsystems, Intel, Angen, Wal-Mart, Federal Express, and Microsoft, to name a few. While there are no magical formulas for reinventing U.S. competitiveness, there are many guidelines suggested directions the U.S. corporate enterprise and governance system should take.

Changes in corporate governance: The unusually high salaries, benefits, and perks of CEOs and the role of corporate boards of directors, shareholders, and top-level managers are being questioned, especially in companies that are not performing. Changes are being made. The General Motors board of directors startled the corporate world by cutting former CEO Stempel's salary by one third and by closing plants and shedding thousands of workers. This move may shake up other corporate boards and move them to against waste and corruption, toward more entrepreneurial policies and practices.

American Keiretsu U.S. firms in industries that have been competiting head-one with Japanese *keiretsu* have realized that the competition is too great to got it alone. As a result, U.S. firm have been forming their own kind of *kiretsu*. Ford has been focusing on its automotive and financial-services business through the strategies of acquisitions, equity holdings, international linkages, and research consortiums. In its vehicle assembly business, for example, Ford has a 25% equity stake in Mazda, 10% in KIA Motors in Korea, 75% in Aston Martin Lagonda and 48% in Iveco Ford Truck of Britain, and 48% in Autolatina in Brazil and Argentina. Fod also is a member of eight R&D consortiums that investigate environmental issues and other innovative projects. Ford also has partners in its parts, production, financial services, and marketing business. IBM also is becoming a kind of American *keiretsu*.

In the 1980s U.S. industries created over 250 R&D consortiums. The federal government has funded $120 million to Detroit's automakers to work jointly on a new battery technology for electric cars. Finally, U.S. firms are following the strategy, "If you can't beat them, join them." Detroit's auto manufacturers and U.S. computer firms have several strategic alliances and joint ventures with their Japanese counterparts. Ford has aligned with Mazda, Mitsubishi in Japan. Chrysler also aligned with Mitsubishi. GM is in an alliance with Suzuki. Honeywell and Nippon Electric of Japan share business dealings, and IBM and Matsushita are partners.

Reinventing American management practices A number of books and studies have offered suggestions for improving U.S. productivity and competitiveness. Among the most notable is Dertouros, Lester, and Solow's *Made in America: Regaining the Productive Edge.* Steiner and Steiner use this source, among others, to summarize the following points offered for U.S. firms: (1) Think globally; (2) balance short-term and long-term thinking; (3) implement global strategy; (4) give high priority to the improvement of production processes; and (5) improve human resource management. Also, government should focus on public policies that strengthen science and technology advantages and increase tax credit for R&D projects.

W. Edwards Deming, the American management guru who, when shunned by the U.S. corporate establishment after World War II, turned to Japan to impart total quality management, continuous productivity improvement, and statistical system control methods. Deming is, after the last four decades, welcomed back by American firms.

American entrepreneurship is also a driving force that our industrial leaders are striving to reward and maintain in the midst changing corporate structures and manufacturing techniques. The challenge is not how to become like the Japanese or any other management system. We cannot. The challenge is how to adopt successful elements from worldclass management systems to our entrepreneurial business practices.

There are no quick fixes that will turn the U.S. economy and corporations back to global competitiveness. Some argue that the United States will never again command the scope and extent of global control of manufacturing and production power it had after World War II; the world economy and politics are too complex and competitive. The United States should, therefore, assume its competitive and cooperative place within thin new economic system. Still, to do so requires the momentous changes, many of which are occurring now, and a major question remains: "Can the U.S. afford to maintain its democratic and Constitutional principles in the face of less-principled international business practices?"

Modified American Management System Based on integration of American and Japanese Practices

	Type A (American)	Type J (Japanese)	Type Z (Modified American)
Employment	Short-term	Lifetime	Long-Term
Decision making	Individual	Consensual	Consensual
Responsibility	Individual	Collective	Individual
Evaluation	Rapid evaluation	Slow evaluation and promotion	Slow evaluation and promotion
Control	Explicit, formulized	Implicit, informal	Implicit, informal with explicit, formalized measures
Career path	Specialized	Nonspecialized	Moderately specialized
Concern for employees	Segmented	Holistic	Holistic

Multinational enterprises as stakeholders

Multinational enterprises (MNEs) are corporations that "own or control production or service facilities outside the country in which they are based". MNEs are also referred to as global, transnational, and international companies.

While MNEs often reflect and extend their home nation's culture and resources, many act as independent nations. This selection focuses on MNEs as independent, powerful stakeholders, using their power across national boundaries to gain comparative advantages, with or without home country support. Common characteristics that MNEs share include (1) operating a sales organization, manufacturing, distribution center, licensing, and/or subsidiary in at least two countries; (2) earning an estimated 25% to 45% of revenue from foreign markets; and (3) having common ownership, resources, and global strategies. since MNEs often span nations, governments, and different types of businesses and markets, their operations are based on a shared network of strategies, information and data, expertise, capital, and resources. MNEs have become the most strategically powerful stakeholders in the race to compete and dominate global industry marketshares.

Many MNEs are more economically powerful than the nations in which they do business. For example, IBM operates in over 126 countries, communicates in 30 languages, runs 23 foreign plants, and obtains over one half its total net income from its foreign business. The 10 largest U.S.-based MNEs in terms of export sales dollars are shown in Figure. Figure lists the 10 largest MNEs headquarters outside the United States. Of these foreign-based multinationals, seven are located in Western Europe and three are located in Japan. America's largest international exporters, as shown in Figure, include Boeing, GM, CE, Ford, IBM, Chrysler, E.I. Du Pont, United Technologies, McDonnell Douglas, and Caterpillar. The foreign-sales share of total sales for the world's largest MNEs, once estimated at one fourth, is now closer to 40%.

The dominant goal of MNEs is to make a profit. Corporations expand and do business across national boundaries to take comparative advantage of marketing, trade, cost, investment, labor, and other factors. At the same time, MNEs assist local economies in many ways, as will be explained below. The ethical questions that critics of MNEs have raised are reflected in the following statement by the noted Harvard professor, Raymond Vernon: "Is the multinational enterprise undermining the capacity of nations to work for the welfare of their people? Is the multinational enterprise being used by a dominant power...as a means of penetrating and controlling the economies of other countries?" We address these questions in the following discussion of mutual responsibilities and expectations of MNEs and their host countries.

Recent crises since the birth of the multinational corporation after World War II have raised international concern over the ethical conduct of MNEs in host and other countries. For example, Union Carbide's chemical spill in Bhopal, India, which resulted in thousands of deaths and injuries, alarmed other nations over questionable safety standards and controls of MNE foreign operations. Nestle's marketing of its powered infant milk formula that resulted in disease and death of a large number of infants in underdeveloped countries raised questions over the lack of proper product instructions issued to poorer, less-educated consumers. Also, the presence of MNEs in South Africa raises criticisms over the role of large corporations in actively supporting apartheid or government-supported racism. Because MNEs have to pay taxes to the South African government, and because apartheid is a government-supported policy, MNEs—it is argued—support racism. Several U.S.based MNEs that operated in South Africa witnessed boycotts and disinvestment by many shareholders. Many MNEs, including IBM and Polaroid, withdrew. Another long-standing moral issue is the practice of MNEs not paying their fair share of taxes in countries where they do business and in their home countries. Through the process of transfer pricing and other creative accounting techniques, many MNEs have shown paper losses—thereby enabling them to avoid paying any taxes. We discuss the ethical concerns that surrounded MNEs in the following overview of two perspectives relating to the arguments for an the criticism of MNE presence in host countries.

MNE perspective

The MNE enters a foreign country primarily to make it profit. MNEs expand globally for a number of reasons; for example, they seek to benefit from currency fluctuations, more available and cheaper labor costs, tax and trade incentives, and use of natural resources. They also hope to gain access to more foreign markets and to create or maintain competitiveness.

MNEs benefit their host countries through foreign direct investment (FDI). Through their direct investment and presence, MNEs (1) attract local capital to projects; (2) provide for and enhance technology transfer; (3) develop particular industry sectors; (4) intensify competition in the country by introducing new products, services, and ideas; and (5) help decrease the country's debt and improve its balance of payments and standard of living. Moreover, MNEs open less developed countries (LDCs) to international markets, thereby helping the local economy to attract greatly desired hard currencies. Also, new technical and managerial skills are brought in and local workers receive training and knowledge. Job and social class mobility is provided to inhabitants. Some MNEs also introduce schools, colleges, and hospitals to their host countries.

The MNE must manage overlapping and often conflicting multiple constituencies between and in its home and host country operations. Figure illustrates some of the major environments and stakeholder issues that must be technically and ethically balanced and managed by the MNE in its foreign location. From the MNE's perspective, managing these stakeholders issues is difficult and challenging, especially as the global economy presents new problems.

MNE executives and managers also complain of what they consider unethical practices and arbitrary control of host country governments. For example, local governments can and sometimes do (1) limit repatriation of assets and earnings of MNEs; (2) pressure and require MNEs to buy component parts and other materials from local suppliers; (3) require MNEs to use local nationals in upper-level management positions; (4) require MNEs to produce and/or sell selected products in order to enter the country; (5) limit imports and pressure exports; and (6) require a certain amount or percentage of profit to remain or be invested in the country. Finally, MNEs always face the threat of expropriation or nationalization of their operations by the host government.

Host country perspective

Arguments critical of the presence and practices of MNEs in host and other foreign locations include the following (1) MNEs dominate and protect their core technology and research and development, thus keeping the host country as a consumer, not a partner or producer. For example, the Brazilian government has entry barriers and laws that have protected the complete control of its own electronics industries from foreign manufacturers since the 1970s. It is also argued that Japan could in the long-term dominate certain critical industries in the United States, and use American labor more as assemblers rather than technology

R&D partners, (2) MNEs destabilize national sovereignty by limiting a country's access to critical capital and resources, thereby creating a dependency of governments and politics on the MNE. (3) MNEs create a "brain drain" by attracting scientists, expertise, and talent from the host country. (4) MNEs create an imbalance of capital outflows. MNEs create production but emphasize exports over imports in the host country, thereby leaving local economies dependent on foreign control. (5) MNEs disturb and disrupt local government economic planning and business practices by exerting control over the development and capitalization of a country's infrastructure. Also, by providing higher wages and better working conditions, a country's traditions, values, and customs are influenced and changed. "Cultural imperialism" is imported through business practices. (6) MNEs sometime destroy, pollute, and endanger host and underdeveloped countries' environments and the health of local populations. For example, the mining of and dangerous exposure to asbestos continues in some LDCs and in Canada.

Obviously, these criticisms do not apply to all MNEs. These criticisms represent concerns of host and underdeveloped country government that have suffered abuses from multinationals over the decades. Tensions in the relationships between MNEs and host countries and other foreign governments, especially in more underdeveloped settings, endure. Whenever the stakes for both parties are high, so will be the pressures to negotiate the most profitable and equitable benefits for each stakeholder. Often, it is the uneducated, poorer inhabitants of underdeveloped nations who suffer the most from the operations of MNEs.

MNE guidelines for managing morality

Guidelines for managing ethical conduct have received detailed attention and work over the past for decades in the areas of consumer protection, employment, environmental pollution, human rights, and political conduct. The driving forces behind the development of these published guidelines include the United Nations, the International Labor Office, and the Organization for Economic Cooperation and Development.

The underlying normative include the beliefs in (1) national sovereignty, (2) social equity, (3) market integrity, and (4) human rights and fundamental freedoms.

The following MNE guidelines are summarized under the categories of employment practices and policies, consumer protection, environmental protection, political payments and involvement, and basic rights and fundamental freedoms.

Employment practices and policies

- MNCs should not contravene the manpower policies of host nations.
- MNCs should respect the right of employees to join trade unions and to bargain collectively.
- MNCs should develop nondiscriminatory employment policies and promote equal job opportunities.
- MNCs should provide equal pay for equal work.
- MNCs should give advance of changes in operations, especially plant closings, and mitigate the adverse effects of these changes.
- MNCs should provide favorable work conditions, limited working hours, holidays with pay, and protection against development.

- MNCs should promote job stability and job security, avoiding arbitrary dismissals and providing severance pay for those unemployed.
- MNCs should respect local host country job standards and upgrade the local labor force through training.
- MNCs should adopt adequate health and safety standards for employees and grant them the right to know about job-related health hazards.
- MNCs should, minimally, pay basic wages to employees.
- MNCs' operations should benefit lower-income groups of the host nation.
- MNCs should balance job opportunities, work conditions, job training, and living conditions among emigrant workers and host country nationals.

Consumer protection

- MNCs should respect host country laws and policies regarding the protection of consumers.
- MNCs should safeguard the health and safety of consumers by various disclosures, safe packing, proper labeling, and accurate advertising.

Environmental protecticn

- MNCs should respect host country laws, goals, and priorities concerning protection of the environment.
- MNCs should preserve ecological balance, protect the environment, adopt preventive measures to avoid environmental harm, and rehabilitate environments damaged by operations.

- MNCs should disclose likely environmental harms and minimize risks of accidents that could cause environmental damage.
- MNCs should promote the development of international environmental standards.
- MNCs should control specific operations that contribute to pollution of air, water, and soils.
- MNCs should develop and use technology that can monitor, protect, and enhance the environment.

Political payments and involvement

- MNCs should not pay bribes nor make improper payments to public officials.
- MNCs should avoid improper or illegal involvement or interference in the internal policies of host countries.

Basic human rights and fundamental freedoms

- MNCs should respect the rights of all persons to life, liberty, security of person, and privacy.
- MNCs should respect the rights of all persons to equal protection of the law, work, choice of job, just and favorable work conditions, and protection against unemployment and discrimination.
- MNCs should respect all persons' freedom of thought, conscience, religion, opinion and expression, communication, peaceful assembly and association, and movement and residence within each state.
- MNCs should promote a standard of living to support the health and well-being of workers and their facilities.
- MNCs should promote special care and assistance to motherhood and childhood.

Frederick states that these guidelines should be viewed as a "collective phenomenon," since all do not appear in each of the six international pacts from which they originated.

The guidelines serve as a broad basis on which all international organizations can design and apply specific corporate policies and procedures in such areas as:

> children, minimum wages, hours of work, employee training and education, adequate housing and healthcare, pollution control efforts, advertising and marketing activities, severance pay, privacy of employees and consumers, information concerning on-the-job hazards and...for those companies with operations in South Africa...as the place of residence and free movement of employees.

The problem remains: Who enforces these types of principles across geographic boundaries when complex situations involve competiting intercasts and power demands?

Ethics and global stakeholder disputes

In the real world of trade and buying and selling, MNEs and host governments will continue to quarrel and litigate over control of high-stakes technologies, intellectual patents, and controversial issues relating to industrial abuses health, physical environments, and cultural traditions. Governments will claim they have a right to, for example, their apartheid laws, while other nations will boycott companies who do business in such nations. Countries such as Brazil may attempt to continue protecting their small to minimize computer firms by imposing laws and regulations over foreign companies that attempt to overwhelm the R&D ability of that nation's computer industry, while Western high-technology producers threaten to leave Brazil if their control is jeopardized. The Jujitsus of Japan and other countries and the IBMs of the United States and Europe continue to debate over what constitutes "intellectual property," whose definition should be used, and what moral and legal criteria should be applied to settle alleged violations.

These examples, "Who is right and who is wrong in ethical dilemmas in which the stakes are high for both parties who are both right? Whose morals and solution should then be followed?"

These questions become even more difficult in international disputes when both sides have valid, legitimate claims, according to their historical traditions, customs, and legal history and practices.

The summary of universally recognized rights of international firms and countries in section 7.4 a starting point for identifying conflicts of interest. After that, advocating a specific ethic usually does not satisfy a solution when cultural, religious, economic, and legal "rights" of two disputes parties historically differ. The conflicting claims must be negotiated.

Thomas Donaldson offered an "ethical algorithm" to help revolve difficult conflicts of interests between international parties. However, this logic appears somewhat cumbersome and even mechanical in real-time experience.

We advocate a more practical exercise that business and legal professionals and accustomed to using, namely a stakeholder analysis. Once the issues, stakes, and priority ranking of shakes are identified, then the two parties should begin to discuss the differing legal, cultural, historical, and social value differences that underlie each party's claims and motivations. The different ethical value systems can be applied as "first pass" to understand the moral nature of the claims, even though other moral traditions may also be relevant to the situation. Using the list of universal rights in section 7.4 provides a starting point for reviewing issues of justice, duty, and moral obligations of the parties, but beyond this exercise, negotiation techniques are required to thrash out assumptions and issues to settle disputes.

Again, there are no quick fixes for resolving high-stakes ethical and economic dilemmas between international players when both sides are "right." Sensitivity to communication and diligence with negotiation techniques that help us understand and consider the differences in cultural traditions, language, and assumptions are required in order to reach what Roger Fisher, in his influential book on negotiations, termed "getting to yes"

4

International Business Management Strategy

The selection, preparation, promotion, and remuneration of international managerial personnel become a matter of signal importance, so likewise the selection of managerial style. In many instances, circumstances compel overseas managers to operate more autonomously than their domestic counterparts; expert staff assistance is not always immediately available. Also, their principal function may be that of training rather than management per se. And, in any event, they are part of an intercultural communications system.

Despite so-called instantaneous communications, such communication is in fact often far from instantaneous, and frequently less than "communication" in the true sense of the word. In a single national setting, many relevant variables need not be made explicit; they are within the compass of the experience of both parties and are implicitly given similar values by both. Hence, their words are understood within a similar context. Not so for an international setting; much more need be made explicit, even the use of words. To communicate by writing is time-consuming and tedious. Yet oral communication is subject to gross misunderstandings. The mind wanders for a moment, the thread is broken. A word is not understood; too late, the conversation goes on. A nuance is lost; a tone of voice misinterpreted; puzzlement in a person's eyes not seen. The probability of such events is multiplied if the conversation is over radio or wire. It is not happenstance that speaking in a foreign language by telephone is more difficult than in face-to-face conversation.

It should be borne in mind that an overseas manager occupies several roles: (1) representative of the U.S. firm, (2) manager of the local firm, (3) resident of the local community, (4) citizen either of the host state or of another, (5) member of a profession, not to mention (6) head of family and all that implies. To the extent that these roles conflict, communication tends to be blocked. For example, if expectations created by the manager role cannot be realized due to the restraints imposed by the representative role, the individual is in a position of role conflict. The resident and citizen roles are likewise likely to conflict. Unless the parent management is sufficiently sensitive to these possible conflicts, the overseas manager's behaviour may be inexplicable and communications become blocked or at least noisy.

An example would be an executive of a U.S. firm sent to India for an extended period of time as financial manager of an Indian subsidiary. Over time he finds himself identifying emotionally with India and grows impatient with the financial restraint placed on the subsidiary by the U.S. parent. More rapid growth, which requires greater parent company financial commitment, is required if the enterprise is to live up to Indian expectations, which objective the young man sees as increasingly important in the broad context of supporting the more liberal approach to rapid national development. He makes vigorous representation to the parent on behalf of the subsidiary. Not necessarily on purely financial grounds, which becomes known in India and improves his status as one who "understands our problems." But because of his apparent inability to influence the parent company, he loses some authority within the Indian subsidiary itself. And, his colleagues back home, knowing far less about India and identifying very little with its problems, refer to our man as "unrealistic" and "Soft". In addition, he himself may realize that he is getting out of touch with domestic developments in his profession, as well as losing contact with professional colleagues ordinarily maintained through attendance at periodic conferences and seminars. He begins to feel uncomfortable. So, likewise, does his family, some members of which are reaching high school age. Even though the Indian subsidiary may be in critical need of his services, the executive may now engage in a homeward-bound strategy. Again, he is making decisions and recommendations for reasons other than the immediate financial profit of the corporation. Perhaps he should; that is not the issue. The point is that unless the parent company management is aware of the pressures and needs to which his various roles can expose him, it may not be in a position to read his communications from India correctly. If one substitutes a qualified local national, one resolves some of these conflicts but intensifies others. For example, what if the financial manager were Indian, and the parent company had no process whereby nationals other than those of the parent country were considered for assignment to world corporate headquarters? Then, if the Indian were ambitious and wished to develop international status in the field of financial management, he would either seek to increase autonomy for the Indian firm or, failing that, leave the employ of the firm entirely. Whatever his action, it is likely that the headquarters management will misunderstand his motivations.

The critical importance of overseas managerial selection is heightened by the greater difficulty in assessing performance and in finding replacements than in a purely domestic situation. Performance measurement is rendered difficult by different factor inputs, differential inflation and foreign exchange rate moves, time delays in reporting, and the external restraints embedded in intercompany relationships (such as pricing, financial decision) over which local management has little control. An internal profit-and-loss accounting is unlikely to provide an adequate basis for judging managerial effectiveness in this situation. The replacement problem is aggravated by personal difficulties involved in international moves and by the severe shortage of management skills in many parts of the world.

How and where do firms find managers for assignment to international operations, whether in corporate headquarters or foreign affiliates? There seems to be little research into current practice. But one such, a 1974 survey of 72 U.S. firms, revealed substantial differences. About two-thirds took on U.S. nationals directly for work in international operations. The balance required previous experience in domestic operations. Just over half reportedly hired foreign nationals directly for management positions in the U.S.; another 20 percent only transferred them from affiliates abroad. The balance employed no foreign nationals in the U.S. Some firms would accept applications for foreign nationals in the U.S., such as foreign graduates of U.S. management programs, for jobs with associated overseas firms: others would not. It was clear that a more internationally-oriented set of hiring policies went together, that is, those firms hiring U.S. nationals directly into international operations also tended to employ foreign nationals in the U.S., and accept foreign applications in the U.S. for overseas positions. Hiring foreign national managers in the U.S. suggested relative absence of national bias at corporate headquarters. Accepting applications in the U.S. for foreign jobs suggested a high level of control by the U.S. parent over its overseas affiliates. One further point came out of this study: of those firms hiring foreign national managers in the U.S., 12 required a permanent U.S. visa; 23 did not. The latter firms were willing to support one's application for a permanent U.S. visa *after* a job offer.

Selection of overseas management

Two decisions are involved in the selection of overseas management: choice of prerequisites (including nationality) and validation of those prerequisites.

Until recently there seemed to be a clear trend for U.S. firms to employ an increasing percentage of local nationals in management positions in associated foreign firms. For example, one report shows that some 70 percent of the managing directors of U.S. subsidiaries in Europe were local nationals by 1969, as were 55 percent of other key executives. Comparable figures for subsidiaries in Latin American were 30 percent and 50 percent. And a 1970 study found a definite trend in the direction of sending fewer U.S. managers abroad. In 1975,

General Motors reported total overseas employment of 168,000, of which only 421 had been assigned to foreign subsidiaries by the Overseas Operations Division within corporate headquarters in the U.S. (Presumably all U.S. citizens).

But the evidence is not all one way. A 1972 study by the Conference Board found that 268 major U.S. corporations then employed 3,455 U.S. citizens abroad. By 1975 the total for 213 of the *same* companies had *risen* to 5,300. Also significant was the fact that the number of U.S. passports issued or renewed for business travel rose dramatically from 40,000 in 1970 to 268,000 in 1974. Obviously, these figures did not mean that the number of U.S. managers on long-term assignment abroad per million dollars of sales or of assets had increased. Possibly not. But at the same time, the number of expatriate U.S. managers seemed to be holding its own. Based on 1972 data relating to 250 U.S. and European firms, Franko related the number of U.S. expatriate managers to the stage of internationalization of the firm. If true, this pattern would conform to the evolutionary model of the control system of the internationalizing firm. It may be that some of the mature multinational and transnational corporations actually plan on maintaining between 5 and 10 percent expatriates or third country nationals in local subsidiary managements. Unilever, the U.K.-Dutch transnational, reportedly does so on the assumption that there are benefits in mixed management, such as providing multinational experience and intensifying corporate socialization for all parties. When General Motors set up its Australian operation in 1948, some 42 U.S. managers and technical specialists were required. Twenty years later, the number had apparently stabilized at about ten.

Franko found that European-based firm maintained their preference for home country nationals through the periods of initial manufacture and, unlike U.S. firms, foreign growth. Both ended up in stage six, however, employing fewer home country and third country nationals.

There is some evidence that there may be national differences in respect to a corporation's propensity to employ local national managers.

It may well be true, however, that these apparent national differences arise more out of the fact that more European and Japanese firms are at lesser stages of internationalization than the U.S. than out of national differences. One would have to control for stage of corporate evolution.

Two reasons are generally given for the employment of local national managers: lower cost and more intimate environmental knowledge. A third reason is the difficulty a nonnational may face in assuming either the highly paternalistic role vis-a-vis employees that is expected of him in traditional society or the egalitarian or subordinate role required in some of the more collectivist societies. Two obvious disadvantages to the employment of local nationals as managers are non-transferability and poor communications. An alternative is the use of a third-country national or assignment without regard to nationality unless relating directly to managerial effectiveness. In some cases, of course, denial of entry visa or work permit may require the firm to nationalize management over a specified period of time. In other cases, the top management must be local, as in the case of a foreign investment in a Yugoslav enterprise in its entirety. In the former case, the director must be a Yugoslav citizen; in the latter, he could be a foreigner. In fact, virtually all directors of international joint ventures in Yugoslavia have been local nationals. In still other cases it is exceedingly difficult to use expatriate managers effectively. A case in point is Japan. In a number of LDCs the development of local management may be legally required by the host government as a condition of entry. And, if some circulation of foreign national managers through assignments at corporate headquarters is anticipated, legal restraints imposed by the *parent* country can become important.

For example, although U.S. firms report relatively little delay in moving foreign nationals into management positions abroad, prior to 1970 months of advance planning were sometimes needed to move non-Americans into the U.S. In some cases this difficulty of entry into the U.S. for alien managers led to employment by a firm of more U.S. nationals in overseas positions than might otherwise have been the case. It has been possible all along for foreign managers to be admitted into the U.S. in training status for a period of two years, or on a temporary permit basis for six months, but the assumption of managerial responsibilities in the U.S. until 1970 required an immigration visa, which often meant a wait of anywhere from 10 to 18 months because the Department of Labor generally declined to certify executives as needed talent."If all countries had the same immigration set-up as America now uses, multinational corporations simply couldn't function." The practice was for companies faced with long delays in gaining entry for much needed talent to fly in executives for short business trips at regular intervals, a procedure that was both expensive and personally difficult.

Fortunately, a 1970 amendment to U.S. immigration law permitted non-U.S. executives employed by a firm over one year to enter the U.S. on a temporary basis in a management or executive capacity in the employ of that firm or of an associated entity. Such visas are granted more swiftly than other types of visas and are valid for three to five years. Obviously, certain questions are begged: What is a manager or executive? What constitutes an associated entity?

Rules controlling entry for managers are sometimes modified reciprocally on the basis of a bilateral commerce, friendship, or navigation treaty or convention of establishment. In the French-U.S. case, there is a 1961 Convention of Establishment, which specifies that those French or U.S national qualifying as "treaty traders" or "treaty investors" will be given permission to reside, to work in a salaried position, and to carry on a business in the other country. Qualifications consists principally of establishing nationality free of bankruptcy, and credit worthiness.

The key question is what are the relevant variables in determining optimum strategy: employment of parent country nationals, local nationals, or third-country nationals?

The use of parent country nationals in key managerial roles may be justified in the following situations:

1. The foreign enterprise is just being established (start-up phase).
2. The parent firm wishes to develop an internationally oriented management for the headquarters.
3. No adequate management is available from other sources.

4. The parent firm has surplus managerial personnel toward which it feels responsible.
5. The parent firm has no one sufficiently familiar with the foreign environment to interpret communications from a non-parent country management, and therefore needs to develop area expertise.
6. Virtually no autonomy is possible for the foreign enterprise because it is integrated so closely with operations elsewhere.
7. High-level technical knowledge and skill of a nature that cannot be protected legally is carried by top management.
8. The foreign enterprise is seen as short-lived.
9. The host society is multiracial, and a local manager of either racial origin would make the enterprise politically vulnerable or lead to an economic boycott.
10. There is a compelling need to maintain a foreign image.
11. The parent firm will be serving largely other firms of the same nationality operating abroad, most of which are directed by parent country nationals.
12. It is felt desirable to avoid involving particular local nationals or families in management, and the use of other local nationals would create dangerous animosities.
13. Local nationals are not mobile and resist assignment elsewhere.
14. A parent-country national is simply the best man for the job, all things considered.

15. Control is weak, particularly in cases where local nationals are highly nationalistic and more responsive to government appeals than would be an expatriate.

It will be noted that several of these conditions are not persuasive in the long run, such as condition 1. In regard to condition 2, there is no reason for parent-country nationals to occupy the *top* roles. In any event, U.S. firms are finding it increasingly difficult to induce their expatriates to return to the United States. "Adequacy" is in part a function of perception of one's superiors; that is, personal confidence. For an individual not known intimately on a person-to-person basis over a significant period of time, personal confidence is hard to come by. hence, one way to build up adequate managerial skills in foreign nationals is through extended assignment to corporate headquarters. Condition three may be limited in time; local nationals may be trainable. Mere unfamiliarity with individual foreign nationals may be a valid reason to send in known nationals for a period of time, though not indefinitely. Condition four is also a limited phenomenon; management can be sloughed off. Condition five will change over time as the parent country nationals are rotated home. Condition six could be argued. Why should parent country nationals perform more adequately? In either case, the manager's role should be carefully defined so as to avoid conflict of roles. Condition seven begs a question: why should parent country nationals be more trustworthy in this regard? In fact, given their greater ease in securing jobs with domestic competitors, the risk of loss of such knowledge and skill may be greater in the case of parent-country nationals. It might be argued, however, that the transfer of skills and know-how decreases a firm's external leverage against possible nationalization. Conditions eight through fourteen clearly seem to demand parent-country nationals under some circumstances. In the case of condition 15, the situation calls for a careful analysis as to the source of weakness and to the costs and benefits of enforcing greater control. What control is required and why is a parent-country national better able to control? Is this ability based simply on familiarity with both the local scene and the parent company? Very likely, in which case the key element here is an effective communicator in both directions.

Perhaps the alternatives should really be though of as representing a continuum over time as individual communication abilities develop—from channel one, to channel two, to channel three, to channel four, to channel five. When the term "U.S.-trained Mexican manager" is used, what one means is a Mexican national who is able to communicate effectively with a U.S. management that includes no particular expertise in understanding Mexico or Mexicans. Channel five is characteristic of the multinational corporation, which has a cadre of international managers of different nationalities who can communicate effectively in all directions.

Because of the competition for such individuals, many firms may find it virtually impossible to move beyond channel three, which can be perfectly adequate system of communications. The trouble is that the need for the person in headquarters who is knowledgeable of things Mexican is often over-looked. Words flow, and management is led to believe that it is communicating effectively with its Mexican management when in fact it is not.

For example, it is reported that:

> About half the existing officers of foreign companies in Japan—mostly the smaller ones—are staffed exclusively by Japanese. One might think that this would solve the problem, but it doesn't. If executives at headquarters responsible for the operation are unfamiliar with Japan's customs and business practices, the indigenous staff is not likely to receive the understanding or cooperation requisite for success and a smooth-running operation.

A Scandinavian businessman speaks of another aspect of the same problem:

> Nowadays there seems to be a tendency towards "over-Japanization" of the foreign company in Japan; i.e., the top management is after the initial stages of starting up business staffed entirely with Japanese executives. It has been observed that this can create serious problems particularly in the communication with the head office overseas. In one actual case, the Japanese president of a joint venture company got so frustrated with this communication problem that he actually resigned and returned to the large Japanese corporation he originally came from. The occasional visitor from the head office cannot possibly understand all the complexities of carrying out business in Japan, and what the Japanese executive in the related case actually wanted was to have an able person from the head office permanently stationed in Japan and with whom he could discuss the various problems on the spot.

The language differences create difficulties not only for the foreigner but also for the Japanese executive in an international company. There are also many other difficulties for both. However, these can be overcome by having a team of two able executives, one Japanese and one foreign, working together to form a very effective and powerful combination.

A dubious reason for employing a foreign national management is to insulate parent company personnel from direct involvement in making extra-legal payments to foreign government personnel.

On the other hand, Lord Cole of Unilever has written,

> It may in some cases be expedient to keep an expatriate in a country to balance the pulls which can be made on a locally born manager and to be available to present cases to government, or to other agencies, which it is often difficult for a national to do without being suspected of lack of patriotism.

A Swedish company (Volvo) reports that it prefers to use Swedish nationals to fill financial executive positions abroad, principally because they are more familiar with the financial and accounting procedures of the parent company. Particularly for firms preparing consolidated international financial statements, this consideration may be important. All in all, generalizations in this area are unwise.

The danger is that the firm will opt for a policy of using parent-country nationals in foreign management positions by default, that is, simply as an automatic extension of domestic policy, rather than deliberately seeking optimum utilization of management skills. For a parent firm inexperienced abroad, the selection of foreign nationals, whether of the host or third country, may be difficult. But a variety of approaches are open: (1) recruitment from among foreign students or foreign alumni of domestic schools of engineering, business, and management; (2) recruitment from among students and alumini of recognized management development schools abroad, the number of which is growing rapidly; (3) application to the files of such organizations as the Institute of International Education in New York City; (4) development of a company-sponsored management training program for foreign nationals; (5) reference to the Home Country Employment Registry of foreign students in the U.S., located at Tulane University; (6) utilization of one or more management recruitment organizations operating in the countries of interest. An increase in management mobility has been noted in Western Europe and Japan. In France and Germany, non state employment agencies are prohibited legally from soliciting or maintaining files of either job seekers or companies in the market for personnel. Management consulting firms, however, are apparently not prohibited from giving advice in this area.

Emerging from a number of studies in various parts of the world is the fact that the businessman is not rated highly in relation to those employed in government services, medicine, law, teaching, or the military. Therefore, an unduly large proportion of the more qualified and achievement-oriented individuals may seek careers in these more prestigious professions, thus depleting the flows into private management. Nonetheless, in that the cost advantage of a foreign over a parent-country national in a management position abroad is often substantial, a firm may justify considerable expense in finding and developing foreign nationals. On the other hand, equally compelling is the need for channeling communications to the parent firm by someone sensitive to the implicit cultural and environmental variables under which the foreign management is operating and equally sensitive to the external and internal environment of the parent firm.

A firm can invest profitably in an individual's development only if he is likely to remain in the firm's employ for an extended period of time. This is an area, incidentally, in which the Japanese permanent employment system contains an advantage. But in societies in which there is high job mobility among managers, whether due to a shortage or other causes, the firm's interests dictate that it invest only in those managers committed to the company and likely to remain in its employment. Herein lies solid rationale for a hiring policy based on nepotism. Friends and relatives of owners and top executives are probably somewhat less likely to exploit the firm for training and development and then leave.

Some have estimated that the turnover rate for U.S. expatriate managers may be as high as 30 percent. "Companies cannot long suffer such an astounding high percentage, given the cost of relocation and training and uncountables in good will and organization."

> A large international company, which draws most of the managers of its international operations from its international division, calculates its turnover as 5 percent to 10percent; but also expects that this percentage will rise sharply when personnel from its domestic companies are sent overseas.

One of the main problems is the apprehension some executives feel when offered and placed in foreign locations. I an overseas assignment a road to advancement or a road to nowhere? Are domestic colleagues the ones who carve up the pie? Where really does an international executive fit into the total corporate picture?

Enough for the pros and cons of the expatriate-local national argument. What of other selection criteria for overseas managers?

There is very little hard data relating certain personal characteristics with overseas management success. One effort to do so was based on a study of 50 expatriate managers operating in U.S.- affiliated companies in the Mexico City area. These managers were asked to rank four abilities most important to success overseas.

The same study reports unusually high expatriate scores in respect to responsibility, moderately high scores in emotional stability, and low scores in sociability. Expatriates scored high in internationalism, but with fairly high variability. The study went on to say,

The executives interviewed were generally well-adjusted to the foreign environment but a rather wide range of acculturation existed, and many examples of acculturation failures were cited. This indicates a very spotty success in the selection and training of expatriates and again points up the need for improved knowledge.

Qualities deemed most important for overseas success by managers of foreign operations in 127 large U.S. firms were (1) independence and ability to achieve results with limited resources, (2) sincerity and integrity, (3) technical knowledge, and (4) a positive attitude toward overseas work, in that descending order. Overseas managers in the same firms specified (1) a positive attitude by the wife, (2) sincerity and integrity, (3) adaptability, and (4) a positive attitude on the part of the manager, in descending order.

Another study, limited to canvassing the opinion of U.S. expatriate managers. Still another study of 70 U.S. based companies came up with the results shown in Table 4.4 All the these criteria can be grouped under: (1) experience in company, (2) technical competence (including managerial), (3) language, (4) area expertise, (5) age, (6) stability of marital relations (including spouse's attitude), (7) personal preference, (8) personality attributes, (9) career plans, (10) sex, and (11) social acceptability. Curiously, the last two are almost never articulated by U.S. managements. Not mentioned at all is physical stamina of both husband and wife.

It is clear that most U.S. managers overseas have been recruited from within their respective firms and that there is a "trend away from using foreign-reared Americans as managerial talent in U.S.- based multinational firm."

For an individual to be versed fully in company policies, procedures and products are often felt to be of prime importance. It is sometimes claimed that a foreign manager, operating at greater distance from the home office and under a severe communications handicap, must have internalized thoroughly the way the company operates and the nature of its products. In fact, however, this may be the easiest prerequisite to satisfy by training and periodic conferences.

Technical competence is, of course, essential if by "technical" skills one refers to skills required to do the assigned job. Warning: the skill-mix for a successful manager abroad may differ somewhat from the parent country model. It is a truism that one of the elements most important in gaining acceptance for foreign management is demonstrated technical capacity. This quality is also important in providing the manager himself—be he or she of parent or of third-country origin—with that degree of confidence necessary to overcome "cultural shock." A person must be genuinely self-confident, although not arrogantly so.

A recent study of the international marketing function of the larger U.S. firms disclosed that 40 percent of the responding U.S. executives listed proven domestic marketing ability as the primary prerequisite for appointment to overseas marketing positions. One quarter cited foreign national status; 16 percent specified an expression of personal interest; only 10 percent, prior formal training; and a mere 2 percent, foreign language ability. Yet, 43 percent of the executive responding specified that adapting to different cultural concepts and overcoming the language barrier were the main difficulties faced by international marketing personnel, and 24 percent said that the chief characteristic favoring success was strong empathy with the cultural environment.

Must a manager know the language of the host country? If we admit the validity of employing parent or third-country nationals under certain circumstances, then language may impose a severe restraint on recruitment. A second language may be most efficiently acquired either as a child or as a mature adult when a specific language need arises. With concentrated effort, a *casual* speaking knowledge of any language may be acquired within six to 12 months by an intelligent adult. With but exceedingly rare exceptions, an adult with no prior exposure to a given language cannot become bilingual in it. The rare exceptions are two: linguistic genius or complete isolation from the mother tongue for a long period of time. The major danger to management is that a person inadequate in the local language will nonetheless attempt to carry on as though he understood, or was being understood, at all times. The local community undoubtedly appreciates the foreigner's efforts to communicate directly, but these efforts should not be permitted to interfere with understanding Pride should not stand in the way of employing a good interpreter.

For the novice in a language, there are at least three serious blocks to full understanding:

1. inadequate knowledge and understanding of the culture and, hence, of words. Many apparently equivalent words do not, in fact, carry the same meaning;

2. the use of words to carry other meanings because they are equivalent in a first meaning, the point being that the words may overlap only for a single meaning. Simply because the English word equivalent carriers the other meanings is no guarantee that the foreign word express the same. Concept clusters vary;

3. the use of metaphors, similes, and analogies.

Even the effective use of an interpreter requires an alertness to these difficulties.

Many nonlocal managers with no prior knowledge of the local language have been eminently successful. The skilled use of competent interpreters, plus coincidental study of the language to the point of being able to keep the interpreter on his toes, may be quite adequate. The pitfall here is the temptation to associate unduly with those speaking one's own language. In many non-Western countries, the U.S. businessman is surrounded by English-speaking "carpetbaggers," many of whom may not be ethnically or culturally part of the major community. He should be wary of becoming too closely involved.

Perhaps of greater importance than ability to use a given language is an awareness of the importance of language as a programmed thinking process. The capacity and structure of a language to a significant degree determine the nature of both thought and emotion and hence, of behavior. Granted, a language changes over time, but for a given experience it is fixed. Associated with this subject is that of the so-called "silent language," in the context of which only a spoken language can be understood. Essentially, the "silent language" consists of signals communicated by means other than words—spatial relationships, timing, movements, sequences. What may be insulting in one culture may be complimentary in another. The point is that *a characteristic of a good manager is a capacity to communicate effectively. How he does it is relatively unimportant.*

As noer has pointed out, an essential ingredient in effective communication has to do with knowing one's *own* cultural bias.

The dynamic nature of cultural values works at both ends of an international assignment. The German manager brought up in the aftermath of World War II has different cultural values from the young German worker. A 28-year-old U.S. technician selected by a 45-year-old middle manager in the United States and sent to work for a 50-

year-old manager in Germany, where the peer group is 28-year-old German technicians, is caught in a crossfire of cultural values before he starts. If he and the individual who selected him are unaware of cultural differences and cultural bias, the chances for a cultural clash are greatly increased.

A cultural clash simply signals a breakdown in effective communication. Individuals are speaking and acting from different premises.

Another prerequisite often specified for the foreign manager is area expertise, knowledge of the market or production area. Several points should be made. Firstly, prejudgment without personal experience can be very misleading. International communications are clogged with misinterpretation, bias, misinformation, propaganda, distortion, and outright lies. Secondly, experience has demonstrated that a man who has worked *successfully* in one national environment different from his own is very likely to operate with similar success wherever employed. Once he has breached an intercultural communications barrier, and once he has felt the essential unity of human society, the likelihood of failure is greatly reduced.

This last point needs expansion. By "essential unity of human society" is meant the fact that human life everywhere faces similar needs and drives. Given a historical input, certain institutions, relationships, personality types, and values emerge. All are functional, that is, rational, within a context. They are constantly changing as interactions slowly alter the historical input. The manager himself is one of these inputs. Once a person views human society in this manner, he always feels "at home" wherever he is. He realizes that bargaining in the bazaar, or elaborate rituals of politeness are not simply quaint old customs, but serve definite functions. This realization does not mean that one is necessarily resigned to the *Status quo.* On the contrary, he is then in a position to deal with his cultural environment more effectively. For example, he knows what is likely to reduce the pressure to bargain. In short, the successful international manager is one who sees and feels the similarity of structure of all societies. The same set of relevant variables are seen to operate,although the relative weights may be very different. This capacity is far more important than possession of specific area expertise, which may be gained quite rapidly if one has this capacity to see similarities and ask the right questions—those that will provide the appropriate values or weights for the relevant variables. Such an individual very quickly locates himself on the social-cultural map.

It could be argued that the manager's success in subsequent foreign environments after an initial success is not because he has learned anything but because he has demonstrated that he possesses a special set of qualities, perhaps most importantly a coherent identity and adequate ego strength. The counter argument is that identity and ego strength may be necessary conditions, but possibly not sufficient. It may be that the learning process in the initial experience shortens the time to relate effectively to a foreign culture in subsequent experience.

Other than nationality, company experience, technical competence, and language and area expertise, there are at least eight other prerequisites used in selecting overseas management either consciously or unconsciously: health, martial relations, career plans and personal preference, age, social acceptability, sex, and personality attributes.

It has been noted by those experienced in this area that an individual's physical health is peculiarly relevant to success abroad. For example, the U.S. Foreign Service rejects candidates with not "*more* than average health." The health of one's family is also important. The point is that adjustment to the different working and living conditions encountered abroad generates psychological and physical strain. Undue worry about one's health, or that of one's family, can well subvert managerial effectiveness.

Virtually all analysts stress the importance of a strong and mutually reinforcing relationship between man and wife. In some circumstances sending an unmarried persons overseas can be risky, particularly in socially sensitive and racially conscious societies. In many, a single person simply will not have the access to families and homes that would a married couple, which may interfere with his or her effectiveness at work. Both husband and wife should have a positive attitude toward the proposed overseas assignment, but an attitude based on accurate knowledge of the working and living conditions they can anticipate.

Career plans and personal preference cannot really come into full play unless overseas job opportunities are posted within the company rather than communicated on an individual-to-individual basis either through formal or informal communication networks.

While there has been some movement toward intra-company job "advertising" in many corporations, the extension of such systems to the international arena is not common. A few companies have instituted programs—often using computerized inventories of employee skills—so that the corporate personnel department can quickly ascertain where qualified candidates are located, even on a worldwide basis. This type of system can be characterized as company-initiated rather than employee-initiated, since the prospective candidates usually do not know of the job opening until they are approached.

The job positing scheme used by the U.S. Texas Instruments (TI) is a different system, in which the initial impetus to apply for a position within the company comes from interested employees themselves. Although oriented primarily to the domestic area, the program is being implemented for jobs outside the U.S. as well.

Management jobs abroad not limited by corporate policy to local nationals are posted worldwide by TI. Intracompany job opportunities in Europe are funneled through the European regional office. A more recent innovation in the TI system is anonymous advertising by employees in search of new jobs, either domestic or foreign.

Influencing preferences for overseas assignment, of course, is the degree to which such assignments are seen as a necessary step on the ladder to the top.

Age may or may not be important to an overseas assignment. Should a Brazilian enterprise be run by a young or more senior person? Obviously, managing an enterprise far removed from headquarters requires great responsibility and maturity of judgment. Within a broad range, no one has demonstrated that these latter qualities are closely related to biological age. In more traditional societies, of course, age may be an important status symbol, which fact may then become relevant to selection of management. Age may also be relevant if an individual's overall management career is considered to be a prerequisite for selection. Is a foreign assignment considered to be preparation for promotion or is it a dead end? If the latter, the parent firm may push its undesirables overseas. Very frequently, U.S. firms with policies of employing local nationals in overseas management do not consider these managers transferable, either to third countries or to the United States. Therefore, their career horizons are limited to the local enterprises. A few U.S. firms now require foreign experience for promotion to corporate level. If this be the case, career expectations may be an essential prerequisite for selection of a manager for a foreign enterprise. Indeed, a tendency seems to be evidence among firms operating internationally—U.S., European, and Japanese—to make foreign experience a necessary step on the ladder to a top corporate position. The giant Japanese firm, Mitsui K.K., whose personnel policy is described in Case G, appears to be an example.

In the list of prerequisites we have included social acceptability, by which is meant the reflection on the part of the manager of those social characteristics identified by his or her local colleagues and subordinates with a manager in that society. Particularly in a traditional society, where ascriptive factors, rather than demonstrated ability, predominate in establishing authority, care should be used to select one who possesses at least some of the characteristics, whether they be defined in terms of college degrees, knowledge of the fine arts, or manner of behavior. For a parent country or third-country national, family background may not be important, but if a local national is involved, social status may be a relevant variable, however social status may be defined in that particular society. Indeed, a more efficient organization may result than if one ignored such considerations and merely appointed the most *technically* qualified person.

Almost never mentioned in the literature is women's place in international business. In certain overseas managerial roles, particularly sales, a woman may have a distinct advantage. She is more likely to be treated with deference, may find it easier to gain access to distributors and customers, and may be more frequently invited into their homes. A case in point is the sale of pharmaceuticals in Western Europe and Latin America. Possible relevant variables are the area, the function, and the product. National differences in the degree to which women are active in business are remarkable. For example, in Switzerland women constituted 47 percent of all those in business in 1966; in Japan, 4 percent. Other country ratios were: France, Germany, and Italy, 22 to 24 percent; Australia, 15 percent; Mexico, 12 percent; Canada 11 percent; Britain and South Africa, 9 percent; Sweden, 8 percent; and Spain, 6 percent. More recent statistics might reveal a tendency to converge.

Even more seldom is race mentioned by researchers or practitioners as relevant to the selection of an overseas manager. For example, is a black American more likely to be more effective in black Africa than a white American or a Nisei in Japan? There seems to be no research on the subject, although some experienced observers express doubt. It is possible that such individuals would be viewed with more suspicion—if not hostility—than one not racially identified with the host country population. It is known that some of the Japanese firms established in the United States have employed Nisei.

Even if we specified the prerequisites for overseas assignments, we still must validate certain of them vis-a-vis a given person. The problem arises particularly in the language and area expertise areas, which we have redefined in terms of ability to communicate and capacity to grasp the interrelationship of societies. How does one increase the probability of selecting an individual who will perform effectively in a different culture, that is, one who will be least affected by culture shock?

Culture shock is induced by the removal of familiar cues. People are seen as behaving irrationally or stupidly; institutions, as not being functional. One is confronted by unexpected behavior and institutions and by different values and world perceptions. "When expectations are not fulfilled, stress and dysfunction are found to follow." Such stress, or culture shock, may be manifested in a request for a transfer, the desire to leave a job before completion, dissatisfaction and indifference to work, quarreling, undue criticism, blaming failures on inherent qualities of relevant nationality, adulation of the home country, withdrawal from social relations with local nationals, alcoholism, poor quality work.

Methods for selecting individuals who are likely to be least upset by such a different value system and best able to work effectively include formal tests, training, personal preference, and none of these.

Formal tests are not widely used by companies to aid in the selection of personnel for overseas assignment, and there is some evidence indicating loss of confidence and decline in testing by former users. Even those firms employing tests do not seem to evaluate their predictability and, hence, are not in a position to relate scores with on-the-job performance overseas. One writer claims, without offering any hard data, that "tests have proved to be valuable in at least some respects to psychologists in selecting American employees for assignments abroad." The tests so cited are the F scale, the All port-Vernon Study of Values, the Guilford Zimmerman Temperament Survey, and the Individual Background Survey.

The consensus of the U.S. international practitioners seems to be that testing has not proven very helpful. The most promising may be the "California Test", in that from limited data it would appear that high ethnocentrism is associated with overseas job failure. Various thematic apperception tests (TATs) may be useful in disclosing such characteristics as prejudice, a tendency to evaluate individuals in terms of stereotypes (or generalities), and compulsion to see things always in terms of absolute universal values. These characteristics would seem to be undesirable among international managers who must deal with multinational situations, for they are likely to make them unable to see the cultural relativity of either personal behavior or corporate strategy. Success in a special training course for a particular assignment, including language, may be an indirect measure of ability to adapt and to relate oneself to a different culture, and may provide as well an insight into motivation. But much, of course, depends on the quality of the training. The weight given to personal preference in the selection process depends on the reason for the preference; a keen interest in new and challenging social experience is very different from a mere desire for the glamour of the "international jet set." Possibly, one should be wary of those who speak of peoples and nations in broad generalities, who pass easy judgment as to the right or wrong of the acts of others, who "love to travel," who show little concern for their personal family responsibilities. or who are extremely extroverted. The personality of the wife and the quality of the husband-wife relationship are also of critical importance. There is evidence that many failures abroad are due to the inability of the wife to adjust satisfactorily or of the marriage relationship to sustain the compression of isolation from one's own culture.

All in all, there seems to be no substitute for the in-depth interview of both husband and wife by one of more persons intimately familiar with the problems of intercultural movement, that is, one who has experienced them himself. "Mobil's four-hour environmental interview" is most revealing. The Mobil interviewers first seek for above-average technical competence and solid marital relationship. The interviewing process includes the presentation of a complete and accurate description of the overseas work environment, and the requirements of the job. Interaction between husband and wife is observed in the process. To hurry the process up would be to sterilize it; hence, the four hours. In addition, the applicant undergoes at least one functional interview confined to a job's technical aspects. The job offer is made after the lapse of a few days, and the applicant is permitted about two weeks to respond. The offer spells out the precise terms, such as base salary plus premium less U.S. tax and other relevant factors.

The organizations, business and otherwise, with long success records in recruiting for difficult overseas assignments seem to depend very heavily upon similar in-depth interviewing, not by professional psychologists but by those with intimate familiarity with the sorts of problems the applicant will face overseas.

One experienced practitioner writes,

It is recommended that a system be designed to

postpone an expatriate's acceptance of a position until he clearly understands the mechanics of his assignment—how he will be paid, how his taxes will be handled, and what will happen to him when currency relationships change.

Many multinationals are utilizing the "letter of understanding" concept to finalize the selection process. A letter of understanding is a summary of all the terms and conditions of an international assignment. It serves not only as a communications vehicle but also as a record of the details of an expatriation transaction.

At the top of a series of recommendations made in a report sponsored by the South African Institute of Race Relations appears the following:

> If United States companies are to engage in a serious attempt to effect social change in South Africa, they will have to exercise the greatest care in the selection of top management. The men at the top would not only have to be thoroughly versed in modern management and labour relations techniques, but also imbued with a sense of urgent necessity for evolutionary advance towards a more just society if sporadic violence and ultimate revolution are to be avoided. It is clear that they should have a thorough grounding in the problems of intergroup relations and that they should be well acquainted with the realities of the South African situation.

Whatever the criteria used in selection, or the screening mechanism employed, expatriate U.S. managers are reported to be somewhat more educated than their stay-at-home counterparts, exhibit a somewhat higher career speed (difference between the executive's age when first entering business and when achieving major executive status), are several years younger, and demonstrate lower interfirm mobility. There is also some indication that the average U.S. top overseas manager is more satisfied with respect to Maslow's hierarchy of needs (security, social esteem, autonomy, and self-actualization) than his or her domestic counterpart, with the one exception of social esteem. Overseas *middle* managers are more satisfied except in respect to security and social needs. The lower satisfaction of social need probably rises from the more limited opportunity for social contact overseas, particularly given the inadequacy of preparation in the typical case. The lower level of satisfaction in respect to the need of security possibly arises because the individual perceives himself as out of the mainstream of company life, which understandably would be more acute for a middle manager than for a top manager.

A 1976 study based on data provided by executives in 33 major U.S. based international companies concluded:

The limitless variety of human personalities makes it virtually impossible to set out the ideal, or even the optimum, characteristics for foreign service. But most of the executives contacted indicated that what they find preferable is the person who is positive-even buoyant-about the assignment.

They also look for evidence of successful exposure to many different levels of society;an intellectual curiosity; and a talent for participating and sustaining group activities. The candidate who approaches the interviews in a wary, tense manner, whose manner is overly formal, painstaking and awkward, whose interests do not extend far beyond his profession, his home, family, and a small circle of friends, is less likely to succeed in foreign assignment, according to the executives interviewed.

There are elements of this conclusion with which one might quarrel. The buoyant, back-slapping, extroverted, group-oriented type may not be the appropriate choice in a number of situations.

A 1971 inquiry into the practices and policies of 77 U.S. managers of foreign operations reported that 60 percent agreed with the statement that "the over-seas American must have a broader and deeper professional training than he needs to perform the same kind of work in his familiar home environment". Only 26 percent disagreed. The generalized need may be there, but precisely what sort of training or preparation is the best? And, let it be noted that many international executives have observed that the cardinal quality for successful management in many countries lies in the manager's ability to obtain the necessary permits, licenses, and approval from government. All else is secondary.

Preparation fo overseas assignment

Very few U.S. firms appear to provide special training for managers slated for overseas assignment. A 1969 survey of 127 large U.S.-based international firms indicated that only 33 percent had any sort of predeparture training. Of this 33 percent, only 41 percent (13.5 percent of the entire sample) offered language training for assignments in non-English speaking countries. Some 73 percent of the companies reported a time span of three months between selection for an overseas assignment and departure. Another survey of 50 U.S.-based companies revealed that 24 conducted regular in-house programs, largely in language training. This study concluded. "On the whole, less is done than might be expected in terms of providing environmental training prior to assignment."

In an opinion survey of foreign operation managers and overseas managers as to the value of various types of preparation for working overseas, the subjects mentioned most frequently were language, living conditions, economic environment, and customs. Other areas given considerable value were business law, government and political structure, and geography. But of the 127 firms surveyed, only three exposed their prospective overseas managers to anything other than language and customs. A 1976 survey of the practices of 33 large U.S.-based corporations revealed that only half had formal programs, and about one-third called upon outside consultants for assistance in their implementation. Of the 33 companies, 16 required at least some language training.

Although virtually all commentators on the subject speak of the need to prepare a wife or husband for overseas experience, only 32 percent of the 127 firms surveyed in the 1969 Ivancevich study even asked the whether they wished to go abroad and an even smaller number allowed spouses to participate in predeparture training. This finding was supported by a completely separate study that concluded,

It seems to us that the greatest weakness of the selection process as now practiced by people in charge of selection at the twelve companies review lies in the failure to realize that an assignment abroad is a family venture. Yet, in another study, the U.S. managers of foreign operations overwhelmingly agreed that families should receive training or orientation prior to going abroad.

There are many reasons for omitting formal training prior to overseas assignment; specifically, (1) the temporary nature of many such assignments, (2) lack of time because of the immediacy of the need for the employee overseas, (3) the trend toward employment of local nationals, (4) doubt about the need for special for special training, and (5) parallel doubt the effectiveness of existing training programs. Nonetheless, a argument in favor of special cross cultural training is made by Shaw and Miccio. Van Zandt reports that "so different is the [Japanese] culture... that it generally takes about three years in residence, and faithful attendance at ...training seminars before the average Westerner develops confidence in his ability to do business in Japan. The seminars to which reference is made are conducted by the American Chamber of Commerce in Japan. Teague wrote in 1976, "It is becoming more and more apparent that American business in foreign lands will have to give more attention to adapting to local styles in product, method of operation, and approach.

There are a few formal programs within the U.S. designed to improve the effectiveness of the international manager, posted to an overseas job or occupying a spot at headquarters within the international channels of communication. The best known of these are the American graduate School of International Management in Glendale; Arizona; the Institute of the Business Council for International Understanding at the American University in Washington, D.C; and the Monterey Institute of Foreign Studies in Monterey, California. In addition, such organizations as the Institute of International Education and Overseas Briefing Associates organize orientation programs that are on specific countries and are tailored to particular companies. Such organizations as the Asia Society, the Japan Society, and the Middle East Institute likewise periodically mount briefing sessions for businessmen. One of the more highly developed located elsewhere seems to be the Institute of International Training and studies near Fuji, Japan. Created by the Ministry of International Trade and Industry, the student body consists of 120 young corporate executives (average age about 30) who are sent by their respective employees for an intensive year-long, full-time course of study. It consists of intensive English language training plus U.S. area study, general management training, international management study, a second language plus relevant area study, and, finally, a two-month study tour of some part of the world. Japanese industry is thus deliberately creating a trained cadre of international managers. Communication skills and the demonstration of the cultural relativism of management policy and practice receive full treatment. There is nothing in the United States or Europe that can compare in quality and intensity. The major oversight is the isolation of Japanese wives from this sort of preparation, although, if traditional Japanese practice continues, few will live overseas with their husbands any event. Another well-known institution is the Center for Education in International Management in Geneva, Switzerland. One should also note the course on directing foreign operations offered by the Administrative Staff College in Henley-on-Thames, England.

In a study of 403 Americans working in Asia, it was found there was a high order of consistency in their ranking of training needs.

With the hypothesis chat Asians rank these training needs quite differently, the same question was put to 212 English-speaking Asian nationals with whom the Americans had worked. The rankings were remarkably similar for the first three, as can be noted in Table 4.8. The ranking of "orientation for service"reflected the greatest disparity. The author comments:

> Apparently the motivation of Americans for working overseas appears somewhat more important to the Asian nationals than it dose to Americans already overseas. The Asian nationals agree with findings of Cleveland, Mangone, and Adams that "belief in mission" is one of the five elements most relevant to success overseas.

The low rating by both groups of language ability should be noted.

An open-ended question asked the Asian respondents to identify the most needed areas of training in an orientation program for Americans preparing to work overseas. Typical comments were:

Taiwan: Attitude of humility. The greatest hindrance to working successfully overseas is the attitude of intellectual, cultural, and religious superiority. Although Americans are sent out to help, and possibly to change the lives of other peoples, they should also be ready to learn, to receive, and to be changed.

Philippines: Americans must not confuse a sense of service to the people with the imposition of their way of life; i.e., the development of other peoples does not necessarily mean their Americanization. I find most Americans I have worked with technically competent but terribly presumptuous, carrying around with them a tragic sense of "know-it-all" or self-superiority. A deep sense of partnership with local peopel and fellow workers is essential in their preparation.

India: Change in attitude. Most of them behave as if they are superior human beings, although we do not believe they are. Some of them who are in the technical fields are not experts and they should be prepared to learn from their colleagues... Americans who are undergoing orientation courses should be made to believe that Indians are intellectual.

Promotion of overseas management

Three strategies are possible in the promotion of overseas management: national, binational, multinational. Valid considerations for the selection of an optimum promotion policy include:

1. legal restraints on emigration and employment of aliens.
2. family participation in ownership and management of an associated foreign enterprise, which may result in conflicting loyalty if promoted to another associated firm;
3. inability to set up a consistent worldwide remuneration strategy;
4. degree of autonomy of associated firms in that the parent may not be in a position to dictate career paths;
5. preference on the part of key managerial personnel;
6. relative cost per comparable management-year for the various options;

7. ownership of the parent firm
8. relative size of foreign and domestic market;
9. direction of major flows of technical development and skills;
10. availability of parent-country nationals able to interpret communications from abroad;
11. involvement in foreign legal problems, thus requiring skills not available locally;
12. relative importance of foreign-source financing, thus possibly requiring special skills.

Insofar as U.S.- based international companies are concerned, there seem to be relatively few non-U.S. nationals in top corporate positions. But their number would appear to be growing, although admittedly the subject has not been well researched. A 1974 study of 62 U.S. corporations found that 47 hired foreign nationals for management positions within the United States.

In a *Business International* study of 77 U.S.-based firms in 1970, only 14 were found to have rotated executives systematically through foreign and domestic posts, and only three indicated that it was stated corporate policy that to advance in the firm both domestic and foreign experience were necessary. These responses were softened somewhat by frequent observations that such practices were desirable.

But another study seems to point to a growing trend in that it reports,

> Personal experience of international operations is becoming increasingly important for the senior

> managers in the central office. Many presidents of multinational enterprises... were in charge of international divisions earlier in their careers.

The authors of the study from which the above was extracted go on to opine, "The experience of senior executives in international business can help greatly to reduce the communications problem that exists between domestic and foreign units."

The multinational promotional strategy is particularly difficult for Japanese-based firms. The realization of this fact may be one reason that the Japanese generally seem to be internationalizing through the joint-venture and contractual route rather than through the creation of a family of centrally-controlled and integrated subsidiaries. Kobayashi writes,

> Despite the good will and intention to promote the locals in the overseas market, Japanese executives seem to experience a strong mental resistance when we discuss the stage of promoting the locals to managerial positions in their headquarters' organization. This is largely due to the closed culture of Japan and the resulting deficiencies of linguistic ability of many Japanese executives.

Kobayashi feels that this situation may change in that a few Japanese corporations have bought out companies abroad, particularly in the more developed countries, and have retained the foreign managements. Consequently, there are examples, albeit very few, of large Japanese-owned companies presided over by non-Japanese executives. He feels that ultimately these executives must be appointed to "top board positions" in the parent Japanese companies.

It is generally recognized that if the firm locks its foreign managers within their respective national firms eventually one of three things happens: (1) as the maturity and stature of the local management increases vis-a-vis that in headquarters, it becomes increasingly difficult for the headquarters to control, hence, local autonomy increases; (2) as competent, ambitious, foreign nationals hit the promotion ceiling, they leave the firm; (3) the company breaks its nationality policy and creates a multinational management. This last process is possibly accelerated—if not made compelling—if parent company equity is owned in significant amount by local nationals. It has been responsibly predicted that within a decade or so the headquarters of any firm operating internationally will "resemble a veritable U.N., peopled by dozens upon dozens of nationalities; the battle for the presidency will be a multinational one.

There are some demonstrable differences in promotion policy from country to country. An example is the difference revealed by a 1968 survey of 138 business executives in Mexico selected from the largest business firms in Mexico. It was found that the "Mexican firms prefer to bring a man from outside who has had some experience in management and make him president or vice-president." On the other hand, American firms in Mexico appeared "to emphasize hierarchical mobility and promotion from within more than the Mexican firms."

Remuneration

Although an exceedingly complex subject, the choice of basic strategies relating to the remuneration of international management is limited to two: (1) multiple or (2) an international base plus a variety of extras.

Commonly included among such extras are a cost of living differential, an expatriate bonus to compensate for being away from home, and a number of personal adjustment payments.

It should be noted that the salary differential between expatriates and local national managers is likely to vary according to job level, narrowing as one ascends the managerial pyramid.

In some socialist countries the relationship between cash salaries paid to management may be a very low multiple of the wages paid to labor, not infrequently only three or two. However, there may be a much greater difference if all of the goods and services received by managers are taken into account, such perquisites as use of a car, large and well-located apartments, and access to special consumer goods denied the ordinary citizen.

A special problem arises in the international area due to the need (1) to provide inducement to leave the home country, (2) to maintain a home-country standard of living, (3) to facilitate reentry into the home country, (4) to meet the requirements of children's education, and (5) to maintain social obligations vis-a-vis friends and family. The obvious cost of these many payments to already highly paid U.S. or Northern European managers constitutes pressure toward the localization of management, or the employment of third-country nationals.

For example, a 1973 survey showed that the average American assigned to Paris received, in addition to his $18,000 base salary, an overseas premium of $2,411, a cost of living allowance of $4,693, a housing allowance of $5,503, an education allowance of $4,600, airfare for a third child in a U.S. college of $879, and home leave transportation every second year for an annual average of $1,100. The total allowance worked out to be $19,186, for a gross annual cost of $37,186. A frequently-used rule-of-thumb is to multiply a U.S. salary by 2 1/2 to derive the total cost of the employee in an overseas assignment.

Almost inevitably, at some stage both parent-country nationals and foreign nationals are employed as managers within the same overseas enterprise. Additionally, there is a tendency to limit the use of parent-country managers more and more to start-up teams or for trouble shooting, which means transfer from one foreign assignment to another. Finally, as enterprises develop, and correspondingly their managerial personnel, nonparent-country nationals may well be shifted, including periods of assignment to the parent country. Therefore, a purely national wage policy becomes inoperative, for otherwise personnel cannot easily be transferred; they may refuse assignment to a post promising less total emoluments. Complicating the problem further are such factors as exchange controls and currency of payment, national social security payments, exclusion from one's own social security system, and diverse rates of taxation of personal income.

For illustrative purposes only, the compensation policy set up by one U.S.- based international firm is described. *For* U.S. *personnel overseas,* this firm paid a base salary equal to the U.S. salary, added to which was an expatriate or overseas bonus, a cost of living adjustment, and several personal adjustment payments. American personnel were paid generally in local currency an amount equal to that paid to comparable local nationals, the balance being paid in dollars. In order to avoid income tax, local social security taxes, and foreign exchange control difficulties when the U.S. national wished to pay dollar obligations or create dollar savings, this dollar salary was generally not reported to the host government and was frequently paid into a Swiss account to the credit of the employee. *Local nationals* were paid the going local wage with no extra payment or dollar component. *Third-country personnel* were paid a base salary equal to that paid for a comparable position in the place where hired, plus a cost-of-living differential for which the place of hiring was used as the base. Income in excess of comparable local salary might be paid in the currency of country of origin.

The problems inherent in such a system are manifold and include the following:

1. It assumes that an individual's consumption function conforms to the average.
2. U.S. nationals receive more for the same job than either third-country or local nationals.
3. Unreported "of-shore" income may be illegal vis-a-vis local tax authorities, and it cannot be shown as a cost against the local firm's taxable income.
4. The value of off-shore income in the eyes of local nationals is very great and can set up tension.
5. A uniform, company-wide pension scheme is difficult to institute.
6. The transfer of local nationals often means higher cost.
7. Once having enjoyed higher income elsewhere,

employees may resist reassignment to a lower income post, including their home country, even though costs may be lower.

8. The necessarily arbitrary nature of expatriate bonuses and cost-of-living differentials sets up tensions.
9. Absence of local authority over salary structure may cause friction.
10. A company-wide profit-sharing system is virtually impossible.
11. Inclusion under the U.S. social security system must be considered.
12. Maintaining acceptable salary and benefit ratios among various levels of management and of labor may be desirable.

It is of interest to note that a few firms have a policy of reducing overseas allowances after a period of time. The assumption is that as time passes the transferee approaches the buying habits and customs of the local inhabitants, thus rendering the initial cost-of-living allowance untenable.

A general policy followed by a few firms is that of paying an international base salary without regard for nationality or place of hiring, plus whatever expenses are incurred by reason of employment with the company, including a cost-of-living differential. Each national enterprise may have its own pension plan in which local nationals continue to participate regardless of where they may be assigned. The entire base salary and cost-of-living differential is paid in the currency of one's citizenship directly by the employing enterprise. In case foreign exchange controls operate, the local firm must negotiate with the host government for currency exchange by its nonnational employees of a certain portion of their respective incomes. Special adjustment payments may be made directly in the relevant foreign currency by the parent company. Thus, an international management cadre consisting of career foreign service executives is created. Formerly commonplace in the large European firms, one suspects that as firms become truly multinational there is likely to be little or no distinction between foreign and domestic managers. Above a certain level, all will be placed on a global salary scale, subject only to cost-of-living and tax equalization allowances. Any pension and profit-sharing rights will be in respect to the consolidated corporate family. In poorer countries, of course, such a scheme has the effect of widening the disparities in income distribution.

As is well known in the United States, there are significant tax benefits for employees where deferred compensation is provided under a retirement plan qualified under the Internal Revenue Code of 1954 in that personal income tax is deferred until the income is actually received, at which time one's tax rate is likely to be substantially lower. Among the conditions a qualified plan must satisfy is the provision that its benefits extend to 70 percent or more of all eligible employees. Prior to the Employment Retirement Security Act of 1974 (ERISA), *all* employees of a corporate employer, regardless of citizenship or country of residence, were considered "employees" for the purpose of applying the minimum participation standards. Hence, if a U.S. corporation operated through a branch overseas, all employees of that branch had to be included. However, if it operated through a subsidiary, the employer was then a different corporation, and the subsidiary employees could be excluded. *But,* if one wanted to include U.S. citizens employed by such a subsidiary, they could be treated as employees of the U.S. parent but only if the minimum participation standards continued to be met including all of the subsidiary's employees. Also, U.S. expatriates would be so treated only if the U.S. parent had entered into an agreement to extend social security coverage to them. ERISA added a provision that for the purpose of applying the minimum participation standards, a corporation's employees would not include nonresident aliens who receive no income from the employer from sources within the United States. For these purposes a foreign subsidiary is defined as a foreign corporation, 20 percent or more of the voting stock of which is owned by a U.S. parent, and any 50 percent-owned foreign subsidiary of such a foreign corporation.

In practice, U.S. expatriate managers are almost invariably kept in the parent company pension scheme. It should be noted that a manager cannot be retained in a U.S. pension scheme unless he is covered by social security; that is, the payments made by the company will not be deductible from taxable income as a legitimate business expense. Coverage by U.S. social security is possible if (1) the U.S. firm owns at least 20 percent of the foreign firm employing the expatriate and (2) if an agreement is executed with the Internal Revenue Service. Meanwhile, by local low, the manager and his employer may be required to contribute to a local social security system from which the employee is unlikely ever to benefit. Not infrequently, local national managers are excluded from headquarters' benefit plans, which fact causes another a symmetry in treatment of expatriate managers as contrasted to the local national managers. Nor are they generally eligible to participate in the qualified pension plan of the parent company. The firm really has three options: (1) set up local national pension plans, (2) pay local national managers from the U.S. payroll and thereby include them within the parent company program, or (3) set up a pension plan in a base company covering all non-U.S. executives. The first seems to be generally preferred. The third-country national may be included either under the pension plan where he is employed or under that within his home country. Unfortunately, many countries do not extend their social security systems to nationals employed abroad as does the United States.

Selelction of management style

There would seem to be at least four significant dimensions to managerial style: (1) degree of subordinate participation in decision-making, (2) degree of calculation as contrasted with impressionism in decision-making, (3) the degree of formality, and (4) vertical consistency. The relevant question for the international firm is whether the establishment of a universally applicable, single style along one or more of these dimensions is optimum.

A continuum of subordinate participation in decision-making would run thusly:

1. Superior makes own decision with no explanation and with little or no thought of subordinate.
2. Superior makes own decision with no explanation but with considerable thought of subordinates.
3. Superior makes own decision, but with fairly complete explanation to subordinates so that they will be aware of why the decision was made.

4. Superior makes own decision with no explanation because of prior knowledge of the attitudes, values, and opinions of subordinates, which he or she has taken into consideration.

5. Superior makes own decision, but fairly complete explanation for the purpose of gaining the support of subordinates.

6. Superior makes own decision, but with fairly complete explanation to subordinates to indicate (1) that he or she has considered their known attitudes, values, and opinions, and (2) to gain their support.

7. Superior makes own decision after consultation with subordinates.

8. Decision is made jointly by superior and subordinate, but is articulated by the superior to his boss.

9. Decision is made jointly by leader and subordinates and is articulated to the superior's boss as a group decision.

10. Decision is delegated to subordinates, but is subject to superior's influence.

11. Decision is delegated entirely to subordinate.

Admittedly, styles 10 and 11 do not tell us how the subordinate makes the decision, who, in turn, may opt for any one of the styles listed.

The depth of management participation may be an important dimension. Participation may be limited to top-management levels, to upper-middle management, to lower-middle management, to lower management, or may be extended to include all employees.

The point is that many studies of managerial style are too simplistic to produce valid findings. They assume either that the degree of participation is the only significant dimension to managerial style or that decision-making style is either participative or not. This latter assumption is like classifying all political systems simply into participative and non participative without recognizing the essential difference between the single party regimes of Stalin and Ataturk or between the multiparty regimes of Sygman Rhee's Korea and Churchill's Britain.

When one considers the variables that must relate in some circumstances to choice of decision-making style as defined by degree of participation, it is obvious that there can be no universally valid superior style. Even to dub one "modern" and the other "traditional," as some authors do, is surely misleading, given the state of present research.

In reviewing all of the major research of a comparative nature relating to managerial attitudes and behavior, Barrett and Bass concluded:

> We interpret all the above studies on superior-subordinate relationships to indicate that there are differences among countries in preferred style of leadership. These differences in leadership styles appear to be largely culturally-based, and at this point of time it would appear naive to advocate one model of leadership style as being optimum for all cultural groups. The widely-advocated American model of participative management may not be optimum for all cultures, and in fact may be dysfunctional in some.

A 1973 survey of 75 expatriate U.S. managers apparently revealed a shift to a more authoritarian managerial style from that practiced in the United States prior to overseas assignment. First, the expatriates, on average, perceived their subordinates overseas as more resistant to change, but more loyal to the company, than their subordinates in the United States. Furthermore, the executives tended to change their beliefs about subordinate employees after assuming overseas assignment. Very few of the respondents felt that U.S. subordinates were lazy, preferred to be led, did not want responsibility, or had to be closely controlled. The number of these same executives associating these qualities to their overseas subordinates tripled. Several of the executives felt that the threat of firing was an effective motivational factor abroad, though not in the United States. And several felt that improving working conditions was an acceptable way of motivating subordinates to achieve higher productivity and was more effective in the overseas case. The author pointed out, "This again concurs that what is good managerial style for the United States does not necessarily apply overseas." "It is evident that the respondents in their present jobs overseas have become more authoritarian in decision-making." "The findings conform to the situational theories of leadership behavior."

There has been little research and writing in reference to the second dimension of managerial style, the use of statistical information in making decisions versus own perception, intuitive assessment, or personal judgment, or in calculation versus impressionism. It has been observed that:

The American executive is number and fact oriented. This is often misleading in that facts and figures do not always contain all that is needed in making the "right" decision. The Latin American and European mind is much more well suited to the uniqueness of international business because they are humanistically oriented as opposed to the American factual orientation.

One study of Mexican managers, previously referred to, reports a difference between managers of Mexican-controlled and U.S. -controlled firms in Mexico. In the former, about 70 percent said that they relied heavily on their perception and value judgment in making important decisions; in the latter, only 40 percent. Giving some validity to the survey was the finding that regardless of types of business, 100 percent of the executives in the sample previously employed by the government indicated that they used perception and a "feel of the situation." It also came out that both the very small and the very large firms, whether Mexican or U.S. -controlled, had a large number of executives who could be classified as impressionists. It was the medium-sized organization that housed the majority of executives classified as calculatives. It was further found that the impressionists were promoted faster than the calculatives. Alpander observed:

In developing countries, such as Mexico, executives need self assurance, and they need to be quick in making their decisions in light of a rapidly changing environment. Therefore, expediency in decision-making by an intuitive approach is tolerated. This intuitive approach is not necessarily an asset in more developed countries like the United States, but it is definitely a characteristic that leads to success in environments like Mexico.

The analysis goes on to conclude that "American firms in Mexico should take into consideration the decision-making characteristics of their executives in establishing recruitment and selection policies, since what is needed in Mexico is the ability to combine knowledge of scientific process with one's own judgment in making quick decisions." He also concludes, "Most of those executives who were classified as calculatives indicated that they could seldom derive a feeling of achievement, or a sense of personal growth, from their jobs."

Very little can be said about the degree to which informal channels of communication from subordinate to superior or from subordinate to others on the same level as his superior are characteristic of enterprises in various societies. The subject seems not to have been researched. But it appears that there may be national differences on this score, in part a function of the status consciousness within a society and the degree to which voluntary, private associations are present. Who belongs to which clubs, associations, churches, and political parties? What sort of off-the-job social intercourse takes place in such organizations may well influence the nature of the subordinate-superior relationship on the job and even the locale or forum in which decisions are made. If A knows that B, his subordinate, can talk freely and intimately with either C, A's boss, or D, who is on A's level, the relationship between A and B is likely to be affected and so likewise the decision-making style. It may be that really important decisions are not made in the office hierarchical context at all but within a more fluid group around the table at the club. In some cases, this circumvention of one's immediate superiors may be institutionalized, as reflected in the policy of some German companies previously commented upon.

A fourth dimension of managerial style is vertical consistency, not only in respect to various forms of participation, but also to the degree of calculation and formality in decision making. To the extent that an elite upper management adopts a particular style that is inconsistent with managerial style at lower levels, lack of communication may become a problem on the interface, at whatever level that may be. An alien management from an industrially developed country operating in a less developed country may find itself precisely in this situation. If so, substantial inputs of patience, education, and training may be required to bridge the gap, or an adaption to the lower-levelstyle by those functioning at the interface. Again, there seems to be very little research bearing directly on this problem.

No discussion of managerial style would be complete without some reference to the Japanese system, which is identified by the phrase *ringi-seido,* literally, "the system of submitting a proposal to one's superior and receiving his approval." The initiative for a decision may be at any level down to middle management, but the formal process starts with the preparation of a written proposal at the middle-management level. The proposal then works its way up both laterally and horizontally. If anyone objects along the way, a meeting is called and the problem talked out until there is a consensus. The process then continues to the top level, at which point the decision is articulated by the chief executive. Four observations should be made. *First,* though certainly time consuming, this style of decision-making means that everyone is fully aware of the details of a decision, and of his respective role in implementing it at the moment of articulation by the chief executive. Hence, implementation is immediate. *Second,* this system may only work effectively in association with two other characteristics of the Japanese managerial system, life-time tenure and promotion by seniority. *Third,* a manager can through the *ringi* system be important without being president. Although many Japanese corporate chief executives are very important and much admired and respected men, one gets the impression that as individuals they are not as important in formulating decisions as, say, many of their U.S. counterparts. *Fourth,* in view of the sociopsychological evidence that decisions made in groups are more likely to be riskier than decisions made individually, it may be that the Japanese system is less risk-averse than the U.S. or European. The individual does not bear the responsibility; the group does.

The idea of collective responsibility is related to a feeling called shu-jo-nu-on. To conform to this concept requires abandoning the idea of individual power domination in favour of cooperative group action where no man's success may be attributed to his brains and the strength of his two arms unaided and alone. The great emphasis on harmony sometimes surprises Occidental visitors; a manager may describe with pride the spirit of concord prevalent in his factory, rather than the profits it makes, even where the profits are high.

In Japanese, there seems to be no precise equivalent for the common phrase, "the self-made man."

In a 1976 survey of Japanese executive opinion, the *"ringi"* system was felt by 42.0 percent to be a very effective way to encourage participation in decision-making and to maintain high morale. Another 21.0 percent felt that it helped to maintain better communication, both vertically and horizontally. Three percent felt that it encouraged the input of creative ideas by the junior echelon of management. Only 22.3 percent reacted negatively.

Finally, attention should be drawn to the Yugoslav system of workers' self-management and to the Chinese system of role exchange. These three quite different systems—the Japanese. The Yugoslav, and the Chinese—all appear to be generating and sustaining a relatively high level of creativity and productivity. The problems inherent in a continuing relationship between a North American or West European firm with a Japanese, Yugoslav, or Chinese enterprise are legion. Experience is accumulating in reference to the Japanese. In the Yugoslav case, the age and number of international joint ventures are so restricted that generalizations are difficult. It has been observed that such ventures are normally managed by a joint operating board on which sit representatives of management of the two contracting firms. This board is required to submit certain matters to the workers' council for decision. These would include distribution of income belonging to the Yugoslav partner, salaries of personnel working for the joint venture, the joint venture's annual economic plan, the organizational structure of the joint venture, and the hiring and firing of workers.

The thrust of this discussion is that the present practice of international firms in the selection, preparation, and promotion of international managerial personnel hardly seems to be the best. The remuneration problem is of more tangible nature and, hence, has been given somewhat greater attention, but the interplay of conflicting laws and regulations and constantly shifting price levels and foreign exchange rates make the creation of an entirely equitable system exceedingly difficult without involving the firm in what would appear unnecessary cost. Finally, it is quite apparent that there is no universally best managerial style. The latter observation relates to the selection and preparation of international managers in that individuals with very different personality attributes, managerial philosophies, and calculative skills may all perform well, but in different environments. The problem lies in matching people to situations, which implies an ability to measure both with something more than random success. Obviously, the measures are imperfect, but such imperfection does not preclude sensitivity to the problem and effort.

This view is challenged by the so-called universalists, those who insist that there is a common pattern of behavior among all managers regardless of the cultural milieu in which they operate. Induced by the discipline imposed by modern industry, this common pattern is seen as a world managerial culture. Differences among managers are thus perceived as reflecting personal, situational, or organizational differences. It should be pointed out that this definition begs a question, for if there is a consistent difference in personal behavior, situation, or organization, the impact of culture may thus be revealed.

A modification of the universalist view is that of the cultural cluster school, in which similarities of managerial values and behavior within multinational cultural areas are emphasized. Most frequent groupings are Nordic-European, Latin-European, Anglo-American, developing countries and Japan.

A third point of view is that managerial behavior is strongly influenced by key environmental characteristics, particularly the economic. Other possibly important factors are size of relevant markets, occupational mix, density of population, level of popular education, prevailing politico economic ideology, social structure, and ethnic-religious homogeneity.

These views may not be as inconsistent as would first appear. That is, the production function and the competitiveness of the international market impose certain pressures on the managerial team of an enterprise wherever located. However, given the general cultural environment of a region, managers within that area tend to react to these systemic pressures in a similar fashion in terms of values and behavior. But, in societies that are unique along some important dimension, managerial values and behavior are likely to be distinctive. Therefore, one may hypothesize that any study designed to demonstrate *globally* either the universality or cultural-relativity of managerial behavior will be inconclusive.

One difficulty in some studies directed to this subject is that they may not have homed in on the really key values and behavior patterns that differentiate managers operating within different cultures. Also, the samples have to be picked with great care. For example, should public sector managers be included in countries in which the public sector industry is a significant part of the total? If they are not, the results of a comparative study could well be vitiated in that among the essential dimensions of managerial values and behavior are those having to do with managerial motivation and organizational goals. These may vary substantially between public and private sector enterprise, and the fact that a society has opted for greater activity in the public sector may be of signal importance. Another possibly relevant dimension is the occupational mix. Certain managerial values and behavior may tend to be associated with specific activities.

Barrett and Bass suggest seven variables in describing management behavior: (1) superior-subordinate relationship, (2) managerial needs or motivation, (3) interpersonal perceptions, (4) organizational goals, (5) perception of equity, (6) decision-making under uncertainty, and (7) managerial values. In respect to the first, the two authors, after surveying the literature of comparative organization, conclude that there are strong arguments against the view that the participative form of management has universal application throughout the world. Without being inconsistent, one can go on to claim that participative management may represent the most highly evolved form of management. That it is not immediately effective in large areas of the world is not surprising. Effective participative management may require that labor and management have consistent goals and similar time horizons, conditions implying a fairly high level of sophistication and material well-being on the part of all concerned.

Managerial needs and motivation, whether measured by a ranking of needs or of life goals, would appear to be remarkably similar around the world but with some significant differences. In order to be more certain of these findings, however, one would have to know (1) whether managers were more similar than nonmanagers, (2) whether public-sector managers differ significantly from private-sector managers, and (3) whether there were significant occupational differences. Perhaps all that these studies tell us is that there is some hierarchy of human need that tends to be universal, at least among secularly educated people no longer directly concerned with daily survival. But these studies do not tell us how those needs are translated into personal or organizational behavior in a given environment.

In fact, what evidence exists would tend to demonstrate significant national differences among managers in respect to interpersonal perception. Also, in respect to ranking organizational objectives, significant differences among managers of various countries seem to have been demonstrated, with the key independent variables being economic. For example, more developed country managers seem to put more stress upon the objectives of growth and competition; less developed country managers, upon the maintenance of satisfactory organizational operations. Also, apparently significant differences have been demonstrated in reference to perceived equity in work rewards. In at least some less developed countries as opposed to some more developed countries, managers appear to be more inclined to give a smaller pay differential to above-average performers and to take into account in setting pay both extenuating personal circumstances and job conditions.

Some research would seem to support the idea that managerial values are perhaps similar cross-culturally, particularly in terms of degree of pragmatism. But the public-private sector problem, the occupational base problem, as well as the linking of values to behavior and organizational characteristics, remain. Also, none of the research suggests that a certain set of values or behavior pattern is associated with the most *effective* management despite environmental conditions.

A 1970 study by Richard Wright based on matched pairs of companies in Chile provides added support for the environmentalist view as against the universalist. In the Wright study, the critical environmental constraints consisted of rapid cost inflation, price control, labor law, and the small market size. Measures of managerial effectiveness used were net profit, a five-year trend in net profit, return on investment, a five-year trend in return on investment, and percentage change in sales and market share. The conclusion of the study was that the locally owned firms were doing better than their American counterparts. A study of the internal operations of the firm revealed that the U.S. firms were operated essentially according to guidelines set down by parent company headquarters whereas the management philosophy of the Chilean firms generally was "based on highly individualized patterns of policies and practices, usually characteristic of the personal value systems of the president and local boards of directors of those firms." These basic differences appeared to affect the relative ability "to adapt to the conditions of the Chilean environment in at least two different ways": (1) the U.S. firms had a more complex and costly management structure and (2) the U.S. firms responded more slowly to rapid changes in the environment.

The evidence accumulates. A study in three very similar factories in France, England, and Scotland concluded,

> Recent work in the field of cross-cultural research on business organizations by psychologists and economists has tended to lay stress upon the businessman as a cross-cultural phenomenon—motivated by the same needs and employing the same methods to achieve those needs. We believe, as the result of this research,

backed up by twelve years experience of management in both countries, that such findings are extremely superficial.

A 1972 Norwegian study came up with some fairly impressive evidence of significant cross-cultural differences in the attitudes of chief executives toward supervisory values and practices. Statistically significant differences among five regions were found in references to the following questions:

1. Are owners more interested in employee well-being than their managers?
2. Must successful leaders be exceptionally self-confidence?
3. Do successful leaders direct subordinate in exactly what they should do and how to do it?
4. Do successful leaders involve as many people as possible in making important decisions?
5. Are major policy decisions made by a committee superior to those made by the chief executive alone?

Significant differences were not found on some subjects. For example, executives in all areas were in strong agreement that successful leaders were interested in the ideas of these subordinates. Response from all areas was neutral in respect to whether subordinates wished to take on more responsibility than they are able to handle. All were in agreement that if subordinates see the likelihood of promotional opportunities, they will work harder. The overall conclusion: "the above findings suggest that culture does play an important role in determining the managerial philosophy, attitudes, and practices of chief executives."

It should be pointed out that to say that the most *effective* style of management, however this may be defined, may vary with time and place is not to say that there may not be a global convergence of managerial style in terms of effectiveness over time. This evolutionary convergence is a legitimate problem for the organizational theorist, but the practicing manager must respond to the environmentally imposed requirements of a particular time and place. He should, however, be aware that the style that is effective at a particular time and place is not necessarily the most effective at a different time and place.

Organizing a mexican corporation

Briefly the following furnishes an idea of the steps required in organizing a Mexican corporation. Legal counsel, particularly one with a thorough knowledge of Mexican laws, and a close acquaintance with Mexican government officials, is extremely important. The correspondent of the Thompson and Root Law Firm is Basham, Ringe & Correa of Mexico City. Chase Manhattan National Bank of New York recommended Hardin & Hess of New York, who have an office in Mexico City.

In the latest *Overseas Business Report,* put out by the United States Department of Commerce, it is suggested that a corporation, or "Sociedad Anonima,"is the most usual type of business organization, and the one most likely to meet the needs of United States interest. Mr. Thompson agrees to this.

Briefly, the Articles of Incorporation, which must be recorded in the Public Resister of Commerce, are not too dissimilar from the requirements of many states of this country, except, perhaps they go more into the nationalities and domiciles of the natural or corporate persons who constitute the corporation.

A minimum of five members is required for the formation of a corporation, and each one of these must subscribe to at least one share of stock. It is preferable that one or more of the members have Mexican nationality.

The capital stock of a corporation must not be less than 25,000 pesos and must be fully subscribed. At the time of organization, at least 20 percent of the capital stock must be paid in cash. If property is conveyed to the corporation at the time of organization in payment of capital stock, an appraisal of the value of such property is required. In such case, the shares of stock are deposited for two years, during which period they cannot be sold or transferred.

Shares of stock may either be bearer shares or registered shares. Shares of the same class must be of equal value and must confer equal rights. However, the Articles of Incorporation may provide for different classes of shares with special rights for each class, provided that no member is excluded from participation in earnings.

No dividends may be paid to holders of common stock until a dividend of at least 5 percent has been paid to holders of stock having limited voting rights.

The customary officers of a corporation are the board of directors, a general manager, and an examiner. They may or may not be shareholders.

The number of directors usually is from three to five. When there are three or more directors, minority shareholders representing 25 percent of the capital stock have the right to elect one member of the board Directors' meetings may be held either in Mexico or in a foreign country.

A general manager may be elected by the board of directors, or at a general meeting of the shareholders.

An examiner must be named at the first meeting of the shareholders. He is presumed to be the direct representative of the shareholders, and he has the right of intervening in their behalf, independently of the directors, in the event that the directors should fail or refuse to comply with their duties. Minority shareholders having 25 percent of the capital stock have the right to elect an examiner to represent their interests.

Meetings of the shareholders may be either general or special, and must be held at the domicile of the corporation.

It appears that the Mexican government will favor the organization of a corporation where one or more shareholders are Mexicans. If Mexicans are shareholders, it may be well to consider the issuance of a special type of share to give the Mexican shareholders their proportionate share of earnings but retain in the American shareholders essential controls and perhaps preference as to assets in the event of liquidation.

Taxation of business enterprises

Business enterprises, whether sole proprietorships, partnerships, or corporations, are subject to a global income tax. This means all income of a business enterprise must be included in its annual tax return except dividends received from Mexican corporations and earnings of funded pension plans approved by the income tax department.

The former tax on distributable profits was repealed when the present law was enacted because it was regarded as an impediment to the reinvestment of profits in productive activities. Profits are thus taxed only when the dividends are actually paid. However, all profits of branches of foreign corporations are subject to the dividend tax mentioned above, whether or not these profits are actually remitted. Dividends paid by one Mexican corporation to another, and the issuance of stock dividends, which represent capitalization of retained earnings, are riot subject to the tax.

The reinvestment of earnings is automatic, and prior authorization is not necessary to secure an exemption from taxes on retained earnings. Losses which are incurred in any one year can be charged against profits earned during the five years immediately following.

The capital gains tax is not applied on sales of real property when the property sold has been held for ten or more years. However, when capital gains are realized on real property held for a lesser period, the capital gains tax is applied at a proportionately reduced rate, that is:

Up to 2 years	100
From 2 to 4 years	80
From 4 to 6 years	60
From 6 to 8 years	40
From 8 to 10 years	20

The corporate income tax is a graduated tax with income up to 2,000 pesos being entirely exempt. Income between 2,000.01 and 3,500.00 pesos is assessed at the rate of 5 percent and income between 3,500.01 and 5,000.00pesos is assessed at 75 pesos, plus 6 percent on the excess over 3,500.00 up to 5,000.00. Income taxes are then increased on a graduated basis to the point where the tax levied on income of 500,000 pesos and upwards is 210,000.00 pesos plus 42 percent on the amount in excess of 500,000 pesos.

Expenditures deemed to be ordinary, necessary, and in proportion to the size of the business, plus those deductions specifically authorized by law, are allowable costs. Capital expenditures are not deductible. The principal business deductions include cost of goods sold; cost of manufacture or assembly of goods sold; wages and related payments; bad debts, when proven uncollectable or when the statute of limitations for collection has expired; rental payments for real property if used for the business; interest on borrowed capital; insurance and bond premiums if paid to Mexican insurance companies; charitable donations to government-approved recipients; and payments of royalties and technical assistance fees.

The straight-line method of depreciation and amortization, at fixed annual rates, is provided for. However, the Ministry of Finance is authorized to approve higher rates of depreciation as an industrial incentive. The maximum annual depreciation rates are:

Buildings and component parts of buildings 5%

Machinery, equipment, and other tangible property not included in the following category 10%

Transportation equipment, machinery for the construction industry, and cooperate for the wine and liquor industries 20%

A maximum of 5 percent is allowed for amortization of intangible fixed assets and deferred charges. Types of expenditures allowed include expenses incurred in forming a company and payments for franchises, patent rights, trademarks, and literary and artistic copyrights. No deductions are allowed for amortization of goodwill.

Gross income earned in Mexico by nonresident corporations or aliens is taxed without deductions for expenses of any kind. Such income is subject to withholding by those who make such payments and includes: (1) a 20 percent withholding tax on technical service fees; (2) 10 percent on interest paid to foreign banks; (3) 20 percent on occasional commission income; (4) the progressive business tax on royalties of all types.

Tax concession

It may be possible for Docker to secure one or more tax concessions. Under Mexico's Law of Industrial Encouragement, the Mexican government may grant tax exemptions to industries than manufacture or produce goods not produced in Mexico; industries that manufacture goods not produced domestically in sufficient quantity for consumer needs; industries "providing services for economically important activities"; assembly operations provided these use Mexican-produced parts that represent as least 60 percent of their products' direct cost; and industries exporting their own finished or semifinished manufactures, provided at least 60 percent of the direct production cost of such products represents Mexican manufacture.

Industries within these classifications are eligible for five-year, seven-year, or ten-year reductions in respect to, or exemptions from, the following taxes: import duties and the surcharges thereon, stamp taxes, the gross receipts tax, and the income tax. The Industrial Encouragement Law limits the income tax reduction to a maximum of 40 percent of the tax.

Among conditions frequently stipulated in the concessions granting the tax exemption mentioned above to foreigners are those requiring that: (1) the firm have a majority Mexican capitalization; (2) foreign technicians remain in Mexico for a limited period and train Mexican replacements; and (3) payments abroad for the right to use patents, trademarks, technical assistance, and the like, whether in the form of royalties, shares in production, sales, or profits be limited to a percentage of the firm's sales, which percentage shall be determined jointly by the Ministries of Industry and Commerce and of Finance and Public Credit.

Also, the Mexican tariff provides for reductions up to 75 percent of the regular import duties for firms that import certain specified types of machinery or equipment to establish new industrial plants and expand or modernize existing plants. Prior authorization must be obtained from the Ministry of Finance for such duty reductions, and approval is not granted for the importation of types of items similar to those made in Mexico or which can be substituted by machinery produced in Mexico.

The income tax law provides for the granting of authorization to use a method of accelerated depreciation for firms which make new investments in machinery and equipment.

Firms producing manufactured goods for export may obtain subsidies from the Ministry of Finance in the form of reductions on income taxes, on the gross receipts tax, and on duties applicable to imports of raw materials and components, provided that the finished goods are in fact exported. Prior approval must be obtained from the ministry for such arrangements.

A subsidy in an amount equal to the federal portion of the gross receipts tax is granted to manufacturers in the interior on the initial sale of their goods within 20 kilometers of the U.S. border and to the free zones. The subsidy, designed to promote sales to the border areas, also includes a 25 percent reduction of railroad freight charges. Firms interested in obtaining the above benefits must be registered with the National Border Program Agency.

Under the Mexican border industrialization program, Mexican and foreign firms that establish processing plants on the Mexican side of the border are permitted duty-free importation of machinery, raw materials, and components provided all their end-products are exported. Exports made by such firms are duty free as well. The program is designed to attract foreign firms, mostly from the United States, to provide the jobs for the surplus labor located along the border areas.

Additionally, special export incentives are available in the form of import duty rebate. To qualify, the firm must utilize at least 40 percent domestic components. When integration reaches the 50-59 percent level, the firm can qualify for a 67 percent rebate. When it reaches 60 percent, a 100percent rebate is possible. Import tax rebates are also available on products sold in the northern border zone and in free zones for those manufacturers showing a cumulative increase in sales of at least 15 percent over the preceding year.

The question remained as to whether it was better to establish a new business or to purchase an existing one. From a tax exemption standpoint it appeared advisable to establish a new business. On the other hand, Jefferson Thompson stated that one Diaz Porfino, an influential Mexican citizen, was manufacturing furniture. It was suspected that in the event Docker opted for a new business Porfino's influence might be brought to bear, with the result that Docker's project might be deemed prejudicial to the interests of an already established manufacturer. Mr. Roberts, a second vice-president of Chase Manhattan National Bank and formerly a businessman in Mexico, stated that in his opinion it would be better to purchase an existing business. Shortly after receiving the above information from Mr. Steel man, L. D. Docker made a short visit to Mexico to look over the situation at firsthand. He came back favorably impressed with Poirot's operation and the Mexican market.

5

Guidelines for Global Business and Legal Aspects

In today's era of rapid technological change and increasing international competition, the world enterprise occupies a uniquely sensitive position. Operating in a diversity of national environments, allocating resources and making decisions in the light of global alternatives, it must cope not only with a more elaborate set of organizational variables but with a far more complex and sensitive array of external factors than a domestically oriented business. Its sheer size relative to some of the national economies in which it functions often magnifies the economic consequences of its decisions.

Particularly where the tides of nationalism are running strong, the political impact of these decisions-and the burden of responsibility on the decision maker-may be heavy indeed. To assure the long-term profitability of the organization, top management must be sensitive to the complex interrelationships between the world enterprise and each of its national environments. Without this awareness, it cannot hope to plan the future strategy of the enterprise so as to maximise growth and profitability.

Since the end of World War II the multinational company has truly come into its own. The lure of overseas markets has brought about an upsurge of international activity among producers of chemical and pharmaceuticals, automobiles, synthetic fibres, electronic equipment, and a long list of other products. It has been estimated that thirty of the top fifty American companies, and twenty-six of the fifty largest enterprises else where in the world, could be ranked as truly international companies-an estimate that is probably conservative if we define, as some experts do, an "international company" as any enterprise with 20% or more of its assets invested abroad. And an informed American observer has speculated that two decades hence 600 or 700 of the largest multinational companies may be doing the major part of the world's business.

Impact of world enterprise

Such figures, however, hardly begin to suggest the manifold ways in which the plans and actions of multinational companies, large and small, affect the host economies in which their subsidiaries operate. Most concretely, there is the injection of capital into the host country, initially from direct foreign investment and later from the reinvestment of local earnings, which tends to mobilize domestic capital for investment in related enterprises and stimulate business activity generally. There is the further benefit of foreign exchange earned by the subsidiary in exporting some or all of its production and, conversely, the unfavorable balance-of-payments effects of repatriation of profits and of raw-materials imports by the foreign-owned enterprise. Beyond its immediate financial impact, the effects of foreign investment are felt throughout the host economy in the form of additions to local resources of knowledge and know-how, competitive pressures, and higher employment.

Initially, at least, the multinational enterprise brings into the host country a cadre of managers and technicians whose knowledge and skills are transferred, in the course of time, to the domestic nationals whom they train. These nationals will, in many cases, ultimately take over responsibilities for local operations; training a new generation of managers and technical workers in their turn. If there is mobility of employment in these occupations, these effects may soon spread to other sectors of the host nation's economy.

The importance of such an injection of managerial and technical knowledge in a developing nation is well illustrated by the case of Africa's only alumina refinery, a $150-million plant operated in Guinea by FRIA, an international consortium of European and American aluminum producers. FRIA's manpower training program, begun nearly two years before its plant went into full operation in 1960, has trained hundreds of African technicians and managers, many of whom were illiterate when hired. By 1962, the company was employing, along with 400-odd European expatriates, more than 900 Africans. The number of its African professional workers had risen from ninety-seven to 476, and its African foremen from two to thirteen. More than twenty Africans, by completing a two-year vocational training course, had become eligible for journeyman and craftsman positions, and some 200 workers had learned to read and write in the company's literacy classes. By 1963 almost the entire initial work force had been upgraded.

Again, the production techniques employed by a

foreign subsidiary may benefit local industries in developing nations. Latin America is replete with examples: the improved cotton-ginning techniques and the advances in vegetable-oil refining, handling and transport introduced by Anderson, Clayton & Company into Brazil; the advances in Peruvian fishing methods traceable to the influence of Wilbur-Ellis, the American fish-packing company; and the pre-shrinking of textiles that is now commonplace in the Peruvian textile industry, thanks to the use of the process by a local subsidiary of W.R. Grace and Company. Comparable effects can sometimes be traced to the marketing activities of a world enterprise. Thus, improved paperwork and office procedures have been brought about by the efforts of International Business Machines Corporation to market its computers to the managements of large banks and insurance companies around the world.

No less important than the immediate infusion of knowledge and skills by a world-enterprise subsidiary are its competitive effects.

When a highly efficient foreign producer enters into direct competition with local industry, some inefficient producers may be forced out of business. At the same time, the foreign operation may tend to bid up the price of local capital and labor, adding to the cost pressures on indigenous producers in other industries as well. Though painful, such effects frequently benefit the economies of the host nations in the long run by forcing local producers to improve their efficiency.

A further important impact of multinational enterprise on the host country is, of course, added employment. The dimensions of this contribution are suggested by a U.S.

Commerce Department study that put wage and salary payments by foreign subsidiaries of U.S. based companies at $6.9 billion in 1957, roughly the equivalent of the total private consumption of Belgium and Luxembourg. Overseas payrolls of U.S. based companies in that year totaled an estimated 3.2 million persons, better than nine-tenths of them local nationals. Roughly 930,000 foreign nationals in that year were employed by U.S. subsidiaries in Latin America, over 1 million in Europe, more than 230,000 in Asia, and nearly 100,000 in Africa. Considering the growth of overseas investments by U.S. companies since then, it is safe to assume that the current employment figures are a great deal higher.

Bowater in appalachia

An interesting example of the contribution of a multinational company to the solution of a local unemployment problem can be found in Calhoun, Tennessee, near the southern tip of the economically depressed Appalachian region of the United States. There Bowater Southern, a subsidiary of the giant British paper company, employs some 1,3000 local workers. In addition to its payroll of about $10 million per year, Bowater Southern pumps approximately $11 million annually into the region's economy by purchases of wood from private landholders.

Besides the local nationals it employs directly, of course, the world-enterprise subsidiary tends to create more jobs in supplier companies and related business. In turn, this added employment enhances consumer purchasing power, stimulates demand, and creates further support for future economic expansion. An example of this can be seen in Volkswagen's Brazilian operation, which employs over 10,000 people directly and stimulates the employment of thousands more through the myriad industries that supply Volkswagen with automotive components and accessories. A further illustration is that of Royal Dutch Shell, whose Venezuelan subsidiary, Compania Shell de Venezuela, besides giving work directly to over 9,000 local nationals, helps create countless other jobs by local purchases of goods and services. These totaled nearly $37 million in 1964 alone.

Long-run compatibility vital

In outlining some of the major effects of multinational enterprise on national economies, I have not meant to imply that the managers of such enterprises should, or indeed could, invariably plan their corporate strategy in such a way as to maximise the immediate economic benefits to the host nations. The basic purpose of a multinational company, like that of any other private business, is the utilization of resources to maximise profit. Its health and survival depend, ultimately, on the vigor, constancy, and intelligence with which it pursues this purpose. But though it cannot invariably act in harmony with the short-run needs of the host economy, the interests of the world enterprise must at least be compatible with those of the host nation over the long run.

Nothing is more basic to the maintenance of a favorable international investment climate than a convincing and continuing demonstration by world enterprise that it can, over some considerable period of time, contribute important and continuing benefits to the economies of the host nations. Indeed, in negotiating with the host government for the protective incentives that are so often a *sine qua non* of profitable investment in a developing economy, the company must generally be able to demonstrate in great detail the nature and dimensions of the long-range benefits its investment may be expected to bring. Thus, in an era of growing nationalism in many areas of the world, the very self-interest of the multinational corporation obliges it to operate with increasing sensitivity to the self-interest of its hosts and to the effects of its activities upon them.

The acute need to harmonize potentially divergent interests has focused attention on the value of detailed, realistic company planning based on adequate information. Effective planning by the multinational corporation inherently acts as a stabilizing force. By shifting the focus of corporate energies from the pursuit of short term profits to the building of long-term profitability, it reinforces the mutuality of interest between the local subsidiary and the nation in which it operates. This in turn tends to dissipate the specter of a powerful foreign enterprise, unpredictable in its behavior and unresponsive to local control.

Above all, the complexity of the risks, requirements and opportunities in the international field lends real urgency to the need for institutionalization of planning in the multinational corporation. Nowhere is it more difficult to develop a planning system that will integrate the separate contributions of many corporate executives into a single set of formal plans for the corporation and its individual units. Yet the special requirements of planning in the multinational enterprise have until quite recently received little attention.

The three faces of planning

Planning in the multinational company may be viewed as the process of developing a program for future action through rational assessment of company potentials, evaluation of market opportunities in the light of the relevant economic, social and political variables, and selection of alternatives on the basis of expected risk and return. The results of this process are a hierarchy of interrelated plans that define the business or businesses in which the company will engage, identify specific goals to be achieved, and set forth the means of achieving them. These plans may be classified as strategic plans, interim plans, and operating plans.

The *strategic plan* envisions the kinds of business in which the company will engage in its various national environments, defines the role its expects to play in the countries where it operates, and sets forth its long-range objectives. A manufacturer of consumer durable, for example, might have as its goal the production and sale of a full line of home appliances throughout the world. Its strategic plan might stipulate:

That the company will maintain control of its market and will create a marketing organization wherever a profitable potential exists.

That as overseas market volume develops, production will be shifted from the company's domestic plants to foreign manufacturing facilities, to be strategically located with respect to production and distribution economies, long-term competitive strategy, and relevant political considerations.

That the company will expand its operations by reinvestment of earnings where feasible, but may speed its growth by acquiring existing overseas marketing and manufacturing facilities if it can do so economically.

That the company will seek to build a long-term position in each of its national environments by pursuing policies that will tend to identify its subsidiaries with local interest: employment of local nationals in supervisory and managerial positions wherever possible, establishment of technical training programs in less-developed areas, and responsiveness to local economic considerations and balance-of-payments considerations when making decisions on repatriation vs. reinvestment of earnings-even where no specific commitments have been made.

The function of strategic plans is to show how the basic corporate objective is to be achieved. Thus, their defining characteristic is content, not timing. Although almost all long-range plans are strategic in nature, the converse is not necessarily true. For example, an opportunity may develop to modify corporate strategy by an acquisition that moves the corporation into an unrelated business, or a new national environment, but is nonetheless consistent with corporate philosophy and objectives. Such a short-term move, being strategic in nature, naturally becomes a part of the strategic plan.

Within the framework of the strategic plan, which may extend from ten to twenty years ahead, an *interim plan* specifies more detailed targets and goals for the years immediately ahead. Depending on the nature of the business and the practical reliability of the forecasts for the various host economies, the interim plan may extend from three to ten years ahead; five years is probably close to the mean.

For example, within the context of the strategic plan just hypothesized, an interim plan might commit the company;

To expand its sales in its existing markets by 50% during the next five years.

To enter and develop six new major markets, selected on the basis of size, probability that the company will be able to compete in them successfully, available labor and capital resources, and likelihood that the operation would make a needed economic contribution to the host economy.

With respect to each of these new national markets, the interim plan would specify, in the form of detailed objectives and action programs:

The market-share target.

The products to be used to enter the market.

The methods of market entry and development

Finally, within the context of the interim plan, an annual operating plan sets forth precise, detailed objectives for the year ahead, designed to bring the company the first part of the way toward its interim and long-range goals. Translated into financial terms, this operating plan often becomes a budget for the ensuing year.

These three plans-the strategic, the interim, and the operating-comprise th total corporate planning effort, which is reviewed and revised annually. As new opportunities for growth or diversification emerge, appropriate modifications can be made in the strategic plan. The interim plan, governed by the strategic plan, can be adjusted to take account of opportunities or problems that are foreseeable during its shorter time span. Within this context, a new annual operating plan will, of course, be established each year. Thus, each year's operating plan will automatically reflect any changes that may have been made in the interim plan.

The integrated planning system comprising these three types of plan should go beyond the effective management and growth of the businesses in which the company is currently engaged throughout the world. It should also provide for the constant exploration and development of new products to round out the company's line of new businesses and diversify its interests. To strengthen the enterprise and maximise its profitability, strategic planning and interim planning are necessarily concerned with global diversification goals as well as with new goals for the present business. Inside the frame-work of the interim plan, moreover, the operating units will be concerned with product diversification in their own areas of responsibility.

Five additional planning precepts

The relationships I have outlined among strategic, interim, and operating plans are more than familiar and convenient abstractions; they are the practical foundations of the planning structure in a wide variety of large, outstandingly successful companies. But though domestic and multinational business planning rest on the same broad conceptual foundations, unique problems and complexities confront the planners of world enterprise. In consequence, five precepts of corporate planning take on special meaning for the multinational company;

1. The overall corporate plan should be total and comprehensive. It should cover every aspect of the

business over the long, medium and short term, including the economic roles of the subsidiaries in their respective national environments, and it should give due weight to political factors at work in various host countries. Particularly in developing nations, these hard-to-quantify political factors, which most domestic U.S. companies can afford to ignore, can and do crucially affect the fortunes of foreign-owned business operations. Finally, the plan should properly relate each element of the business to the others, domestically as well as internationally.

2. The components of the overall corporate plan should be functionally integrated. Especially for a maker of consumer goods, this can be an exceptionally intricate task. In such companies, the basic marketing planning effort must normally be done at the country level so as to take into account varying local conditions and requirements which headquarters planners cannot know at first hand -e.g., different preferences of Danes and Brazilians as to the sugar content of soft drinks. Decisions on sources of supply may also be best made at the local level. Yet these plans, as they are reviewed and coordinated by headquarters planners, will often require modification in the light of overall corporate strategies.

Broadly speaking, the overall marketing plan will serve as a base for the production plan, which in turn will affect the financial plan dealing with capital requirements and capital expenditures. The research and development plan will take into account the long-term objectives of the company as specified in the strategic plan, as well as the immediate short-term marketing goals of the various subsidiaries. The personnel plan, designed to provide for the manpower needs of all parts of the enterprise, may range from such questions as technical training at the local level of to the rationalization of management compensation throughout the enterprise so as to permit international transfer and reassignment of key personnel. It in turn will be affected by the production and marketing plans. And the financial plan, developed with due consideration of the company's net economic contribution to the countries in which it operates, will specify how cash flow and profits will be apportioned to provide for the needs of current operations and for possible future diversification.

3. The plans should pinpoint responsibility, Each organizational unit that can be expected to accomplish a goal should be responsible for its own plan. This plan will later be combined with the plans of other units in a total divisional plan, and the divisional plans in turn will be combined in a corporate plan. Any manager can be expected to discharge his cost, service or financial responsibilities most effectively when he is made to do his own planning. For this reason, it is essential to push the responsibility for planning as far down as possible in the organization. To be sure, local managers may at first need to be educated in the techniques of formal planning. Yet without their participation, the chief executive will find it difficult to locate the real problems within the organization, determine how vigorously its opportunities are being pursued, or measure the performance of individual subsidiaries against the plan.

4. *The plan should be dynamic.* Beside providing for the effective and efficient operation of the current business in all its national environments, it should set

forth programs for new or improved products, new or expanded markets, production improvements through better economy or cost reduction, more effective use of cash flow, and improved personnel standards through new techniques of recruitment or personnel development. Moreover, it may well establish diversification targets. To supplement and protect its existing business, to shift financial resources into faster growing business areas, to add new glamor to corporate stock in the hope of raising its price-earnings ratio, to use corporate strengths more efficiently, or merely to hedge against economic and political uncertainties, the company may find it desirable to move into entirely new businesses. It may wish to diversify its investments so that some of its businesses will be growing when others may be in difficulty. Again, it may wish to spread its investment risk among a number of countries to minimize the effect of political difficulties in any one nation upon the fortunes of the corporation. This kind of planning is especially demanding in the multinational enterprise because of the extraordinary vulnerability of any multinational diversification program to policy shifts as minor as a tariff adjustment by any one of many national governments.

5. The plan should incorporate both qualitative and quantitative standards. Goals and operating programs should be stated as vividly and concretely as possible, e.g., "establish a dominant position in freeze-dried foods by 1975", "cut our customer-service time to lowest in the industry by 1972"; "become the top company in a foreign market by 1978."These goals and programs should then be quantified, in a budget

and financial forecast, in terms of volume and return-on-investment objectives reflecting the varying costs and risks of the respective countries of operation. These financial objectives, in turn, become the yardstick against which to measure the achievement of the unit operating plans. 4 Financial results will gauge the success of the units in meeting their operating plans; it will be immediately apparent from the variances in volume and profit when a units is exceeding or falling short of its operating goals.

Information is vital

Clearly, planning in a successful multinational enterprise is a way of life. It cannot be confined to top management alone or to a small specialized group. Rather, it involves everyone who bears leadership or executive responsibility for the effective operation of any unit of the enterprise. To ensure that all elements of the organization carry out their planning responsibilities in a consistent and coordinated manner, that all plans are properly geared into the corporate planning cycle, and that all are compatible in content and properly supported with data demands not only an effective planning structure but an adequate, current, and meaningful input of planning information. The optimum planning structure for a given company is almost always so intimately related to the nature and organization of the business that generalizations are likely to prove treacherous. Such generalizations are, in any case, beyond the scope of this chapter. The information requirements, however, may be usefully summed up under two heads: accurate assessment of the corporation itself, and alertness to the forces at work in the national environments where it operates. Effective assessment of the company's internal strengths and weaknesses calls, in turn, for three categories of data:

Economic: A continuous record of existing product lines; their current, past and projected growth; their competitive market position; and their contribution to profits. Areas of potential vulnerability and potential growth in existing product lines must be identified. Related product opportunities, especially for vertical and horizontal integration, should be evaluated.

Operational: An inventory of operating strengths and limitations. This requires a continuous critical examination and assessment of all operating activities to identify the areas in which the company is performing well and those in which its capabilities are inadequate. Such an inventory might, for example, reveal a deficiency of marketing skills in a corporation with outstanding research and development resources and a superb capability for low-cost production, but-thanks to a unique product line-without any real experience in competitive marketing. An operational inventory of this kind helps a company build on its strengths while correcting its weaknesses or limitations. It also serves as a valuable guide in a corporate diversification program, by indicating how the parent corporation can effectively supplement the strengths and weaknesses of the company being acquired, or strengthen its capacity to absorb additional product lines or businesses.

Financial: A detailed current portrait of the corporation's financial position and capacity in each of its national environments. This is always important, but never more so than when management is preparing to embark on a program of expansion and diversification. Many aspects of the company's financial position might constitute significant advantages or real drawbacks to such a venture. A large cash surplus and no debt, providing a great reservoir of capital, might encourage ambitious expansion. A high debt ratio, restrictive covenants in borrowing agreements, and a declining cash flow might argue for postponing the program until the company had succeeded in reaching a stronger financial position. There may be reasons for or against the issue of additional common stock. Financial conditions always bear importantly, and often decisively, on the nature and timing of the steps the company should take in carrying out its strategic plans.

The internal information needs I have outlined are, of course, by no means peculiar to multinational business. They are common to all corporate planning; their increased complexity in the multinational enterprise is a function of the special communications problems that are involved in operating a multinational enterprise, as well as of its characteristically more complex structure.

Likewise, every corporate planning effort requires accurate knowledge of the corporate environment. In the multinational company this requirement is singularly difficult to meet because of the dearth of accurate, readily available market intelligence in many countries. Yet knowledge of the national environments in which it operates is indispensable to the sound and profitable development of world enterprise. It constitutes, in fact, an unprecedented challenge to the skill and vision of corporate leaders and planners in the next few decades.

By the year 2000, most of the world's 6 billion people will be pressing toward the common goal of economic development. When to take economic advantage of the great potential opportunities in these markets, and how to operate in them, are problems of great magnitude and complexity. The changing nature of competition, worldwide, must be understood. New technological developments that may threaten a part of the corporation's product line or provide an opportunity to strengthen its market position anywhere in the world must be identified and analyzed. An understanding of demographic change, of changing consumer tastes, and of changes in consumer purchasing power in all the company's diverse national market must be developed. The potential effects on the business of government policy and the probable impact of economic blocs need to be analyzed. Potential business opportunities everywhere in the world must be analyzed with skill and discernment if the company is to take the best and most profitable long-term position in all its world markets.

But it is not only in the interest of multinational enterprise itself that the challenge be met effectively. The issue is not one of private commercial advantage, nor even one of national self-interest. For only if its managers plan with vision can multinational enterprise prosper. And only if it prospers can it effectively promote the growth of the developing nations and contribute its full share to the collective economic strength of the free world.

The legal climate for investment

The Increasing Investment abroad in manufacturing and service industries and the need for massive transfers of private capital and technology to developing countries require preliminary appraisal of the legal climate of the country of investment to assure a minimum level of certainty and stability.

Questions of investment incentives, repatriation of profits and capital, requirements of local majority ownership or compulsory use of local nationals and materials, tax policies and guaranties against non-business risk, all are important elements of the investment climate. Capital financing of a foreign enterprise needs the formal structure of laws and legal institutions relating to business organization, banking and insurance, commercial contracts and credit instruments, labor relations and business taxation. Transfer of technology and product identification depend on legal effectiveness of contracts—turn-key, technical assistance, management, licensing and on remedies available for defense of industrial property rights—patents, trademarks and know-how.

Beneath this formal structure necessary for economic regulation and protection of foreign direct investment, a favorable legal climate must contain an infrastructure of attitudes, beliefs and assumptions expressed in legal norms. A first element is a developed legal system at least national in scope, a well-defined and organized body of rules relating to governmental as well as private activity with established institutions, and a professional class and procedures for administration of those rules. It is difficult to conceive of a developed country without a developed legal system. It is easier to point to developing countries with developed legal systems or to developing countries with developing legal systems.

An essential element is minimum degree or acceptance of the legal system by the country's population. The anchor of a legal system is not its inherent excellence but the extra-legal factor of a people's civic or social consciousness implying a willingness to abide by collective decisions.

Perhaps the discernible gap between the developed

legal systems in Latin American countries and effective administration of justice may be explained by the emphasis on *individualismo* and *personalismo*. A substitute for this social trait was formerly found in the Crown, the Church or some other symbol of legitimacy—an article of faith which, by remaining unquestioned, furnished the pivotal connection for acceptance of law by society.

Closely related to the issue of civic consciousness is the literacy rate of the population. As pointed out by the President of the World Bank, "Four or five thousand years after the introduction of the written word, more than a third of adult mankind still remains illiterate." Many countries in Latin America, Africa and Asia have "received" a developed legal system without the literate capacity necessary to participate in any of its process, particularly outside of urban centers. In such countries law tends to become the exclusive province of a small group and even the most advanced legislative enactments remain dead letters on the books. Modern codes and law written with the assistance of foreign technical experts await years of infrastructure development to become truly effective.

Other factors

Numerous other factors affect a country's legal climate for private foreign investment: exaggerated nationalism leading to discrimination against the rights of aliens; a mixed economy strongly oriented toward public ownership of productive facilities and generally cool toward the protection of private property rights; political instability, creating uncertainty in long-range investment planning. These factors, however, as well as determination of the stage of development of the legal system, the population's rate of literacy and willingness to accept collective decisions, point to the key issue of appraisal of a country's legal climate: the effectiveness of its legal institutions, professional class and procedures.

Aside from a few Stone Age aboriginal territories, every part of the world today has access to and the opportunity to import the latest models of legislation. By treaty or by internal enactment, a developing country can buttress its incentives for investment with freely available shipping laws, mining codes, patent laws and negotiable instrument legislation. The problem of their special application remains.

In view of the range of governmental participation in economic activity, a vital issue of contemporary legal life is the extent to which administrative authorities are or can be subjected to procedures for review of their actions. With the emphasis on exhaustion of domestic remedies as a condition to diplomatic protection, the adequacy of internal protection against arbitrary executive acts in the country of investment is a continuing problem.

In the United States, it is a court, and normally a court of general jurisdiction, which will review governmental action. By the logic of history the judicial power in the United States has developed into the ultimate decision maker of the legal system. No other court system in the world has the gamut of powers ranging from that of annulling legislative enactments to compelling performance by public officers under threat of fine or imprisonment.

As in other countries of the common law system, the judiciary in the United States is conscious of its responsibility for definition and development of the legal system. The legal climate created in the United States by the judiciary is unique in that it does not merely reflect a technique of devising cases by referring to past decision; it embodies a political acceptance of the courts as final interpreters status of the judge is commensurate with the importance of the role assigned. The identity of the individual judge is emphasized, and the views of particular judges are constantly examined and evaluated. They have absolute immunity from damage suits even for intentional violations of individual rights. By elaborate reporting methods court decisions are widely disseminated. The legal climate, Roscoe Pound's "taught tradition," is determined by judicial behavior.

The lawyer trained in a common law system quite naturally assumes that supremacy of the judiciary is a logical and inevitable characteristic of any legal system based on separation of governmental powers. He is troubled and even dismayed at times to discover the different attitudes of foreign legal systems.

In the numerous countries of the world usually described as belonging to the "civil law" system—based on Roman legal idiom and tradition—the judiciary plays a lesser role than in countries of the "common law." Though the status of the judiciary varies in the countries of Western Europe and Latin America, the characteristic of executive dominance is more pronounced. In Latin America, it is not the court decision which gives life to the statute, but the *reglamento*, the executive implementation of the legislative act. In countries that follow the French system, the tendency is to deny the law courts the power to pass on executive action and to maintain separate administrative courts. The German system places greater emphasis on departmental review. Both systems rely on the prestige of a career civil service as a counterpart to the Anglo-American judicial power.

In the modern world of international business, vital decisions will often be made in reliance on the estimated degree of protection afforded by the country of investment. It is not the legal facade of investment incentive laws, tax exemptions and guaranties of repatriation that govern. It is rather the infrastructure of attitudes, institutions and remedies that determine the long-range legal climate.

The problem of identity

The expansion of business enterprise abroad has been accompanied by increasing complexity of legal problems and a correspondingly greater degree of collaboration between the international executive and specialized counsel.

Legal staffs attached to international divisions have become the rule. Individual corporate counsel specially assigned to a company's international operations have become familiar faces in present-day planning. For the thousands of smaller business units operating abroad legal guidance in international operations is furnished chiefly by outside counsel. In the areas of greatest importance to U.S. private enterprise—Western Europe, Japan, Canada and Latin America—the volume of legal business has justified the establishment of foreign offices of U.S. law firms. In Paris alone, more than 22 U.S. law firms are represented by resident partners.

In foreign operations the distinction must be noted between international trade and foreign investment. International commercial and maritime relations generally have tended for centuries to be conducted by merchants or businessmen without calling on lawyers except for litigation. Even in the event of disputes, in the traditional area of trade operations arbitration without lawyers participating is frequently preferred. International trade is based chiefly on the use of standardized forms and practices, a world in which a lawyer, despite his training, is considered more of a layman than his business counterpart. In the area of international trade, in contrast to that of foreign investment, the standardized instruments which contain most of the rules governing the parties, sales memoranda, brokers' notes, bill of lading charter parties, marine insurance policies, letters of credit, all embody familiar clauses which shipping clerks and foreign tellers can be trained to follow.

In those areas of international business activity, particularly developed since World War II, involving the transfer and exchange of technology and direct investment abroad, the reverse is true. Here the individualized rather than the standardized transaction is the rule. While the import or export of goods can be, and usually is, arranged so as to involve the law of a single country, the transfer of technology and direct investment normally involve foreign as well as domestic legal factors.

The presence of the same enterprise in many countries necessarily subjects it to differing laws. Manufacturing, financing and marketing abroad, often involving regional rather than bilateral planning, require the confidence and the ability to handle the laws of more than one country as well as skill in the essential techniques of analysis of legal climate and relevant rules. The businessman or lawyer at one only in a single country's law becomes inadequate. The multinational enterprise demands the multinational mind.

Despite the barriers of language and habit of thought,

the U.S. lawyer accustomed to the complexities of interstate conflicts of rules of law, and the U.S. business executive accustomed to think in terms of regional markets have an advantage over their foreign counterparts in projecting into the international area. The solution of multistate problems is excellent initiation to the consideration of multinational problems.

Corporate forms

The primary step in the approach to foreign business operations is a re-examination of familiar legal-business institutions and conceptions. A look at the corporate forms of business organization will provide some examples of the three-dimensional aspect of international legal planning.

The business world and its legal advisers normally seek the limitation of personal liability of the investing company or individual, accomplished by creation of a separate legal entity. Domestically, the corporation is relied on as the normal and dominant form of doing business, whether giant or small, publicly owned or held by a close few. The "Ince." is ever present in national life. Since, in the U.S. view, corporations are created by state law, by grant of the sovereign rather than the contract of the members, it is a truism that they are identified with the state or territory of the Union where organized. Thus businessmen and lawyers speak of a Delaware corporation, if it was organized pursuant to Delaware law, although all its corporate and business activity are outside that state and the stockholders are non-residents.

In Europe and Latin America, where a single body of national law creates or regulates corporate activity, one can refer to the nationality of a corporation. And because a corporation in many countries abroad is not considered created by grant of the sovereign but by the contractual intent of the members, its nationality is not necessarily defined by that of the country in which it is constituted. Thus a French court has recently held that a corporation organized under Panama law by U.S. stockholders with central management in New York was not a Panamanian national. A corporation not validly constituted opens the path to personal liability of stockholders for corporate debts.

In a case before the German courts suit was brought against the U.S. stockholders of a corporation organized in the state of Washington to conduct mining operations in Mexico with its central management meeting in Hamburg. The stockholders were held personally liable for corporate liabilities on the ground that since the corporation was administratered in Germany and not constituted pursuant to German law, it was an unincorporated association. The Supreme Court of Belgium also held recently that where a company organized under English law transferred its head office to Belgium, it became subject to Belgian rules, such as that limiting the duration of a corporation to 30 years, despite the provisions of English law and the terms of the articles of association.

Pursuant to Italian law if the corporate center of administration or the main business operation of a company is in Italy, even though created abroad, the corporation is subject to Italian law even as to the legal requirements for incorporation. Similarly in Latin America, Venezuela for example, a corporation organized pursuant to a foreign law and with its principal business in Venezuela is considered a Venezuelan national.

Thus the question of the nationality of a corporation is neither academic nor theoretical. Like an individual a corporation may have dual nationality; on the other hand it may be "stateless," a condition affecting its very existence and exposing the members to individual liability. Determination of the nationality of a corporation may have serious tax consequences as well as subject the entity to burdensome regulation or even expropriation of its property, as in the case of the Suez Canal Company.

No pattern

In determining the law applicable to corporate existence and internal relations, no consistent pattern can be discerned. Some countries, such as the United States, the United Kingdom and Brazil, look to the place of incorporation. Others, such as Morocco, look to the place of the registered head office. France, Belgium and Greece look to the center of management. Italy and Egypt apply the test of main business activity. In contrast to domestic practice in the United States, multiple incorporation in various countries of the world may be necessary simply to protect stockholders from personal liability.

In foreign operations it cannot be assumed that ownership by a single person—the one-man corporate entity—is authorized. Even in the United States, some states have specifically refused to recognize the validity of a corporation owned by one person. The North Carolina Supreme Court recently held that where all the stock of a corporations was acquired by one individual, the corporation ceased to exist. A similar rule has prevailed in France, Belgium and other countries following French legal thought. Acquisition by one person, whether an individual or a legal entity, of all the shares of a corporation causes its automatic dissolution, leading to personal liability of the stockholder for the corporation's liabilities. The Supreme Court of Belgium has gone so far as to hold that even though a foreign corporation was organized pursuant to a low that authorized the one-man corporation, such a corporation could not have its existence recognized in Belgium so as to permit it to sue in Belgian courts.

Assuming that the corporation is identified as foreign and that it is validly existing in its home country, the problem remains of its recognition as a legal entity in the country of operations. There is no rule of international law, in the absence of treaty, obligating a state to recognize foreign-created juristic persons. The capacity to sue and be sued as a separate legal entity is the most important incident of recognition. In some countries today, a foreign corporation selling goods may to be able to bring an action in the courts of the buyer in the event of non-payment. Shortly before World War II, when the owner of the Palmolive trademark, a Delaware corporation, attempted to sue an infringer in Mexico, the Supreme Court upheld dismissal of the action on the ground that the Delaware corporation, as such, had no existence in Mexico. The view that "a company can have no legal existence out of the boundaries of the sovereignty by which it is created," expressed in U.S. interstate relations over 100 years ago, still survives in some countries abroad, particularly the developing countries fearful foreign economic penetration.

In the Western Hemisphere it has been found expedient to draft a Declaration on Juridical Personality of Foreign Companies. Parties to the Declaration, in addition to the United States, are Chile, the Dominican Republic,

Ecuador, El Salvador, Nicaragua, foreign "companies constituted in accordance with the laws of one of the Contracting States and which have their seats in its territory." In a similar fashion Article 58 of the Rome Treaty organizing the European Common Market provides that "companies constituted in accordance with the law of a Member State and having their registered office, central management or main establishment within the Community shall, for the purpose of applying the provisions of this Chapter, be assimilated to natural persons being nationals of Member States."

Business enterprise operating abroad must choose a legal form of organization. This brief glance at Pandora's box of international legal problems would indicate that questions of identity, valid existence and recognition of a legal entity operating extraterritorially are not merely theoretical but, often unnoticed, can have serious consequences in foreign operations if not properly resolved as soon as it is possible to do so.

The form of the affiliate

Attention to the composition and form of the business unit which will conduct manufacturing or marketing activities in a foreign country will make a significant contribution to its ultimate success. Tax considerations both at home and abroad play an important part, but in general a major objective is to insulate the parent organization or investor from direct liability for the obligations incurred in the local operation.

To be considered at the outset is whether the business undertaking will be jointly owned with a local interest. Financing and control may depend on the choice of business form. Without discussing their merits, joint ventures, even with both parties ever present, are difficult relationships to maintain. an international joint venture, with the parties widely separated to begin with, is much more difficult to consolidate. Particularly in developing countries, stresses and strains of the simplest business operations tend to result in discord.

Often overlooked, but vital to full protection of the investors' interest, is a detailed study of the problems of eventual liquidation and dissolution. If the joint venture company has been authorized to use an internationally known form name as well as trademarks and has received patent licenses and know-how, the severance may be far more complicated than the creation.

In some countries—Mexico, Japan and India—the impact of legal restrictions may compel organization of jointly owned companies with a minimum percentage of local equity capital. The problem then becomes one of retaining at least veto powers over important decisions and providing sensible procedures for dissolution.

Joint venture forms

A joint venture need not necessarily take the form of a jointly owned enterprise. It may be contractual, the type called in French the *society en participation* and in German the *Stille Gesellschaft*. Again, subcontracting components of the manufacturing process may be a more desirable form of joint operation. As defined in the new French Company Law, the *societe en participation* "exists only as between members and is not disclosed to third parties."

It does not have a separate legal existence and can be established by oral agreement. Each party can retain its name and industrial property rights and in the event of difficulties can terminate the agreement in a manner previously agreed upon without need for formal dissolution of a separate legal entity.

Normally, with limitation of members' liability as a prime objective, the choice of form of doing business abroad will center on creation of an entity with legal existence separate from that of the parent or investor. As Justice Holmes pointed out, "the tradition of the common law is to treat as legal persons only incorporate groups and to assimilate all others to partnerships. The tradition of the civil law is otherwise."

The corporate concept

In U.S. law the term "corporation" embodies the notion of a group treated in law as a person different from its members. Though derived from Latin, the term is not directly transferable into continental law terminology. In French it corresponds to the idea of guild or a professional corps. At common law, a grant from the public authority was necessary to "incorporate." Limitation of liability of members of a corporation was dependent on a concession by the legislature. The civil law countries start from the root concept of *societe* or *Gesellschaft*, "the *contract* by which two or more persons agree to plan something in common ownership for the purpose of dividing the profit which may arise therefrom." Forms of business organization abroad are therefore varieties of *societe*. The general partnership is a *societe en nom collectif*; the limited partnership is a *societe en commandite*. The classical distinction developed in continental law and in Latin America is between the *societes des capitaux* emphasizing the pooling of capital resources and the *societes des personnes* in which reliance is placed on the identity of the members. The partnership, general or limited, is the typical *societe des personnes*.

In most cases the choice of foreign business organization to operate as a subsidiary or affiliate will be between two forms, both akin to the U.S. corporation. In the European Common Market countries, direct investment for manufacturing operations or intensive marketing will be channeled through a *societe anonme* or a *societe a responsabilite limitee*; in German-speaking countries it will be *Aktiengesellschaft* or the *Gesellschaft mit beschrankter Haftung*. Like the private or proprietary company in British Commonwealth countries, the S.A.R.L. requires fewer formalities for formation and operation. The S.A.R.L. has a simple structure with management often centered in a single person, lacking a broad of directors or other supervisory bodies required in the case of an S.A. As international businessmen and counsel have become more knowledgeable and sophisticated, the trend of choice towards the S.A.R.L. or the *Limitada* had become more definite in contrast to the earlier period when the S.A. was regarded conservatively as the most direct counterpart of the U.S. "Inc."

S.A.R.L. preferred

The change in attitude has come from the realization that large corporations, operating as public companies domestically with shares listed on stock exchanges, function abroad through closely held companies. The S.A.R.L. gained in favor as international business found that controlled companies as well as joint ventures with a local interest could operate more effectively through the contractual details inserted the charter of an S.A.R.L. than through more cumbersome mandatory provisions law governing an S.A.

The relatively new institution of the S.A.R.L. originated in Germany in 1892 as an answer to the difficulties encountered by colonial business ventures in complying with the strict German corporation law of 1884. Since then it has been adopted in almost every country of Europe, Latin America, the Near East and North Africa. In each country, however, it has its own distinctive features and varies as much in important details as do the laws in different countries relating to the S.A.

In some countries, the S.A.R.L. is treated as a partnership rather than as a corporation. Thus in Panama, the preferred form is the S.A. because of the partnership nature of the Panamanian *Limitada* and because the S.A. law modeled on Delaware law is extremely simple and inexpensive to organize and operate. In Columbia the Supreme Court has held the Columbia S.A.R.L. to be a partnership, not a corporation, for a tax purposes. The organizational documents of the Brazilian *Limitada* can be drafted so as to make it resemble a partnership.

For the true sophisticate, German practice has developed the "GmbH & Co.," one of the newer and increasingly utilized German forms, particularly as the non-corporate business instrumentality for joint ventures. Despite the misleading designation, the GmbH & Co. is not a GmbH at all. It is a German limited partnership, a *Komanditgesellschaft* (KG) in which a GmbH acts as general partner and manager. As managing partner of the KG, the GmbH's liability to creditors is unlimited. But since the GmbH is itself a corporate form, members in turn are not liable beyond their investment in the GmbH. The analogy in U.S. business forms would be a limited partnership with a corporation as general partner.

A European company

Another new form is the proposed European company. This would be a company subject to uniform rules throughout the European Common Market if established in a Common Market country. The proposal is presently being considered by the Common Market authorities following the French government initiative in 1965. It is significant that no one has advocated any form for a European company other than the S.A. In the Europe of the future, it would be as if the United States had a Federal uniform law for corporations in interstate commerce in addition to the state-law entities now used. An example may be found in the Dominion Company of Canada, a form organized under Dominion law which exists side by side with companies created under Provincial legislation.

Since creation of a European company would require either a uniform law enacted by all the countries of the Common Market or a treaty independent of the Rome Treaty, a certain degree of skepticism is warranted with respect to early adoption. However, as a result of Common Market thinking, a movement to revise company laws is making headway in Europe. Germany and France have recently adopted new laws. In Italy, Belgium and the Netherlands, reforms are in preparation. Harmonization of company law in Europe is being effected at this stage more by internal changes than by any strong urge to create a new and perhaps unnecessary superstructure of business organizations. The organizational alternatives are all complex, but a thorough understanding of their implications by responsible executives is essential to any multinational operation.

The language barrier

To the international business executive and his legal adviser the language barrier poses a constant and elusive problem. At critical points in the management decision process, the area of uncertainty resulting from language differences remains an effective circuit breaker in the transmission of ideas. In formation of contracts, in preparation of corporate documents, in negotiation and settlement of disputes by arbitration or court proceedings, in any reference to foreign laws or concepts, the language factor is ever is ever present.

The international business community has found various ways of assisting the meeting of minds. An example that readily comes to mind is the increasing use of standardized international instruments containing their own definitions in various languages or referring to uniform definitions of terms. Perhaps the most tremendously expanded development of English as the international language of commerce, diplomacy and science.

In this century English has become the most widely spoken language on earth. It is only fifty years since English was first accepted as the authentic language counterpart of French in the Treaty of Versailles. Today, it is the language medium of exchange used in trade agreements between Peking and members of the Soviet bloc and in cultural agreements between Egypt and Indonesia. Nearly one in ten of the world's people use English as their primary language and nearly one in for understand it to some degree. The American abroad may be forgiven for assuming hat the language problem is simply one of spreading even more the use of a language already so widely accepted as a means of communication.

In practice, the chief problem today is in the area of transference of legal ideas. To the businessman a contract or a corporate document is essentially a set of operating rules to be followed as a matter of mechanics in arranging details of delivery, payment, place and date of meetings and similar details. The lawyer views the same instrument from the moment of its creation through the lens of a judge's or arbitrator's eyes. When foreign legal elements are involved, the lens will have to be at least bifocal. For operations, the contract must be understandable in the language of the personnel who must be guided by it. For settlement of disputes, the same contract or written communication must be presented not only in the formal language of the deciding body, but must be so translated as to carry a maximum burden of persuasion. In counselling on the meaning of a contract, in contract to the advocacy necessary for litigation, the lawyer will rely on the least favorable translation for his legal opinion in order to minimize the scope of the calculated risk.

Translation problems

To mention the language barrier is to refer to translation as the channel of communication. The importance of understanding the purpose of a particular translation is evident. A routine translation, merely to have a preliminary notion of the contents of the foreign letter, may be completely justified, while reliance on an "official translation" of a foreign law or governmental document may be a major blunder.

The businessman is often unaware of the special problems raised by translation of legal instruments. To translate is always to interpret, that is, to embody an opinion as to the legal meaning of the contents. Disputes as to the meaning of words invariably arise in marginal situations when more than one meaning is possible. Translating from legal English is usually more difficult than to express oneself directly in the foreign language. Though English may have become an international language, legal English is the product of a unique set of historical circumstances. As Professor Keeton, a leading English historian, has remarked, "Even today the language of the law is so completely permeated by Norman-French terms that it is impossible to imagine the legal system without them."

To the normally complex problem of ascertaining meaning in a single language, the addition of the foreign language factor multiplies the variables of selection and expands the area of uncertainty. Translation of legal language in contrast to scientific information is not a mechanical matching of words. With the aid of computers, over a million words a month are being translated into English from Russian technical works. In contrast to words which embody physical descriptions, most legal concepts leave room for value judgments. As stated by Professor Philippe Kahn, in fairly extravagant terms, "In translating from the foreign language into that of the court, there is a transfer of concepts, expressing the intellectual life of two peoples, the assimilation of a civilization."

In litigation, a point to be noted results from differences in court procedure. In U.S. courts and arbitration tribunals, generally speaking, the emphasis is on presenting the facts to the judge or jury through the oral testimony of the parties or witnesses in open court. Foreign language documents or laws are normally presented through the oral testimony of experts retained by the parties. In noncriminal cases abroad, parties are generally barred from testifying and translations are most often admitted only when made by "official translators," with knowledge of English as well as their own language tested by the simplest of public examinations.

Use court's language

The vital point to bear in mind is that the process of translation to be properly controlled must be affected during the period of drafting of the instrument. From the point of view of potential litigation, legal instruments should be written in the language of the decisional body which will settle the disputes arising in connection with the instrument. The legal language of that body will govern, regardless of the law chosen by the parties or the language actually used in the instrument.

The German Supreme Court has held that a translator is not the agent of the party who employed him at the time of preparation of the original contract but merely a conduit. If he comments an error so that the contract as signed does not correspond to the real intention of the party who signed it, the latter can rescind the contract. The Supreme Court of France has held that a French judge can disregard the translation of a court-appointed expert translator. The instrument involved was a licensing agreement in the English language, calling for royalties calculated on the basis of a percentage of "gross income." This was translated by the expert as "revenus bruts" and by the lower court as "revenus de toute nature" and "montant brut du chiffre d'affaires." The French Supreme Court held that the lower court's own translation, even if erroneous, could not be reviewed. "The translation of a contract written in a foreign language involves an exercise of the lower courts' sovereign power to interpret written instruments."

Bilingual or multilingual instruments in various counterparts normally contain a choice of language clause, indicating which text is to prevail in case of divergence. Such a clause is truly effective only if the controlling language chosen is that the decisional body. In the French case just mentioned, only a French language contract would have been binding on the court as evidence of the intention of the parties as to the meaning to be given to the term "gross income." This conclusion is not limited to foreign courts. When the 1819 Treaty with Spain was first applied by the Supreme Court of the United States in litigation involving the status of private land grants after acquisition of Florida by the United States, the Court faced the problem of translating the Spanish 'las concesiones quedran ratifcadas y reconocidas." The authentic English text of the Treaty read: "The grants shall be ratified and confirmed." As so read, the Treaty would have left in doubt the ownership of substantial tracts of land. disregarding the authentic English version, the Supreme Court applied its own translation to find the meaning to be "the grants shall remain ratified and confirmed."

The translator

Arguably, a critically important translation of a foreign legal text should not be the work of a single person. Julian Green, the American author who wrote in French, has been quoted as saying, "I am more and more inclined to believe that it is almost an impossibility to be absolutely bilingual. A reading research manual insists that "one can translate faithfully only from a language one knows like a native into a language one knows like a practiced writer." In truly critical and decisive issues of translation and interpretation, the process should be bilateral, from one language by the lawyer familiar with that language and that country's law into the language of the law of the decisional body by a lawyer trained in that legal system.

Finally, it should be observed that just as no contract can be drawn to foresee every contingency, so no translation can eliminate all future disputes as to meaning. Particularly in international business relations, where most disagreements tend to be channelled into the language area to avoid implications of improper motives for non-performance, the translation should be carefully analyzed. There is no simple solution to the language barrier. The need is to examine both sides to determine when a language other than English should be the language of the parties and to be aware of the means of controlling language transference.

Diplomatic protection

In sharp contrast to the laissez-faire period prior to World War I, the changes in ideology and social realignment of the twentieth century have vitally affected the legal framework of international life. In the classical nineteenth-century view, with its concept of private property derived from the image of tangible thinks owned by individuals, the definition of ownership in the French Civil code—"the right to enjoy and dispose of things in the most absolute manner, provided that they are not put to a use prohibited by laws or by regulations—served as a model for the codes of many other countries. In contrast, the view of ownership as a "social function" found in many codes enacted since World War I reflects a rejection of absolute property rights and challenges the distinction between private and public ownership.

At the end of the nineteenth century, the Supreme

Court of the United States could say: "in the memory of men now living, a proposition to take private property, without the consent of its owner, for a public park, would have been regarded as a novel exercise of legislative power." Today, the "nationalization" of private property—its transfer to public ownership—is a common phenomenon throughout the United States and elsewhere.

In international legal relations a similar change of emphasis has occurred. In the traditional view, any taking of foreign property, even for a public purpose, was suspect. Indeed, an echo of this view is found in the attitude of the Soviet High Commander in Austria following World War II. He contended that the Australian law nationalizing the Soviet-held Austrian oil industry violated an alleged rule of international law which bars a nationalizing State from applying such measures to any foreign-owned property.

When throughout the world the public sector of enterprise has expanded with an accompanying broadening of the notion of public use or purpose, the question of whether a government's taking of private property is for such use or purpose has become of minimal importance. The issue today centers not on the power or right of a State to take private property but on whether the taking is subject to indemnification. The measure of compensation is as difficult to define in international relations as in the United States.

Prior to World War I, there was general approval in the West of the view that international taking of an alien's property required payment of prompt and adequate compensation. Such a view could persist unchallenged until met by counter-thrusts from developing countries.

Today, the U.S. Supreme Court decides that our courts cannot pass on issues of Cuba's right or power to expropriate U.S. property because "there are few if any issues in international law today on which opinion seems to be so divided." At a moment when the risk of expropriation is an important factor in management decisions, the executive and his counsel find few legal pillars of support or guidance. Yet foreign investment continues to expand-when permitted by balance-of-payments problems—and the ultimate solution may well lie in the political and economic facts of particular situations rather than in piously hopeful verbalizations.

Type of activity

It is essential to consider the need for governmental protection of multinational enterprises in terms of the nature of their activities. In the extractive industries, for example, affecting a country's natural resources, operations must be conducted where supplies are available. The risk of expropriation must be countered, but the existence of even a sizeable risk cannot act as a deterrent if the supplies are available and a market exists for them. This type of enterprise touches directly the most sensitive spot of developed and developing countries' political consciousness: foreign ownership or control of a national asset to be depleted within a fairly short historical period or alien occupation of a substantial part of the national territory. Whether it is Switzerland barring alien ownership of land, aimed particularly at the West German penetration following World War II, or Peru removing an oil enclave, the sensitivity to foreign dominance is evident.

A second type of enterprise which raises specia problems is the foreign-owned or -controlled public utility

Like the extractive enterprise, its legal relations with the host country are normally governed by a concession agreement, a contract-law of the parties. The risk of expropriation in the utility field is due less to sovereignty-sensitivity than to a belief that public ownership is the only alternative to the overwhelming pressures against a fair rate structure dictated by the forces of inflation and popular resentment against rising prices. In the United States the free enterprise system has accepted regulation of public utilities by government agencies as a means of reconciling private return with public service. In other countries, for many reasons, public ownership becomes inevitable.

These are not the only factors inviting expropriation. Where foreigners come to own or control a substantial proportion of a nation's economy, an "occupation" mentally develops within the country which often finds release in measures of strict regulation of existing and new investment if not outright expropriation. It is significant that in the case of Mexico in 1911, when Mexico's decade of revolution began, foreigners owned about two-thirds of the aggregate Mexican investment apart from agriculture and handicraft, a proportion that may have set all-time records for any country claiming political independence.

The calvo doctrine

The Calvo doctrine, named for an Argentine jurist, is generally regarded as expressing a special Latin American attitude barring diplomatic protection of aliens by their governments, with Mexico its most devoted supporter. Its fundamental thrust is rejection or any minimum international standard of protection of foreign investment, and assimilation of the alien to a country's nationals, on the assumption that by entering the country the alien tacitly agrees to be treated as a national. The Mexican Constitution includes a Calvo clause which requires aliens who wish to acquire lands or concessions for working mines or for use of waters or mineral fuel to agree "to consider themselves as Mexicans in respect of such property, and not to invoke the protection of their governments in matters relating thereto, under penalty of forfeiture of the property acquired."

It may seem surprising to the U.S. business community that Latin American countries attach such importance to diplomatic representations. The U.S. business executive normally finds less reason for close relations with his diplomats abroad than his English or West European counterpart. Despite the popular conception in other parts of the world, including Latin America, that U.S. foreign policy is dictated by the business class, the business community displays a marked skepticism toward the effectiveness of diplomatic protection of private business interests. This skepticism is compounded by their legal advisors' preference for legal rather than political channels for settlement of disputes. Anglo-American lawyers are by tradition and training biased toward equating law with what judges do. The U.S. legal profession generally is unaware of the legal rules which guide the process of governmental negotiations and agreement in the protection of private property.

On issues of discrimination, unfair taxation and generally in matters of "creeping expropriation," the diplomatic channel has been more effective than generally realized, particularly in adjustments with non-communist countries. The protest to the United Kingdom against threatened nationalization of Ford Motor Company facilities in England is a recent example. Even with communist countries diplomatic negotiations have resulted in lump-sum settlements compensating for confiscated property of U.S. nationals.

A deeper understanding of the circumstances in which diplomatic protection is extended is necessary to international business management and their counsel. The vital point is that diplomatic protection must be initiated by the private enterprise which has suffered loss as a result of foreign governmental action. In deciding whether or not to espouse the claim, the State Department must make preliminary determinations of fact and law. In the case of multinational enterprise, a preliminary issue of major importance is own which involves the very use of the term "multinational" since a government can protect only an enterprise with a defined nationality. In matters of foreign private investment, disputes between governments usually involve a corporation. Nationality of a corporation defined by the place of incorporation is not sufficient. Thus a Delaware corporation entirely owned by non-U.S. citizens will not be considered a U.S. national for purposes of diplomatic protest by the United States. A substantial national beneficial interest in the corporation is required.

The present practice of the United States is to consider a claim on behalf of corporations organized in the United States if 50% or more of the voting shares are owned by U.S. citizens. Where a corporation is organized under laws of any country other than the United States, the Department will consider a claim on behalf of the U.S. shareholders if they represent 25% or more of the voting shares. That the United States will espouse a claim under these conditions of beneficial interest by its citizens does not mean that the country to whom the diplomatic protest may be directed will follow the same tests.

In a case presently pending before the International Court of Justice, a central issue concerns the capacity of Belgium to represent a company largely Canadian-owned in a proceeding seeking compensation for alleged expropriation of the company's assets in Spain. The International Court has indicated that the issue of nationality of a person, if raised before an international court or arbitral tribunal, will be decided not under the law of the claimant state but pursuant to customary international law requiring a "real and effective" or "genuine" connection between the private individual or corporation and the claimant State.

Type of claim

A second issue involved in the State Department's decision is the type of claim it is requested to espouse. A claim of the taking of property by foreign governmental act without prompt, adequate and effective compensation is the classical basis for U.S. diplomatic protection. There must be a taking and it must be of property. Before the 1930s, repudiation of the public debt at the Caribbean area. Since that period, forcible unilateral action by the United States has not been considered, except in situations involving national security. The United States will not act as a "collection agency" for its nationals. Yet it will espouse claims of arbitrary annulment of concessions or repudiation of vested rights acquired by U.S. nationals, particularly when such action is accompanied by taking of tangible assets. Aside from the question of protecting property, in contrast to contractual expectations, the problem remains of defining "taking."

Not even all direct takings of property will be protected—for example, seizure and confiscation for violation of customs laws. A direct taking assumes destruction of the property or transfer of possession or control from the private owner. However, many forms of state interference with foreign property rights shop short of a direct taking though they severely limit the investor's ownership rights or impose new and burdensome obligations. Thus enforcement of tax laws, currency devaluation, rate regulation or governmental intervention in company management may in effect be tantamount to a taking. The decision to espouse such claims will be decided by the Department's determination as to their being "discriminatory," "unreasonable," "an abuse of power" or similar phrases for shedding heat as well as light. Each situation will necessarily be adjudged on its special facts.

6

Business Control Strategy

Control may be defined simply as the relationships and devices designed to assure that strategy decision are made by designated authority in conformance with corporate goals, that tactical decisions conform to the selected strategies, and that actual operations in harmony.

Clearly, the administrative structure should be rationalized in terms of establishing and maintaining adequate control over the firm's activities at least cost. Administrative structure may thus be viewed as the network of channels through which authority flows, together with the feedback generated thereby. A distinct but related subject has to do with the *nature* of the flows within the system and the devices used to assure against abrupt changes in the flows.

Therefore, in considering alternative control strategies, several key questions present themselves:

1. Where should decision-making authority reside in the firm in respect to strategy choices relating to foreign

markets or to global allocation of corporate resources?

2. Where should the relevant tactical decision-making authority be located?
3. By what methods should decisions be communicated?
4. By what means should operating performance be reported?
5. What measures of performance should be used?
6. How can decisions be enforced?

One might well ask whether there are problems in this area unique to the firm operating internationally. A listing of the differences between domestic and international control systems follows:

1. Currency differences require a more careful approach to pricing, working-capital management, and selection of funds sources, as well as great care in interpreting the meaning of overseas balance sheets and earnings statements.
2. The foreign manager may have little control over many important decisions made by the parent company, which fact may seriously affect his operating performance.
3. Economic data and historical and industry comparisons are often harder to obtain, even occasionally nonexistent, in the foreign environment, thereby making budgetary goal-setting more difficult.
4. Internal performance data for the foreign subsidiary occasionally is difficult to obtain in the form desired due to the unfamiliarity of most foreign-educated

managers with management accounting techniques in the country of the parent.

5. Informal communication between foreign division manager and home office is less frequent than between domestic division manager and home office, therefore causing greater reliance on the data from the formal system.

Research by Professor Skinner of the Harvard Business School has documented a strong feeling of resentment toward the home office by many overseas managers. This resentment was reflected in charges of undue interference, inadequate delegation of authority, onerous reporting requirements, and lack of understanding and sympathy. On the other hand, be observed that home office executives were often frustrated "by possessing a sense of responsibility which is thwarted by having 'only paper authority' over the field operations." They are held responsible by their superiors for what goes on overseas; yet, they are unable to control the latter's daily decisions and sometimes even their policies. Though the headquarters executives may hold the ultimate power to replace the overseas executive, "this extreme action was not only distasteful but an impractical weapon because of their genuine problem in knowing enough of what went on abroad." Skinner distinguished between headquarters' "involvement" in overseas operations and the degree of "command" exercised over those operations. By the former term he refers to the functions performed by headquarters; by the latter term, to the "how" of headquarters' involvement, from nonparticipant observation to a detailed reporting system and specific orders for conformance. "Both of these elements of control can and should be tailored to the situation," he concludes. He warns against arbitrary classification of management decisions into "policy" of "operations". A home office may be of considerable help in resolving many overseas operating problems, and conversely, local management may be better able to make certain policy decisions. He suggests "the probability that the interpersonal relationship will be improved by...an explicit defining of the role of the home office which would eliminate confusion and misunderstanding and establish a mechanism for regular review and open discussion of the role of headquarters." The difficulty of treating different countries, associated enterprises, and functions differently is admitted, and therefore the "situational viewpoint" seems required in international business.

A more recent study reports that executives stationed abroad often complain that: (1) they feel out of touch with the mainstream of the company; (2) it takes an inordinate amount of time to get information from headquarters; (3) headquarters insists on making decisions that can be better made by those in the field who are closer to the situation; and (4) visits by headquarters' personnel are often "jaunts" that waste valuable time for those in the field.

On the other hand, those at corporate headquarters often complain that: (1) it takes too long to get information from the field; (2) those in foreign subsidiaries get into trouble by making decisions without consulting headquarters; (3) overseas executives become too "localized" to function at peal efficiency when they return from their international assignments; and (4) site visits abroad often waste valuable time because the overseas executives have not adequately prepared for them.

One could plausibly that these conditions are found in all large, complex organizations. "Complaints regarding headquarters-field information barriers, and headquarters interference in local decision making, are certainly not limited to international firms." The Jacques-Farris-Sirota research attempted to clarify the effect on communications of being international by hypothesizing that geographical distance was a key factor in headquarters-field relationships. Message turn-around time is magnified and reliance upon written communication becomes greater, thereby leading to less integration of the overseas executive into headquarters, a feeling of being out of touch, and a decrease in mutual trust and understanding. Resting on an in-depth, questionnaire-based study of companies in different industries, each with many foreign subsidiaries, the general conclusion was that, "By and large, communication was of similar quality between the headquarters of each company and its domestic and foreign subsidiaries." Granted that the overseas executive reported making greater use of telecommunications than his domestic counterpart, and a larger cycle time for written requests to headquarters, these factors will seemed unrelated to feelings about the *quality* of communication. Again, although personal contact with headquarters personnel was less than in the domestic case, so likewise were feelings of being integrated with other personnel at headquarters, and no significant differences in trust and mutual understanding could be found. "Headquarters personnel were perceived, however, as having less influence on operations by the international executives than by the domestic executives," representative perhaps of the greater autonomy of overseas subsidiaries as opposed to the domestic.

In further analyzing their data, Jacques and his colleagues found that two of the four companies consistently scored significantly higher in communication for *both* foreign and domestic operations. The information received was clearer, more accurate, more timely—including their own submitted to headquarters. Characteristics of the "better-communicating" companies were (1) less control by nontop management headquarters personnel over subsidiary operations, (2) greater top management willingness to stand by decisions made in the subsidiaries that diverged from established directives, (3) a greater sense of "teamwork" with *local* colleagues, and (4) less personal contact with headquarters personnel. It was then found that international executives in the better-communicating companies had had more management experience than their counterparts in the other companies, presumably most of it with the company of present employ, and had spent more time at their present location. Another characteristic of the better-communicating firms was their larger involvement in foreign markets.

Inasmuch as effective communication is the key in control, one can thus derive some of the necessary, though perhaps not sufficient, conditions, as in Figure 1.

One problem in the Jacques study was that the accuracy of information from subsidiary to headquarters was measured in terms of perceptions on the part of transmitters and receivers. In fact, how accurately did the messages describe environmentally generated problems? To what extent were corporate decisions based on an understanding of environmental realities? It is generally agreed that the lack of systematic environmental analysis by international companies is an important deficiency. Hence, the information flowing from subsidiary to

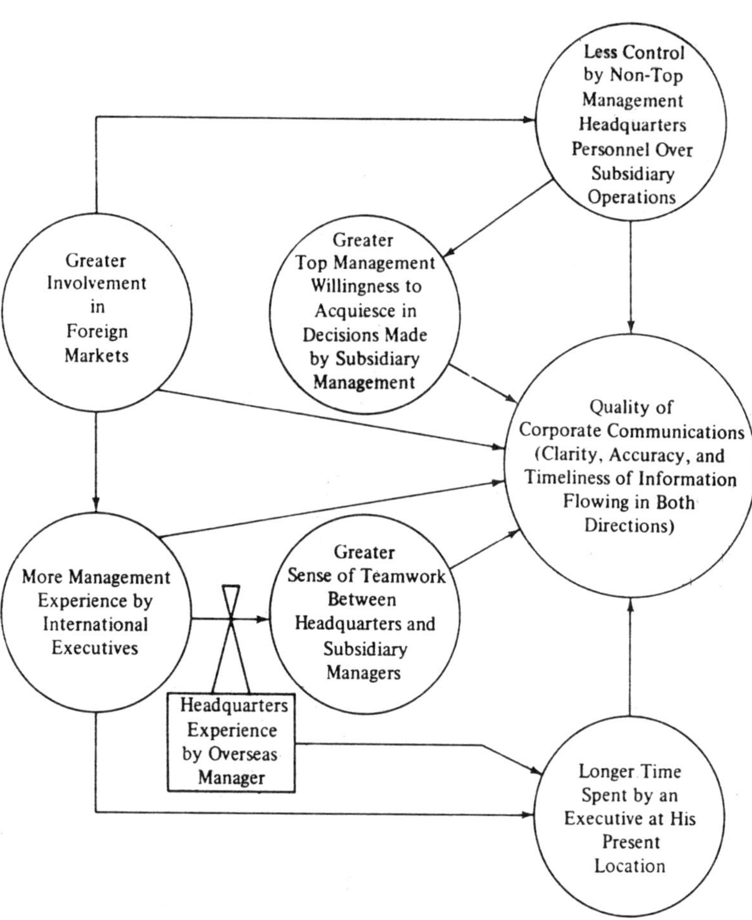

Fig. 1 Some factors enhancing international corporate communications

headquarters, regardless of perception, may not as accurately reflect objective reality outside the firm as it does in the domestic case.

Some concrete examples of this sort of informal communications were reported by another researcher. In one company, foreign employers who had attended a training program at corporate headquarters often contacted friends made during that time in resolving problems; a kind of fraternity had been created by the program. In a second corporation, management had been shaken up recently by a massive reorganization. Instead of following the new official channels, much of the internal business communications moved through informal links based on personal relationships developed within the *formal* organizational structure. Within another corporation was found a large informal network based upon common university experience and membership in the same college fraternity. Many of the links, obviously, are unlikely to appear within an internationally oriented business unless there is opportunity for the face-to-face association of executives from the various regions.

It follows that companies in which the tenure of the relevant managers is relatively long and in which they are promoted by seniority would, all else being equal, lead to the most effective international communication network. The Japanese system, in which there are few intercompany transfers of top managers and in which there are personal ties of long standing, suggests itself. Indeed, the impression one gets is that the international communication network within an established Japanese corporation is so tightly drawn that it is virtually impossible for new managers to be introduced into the system effectively, whether they be Japanese or non-Japanese. Although apparently verifiable by no empirical research done to date, a plausible hypothesis is that as Japanese firms nationalize the managements of their foreign subsidiaries the communications problem will be exceedingly difficult. As much as the local and Japanese management try to have it otherwise, one suspects that the local manager will have a feeling of facing a tightly knit monolithic structure into which he is denied any real access. His frustration is very likely to lead to an erosion of communication and of effective control. This situation suggests why the Japanese have developed the trading company approach, which is discussed in a later section.

As Brandt and Hulbert point out, "Exchange of information between home office and subsidiary management plays a crucial role in coordinating and controlling multinational operations." On the basis of an empirical study of the communications systems used by 63 multinational corporations with subsidiaries in Brazil, the researchers attempted to identify those characteristics of a communication system associated with better understanding between headquarters and field, as perceived by field managers, and to draw comparisons between European, Japanese, and U.S.-based corporations. Among their findings: (1) U.S. companies report to headquarters more frequently than do their Japanese and European counterparts, which appeared to prefer "management by exception"; (2) U.S.-based companies are far more inclined to hold regular management meetings on a regional or worldwide basis; (3) U.S. companies rely much more on personal visits between the chief executive of the subsidiary and his home-office superior.

These differences raise questions about the impact of these differences in communications flows. Rely on research dealing with communications, Brandt and Hulbert identify a number of possibly relevant variables:

Company demographics

1. Firms with more extensive experience outside their own markets should have fewer problems with intrafirm communication.
2. Capital-intensive subsidiaries should be better understood by headquarters.
3. The great the physical and cultural distance,e the less understanding is there at headquarters.
4. The larger the subsidiary's business, the better it is understood by headquarters.
5. The longer the subsidiary's history, the greater the home office understanding.

Organizational structure

1. The greater the organizational complexity in terms of product lines, the more difficult is communication between subsidiary and headquarters.
2. The more levels there are in organizational hierarchy between subsidiary and headquarters, the less the understanding at headquarters.

Reporting procedures

1. More reports from subsidiary to headquarters, and regular responses, should lead to more understanding.
2. Excessive demand for information from the subsidiary can lead to frustration and demoralization of the subsidiary and clog communications with superficial, redundant, and inaccurate information, thus leading to less understanding at headquarters.

Shared experience

1. The more the personal contact between subsidiary and

headquarters, the greater the understanding at headquarters.

2. The more direct overseas experience or knowledge about the subsidiary's operation on the part of headquarters personnel, the greater the latter's understanding.
3. The longer the chief subsidiary executive holds office, the better his communication with headquarters is likely to be.

Brandt and Hulbert found that the nationality of the parent company had the strongest influence on the level of perceived understanding at headquarters. Chief executives of Japanese subsidiaries, it was revealed, perceived that their home offices were much less knowledgeable about Brazilian problems when compared with the perceptions of American and of European subsidiary chief executives. It was felt that the relative newness of the Japanese firms in Brazil was at least part of the explanation. They also found positive correlation between the capital-intensity of the subsidiary and better perceived understanding by home-office management. Likewise, the amount of Brazilian experience by the home officer superior and the chief subsidiary executive's tenure with the company correlated positively with understanding. The complexity of subsidiary operations correlated negatively. But "neither the size of worldwide sales nor the extent of multinational experience, as measured by proportion of sales outside the home-country market had any effect on perceptions of sales outside the home-country market had any effect on perceptions of home office understanding." The authors also observed:

> Although the number of reports sent monthly from subsidiary to home office had no effect on the criterion variable, the use of these reports at home office had a strong impact. The more these reports were read and evaluated, the greater the perceived understanding. In contrast, more reports from home office to subsidiary reduced home-office understanding. Whether this reflects real misunderstanding by home office or the COE's reaction against the barrage of home-office reports cannot be determined. It is clear, however, that merely increasing the information flow without regard to quality will not improve the relationships. In many firms some type of special "international information system" was urgently needed to coordinate and control the constant flow of communication.

The final conclusions: "Home offices clearly need to give more thought and planning to their information systems," and, "Our findings suggest it is easier to build bridges when home-office personnel have first-hand knowledge of the subsidiary's operations, which may well require more than brief visits."

Toyne has pointed out that "the success of a firm depends to a large extent on its ability to organize a cohesive management group who can mobilize the firm's physical resources and exploit opportunities to the firm's advantage." The degree of managerial cohesiveness, almost by definition impacts heavily upon a firm's capacity to control effectively. In an empirically-based study in Mexico, Toyne sought to ascertain whether differences existed between "the managerial belief and need patterns" of Mexican managers of U.S. subsidiaries, Mexican managers of Mexican firms, and American managers of Mexican subsidiaries. Secondarily, he sought to find out what influence industry and company characteristics had "on the degree of change experienced in these belief and need patterns." A third objective was to ascertain if "sociological and behavioral trait differences might influence the degree of change experienced in the managerial belief and need patterns of the Mexican Subsidiary managers because of their exposure to the organization culture of foreign subsidiary operations." But, in fact, only a partial change of beliefs was found in their case.

The overall conclusion of the study was summarized thus:

> The extent that managerial beliefs and needs are transferable is dependent on industry, company, and personal attributes. MNCs and host countries are therefore capable of moderating, not controlling, this transfer process. Grouping foreign subsidiaries by industry and company attributes would enable MNCs to determine how policies and practices at the local level need to be modified to enhance the organization, coordination and control of their global operations.

The company and industry attributes to which reference is made include capital intensity, R&D intensity, and marketing intensity. Personal attributes include education, age, exposure to foreign environments, and managerial position. In other words, all of these factors may impact on the ability of the parent corporation to control effectively a subsidiary's operations.

Location of authority for strategy selection

The local of such authority relating to overseas operations generally depends on:

1. the relative importance of foreign and domestic markets as perceived by management,
2. volume of business and degree of diversity of product,
3. the structure of the firm, such as degree of divisional autonomy, division size, basis for divisional organization.
4. the location of personal interest and expertness within the firm vis-a-vis foreign markets,
5. multinationality of ownership,
6. multinationality of top corporate management personnel,
7. the nature of the planning process.

The degree to which control is centralized is probably related to:

1. extent to which divisions are integrated.
2. amount of personnel exchange and intersubsidiary financing.
3. the degree of divisional autonomy in regard to *domestic* strategy,
4. personal interest and expertise on the corporate level regard to foreign markets,
5. the level of external political pressure to relinquish control,
6. ownership structure.

The latter point leads to the conclusion that corporate goals are relevant. If the principle goal is power maximization, extreme centralization may be optimum; if market share maximization, extreme centralization; if profit maximization, more moderate decentralization; if rate-of-return maximization, somewhat more centralized control. If one holds other factors constant, the priority of corporate goals could perhaps be implied by the level of centralization. No on seems to have researched this interesting hypothesis.

A 1968 study of 153 European affiliates of U.S. companies concluded that there was no general pattern regarding the degree of control exercised by corporate headquarters, even among corporations of the same size and industry. The general conclusions of the study of were as follows:

1. Companies in certain industries tend toward centralized control.
2. Manufacturing subsidiaries are more tightly controlled generally than marketing units.
3. Finance tends to be centrally controlled in virtually all cases; also very commonly controlled are accounting procedures, sales reporting, personnel policy, sources of supply, quality control, trademark and name, and advertising.
4. Subsidiaries with a wide range of products with a variety of markets tend to be more autonomous than affiliates with uniform products and markets.
5. Companies with a few large subsidiaries in a region tend to exercise less control than those with many small units.

6. Distant subsidiaries tend to have greater autonomy, particularly if located in countries with unfamiliar socioeconomic conditions, unstable political conditions, and stringent legal requirements.
7. Joint ventures have considerable local autonomy.
8. Newly acquired subsidiaries that continue to manufacture their old product lines under their former management tend to have greater autonomy.
9. Controls are seldom constant; during early stages the control may be very loose but tighten as the foreign operation grows—up to a point.

"Of the 127 companies whose European subsidiaries and other units...approximately 40 percent imposed strict control, 40 percent had those control, and 20 percent had control that was intermediate, flexible, and undeterminable, or in the process of being change." Nonetheless, a trend toward stricter control generally was perceived by the author. Reasons given for the trend are: (1) development of jet transportation and transatlantic telephone and telex; (2) growth of the European subsidiaries since World War II; (3) the development of the Common Market; (4) the unsatisfactory performance of many subsidiaries.

The same study concluded that strict control is imposed only so long as required, is determined in large measure by management confidence, and depends on the subsidiary's success and the control methods used. Major problems occur because of headquarters' lack of knowledge about conditions abroad, disregard of human factors, delays in decisions from headquarters, cumbersome reporting systems, the lack of knowledge about immediate situations, disregard of local managers' recommendations, and poorly qualified subsidiary managers.

The more important of these relationships are summarized in Figure 2.

Even though greater or lesser participation by the foreign units is possible, in virtually all cases some strategy choices are likely to be retained by corporate headquarters, specifically:

1. What to produce, where, and with what inputs, for sale where, and under what conditions?
2. What R&D to undertake, where, and on what scale?
3. The recruitment, development, and assignment of individuals carrying high-level skills, including managerial, and hence, their remuneration.
4. The negotiation of working conditions with labor.
5. The incurring of large-scale financial commitment.
6. Intrasubsidiary movements of goods, services, and people.
7. The reporting of profits and losses.

Strategy decisions relating to the development and servicing of foreign markets may be made in the domestic operating divisions; in a domestically oriented corporate headquarters assisted by staff office specializing in exports; in an international division; in a regional, product, or functional headquarters; or in a transnational corporate headquarters.

Of recent years there has been some empirical research as to the international centralization of control over certain functions imposed by corporations. For

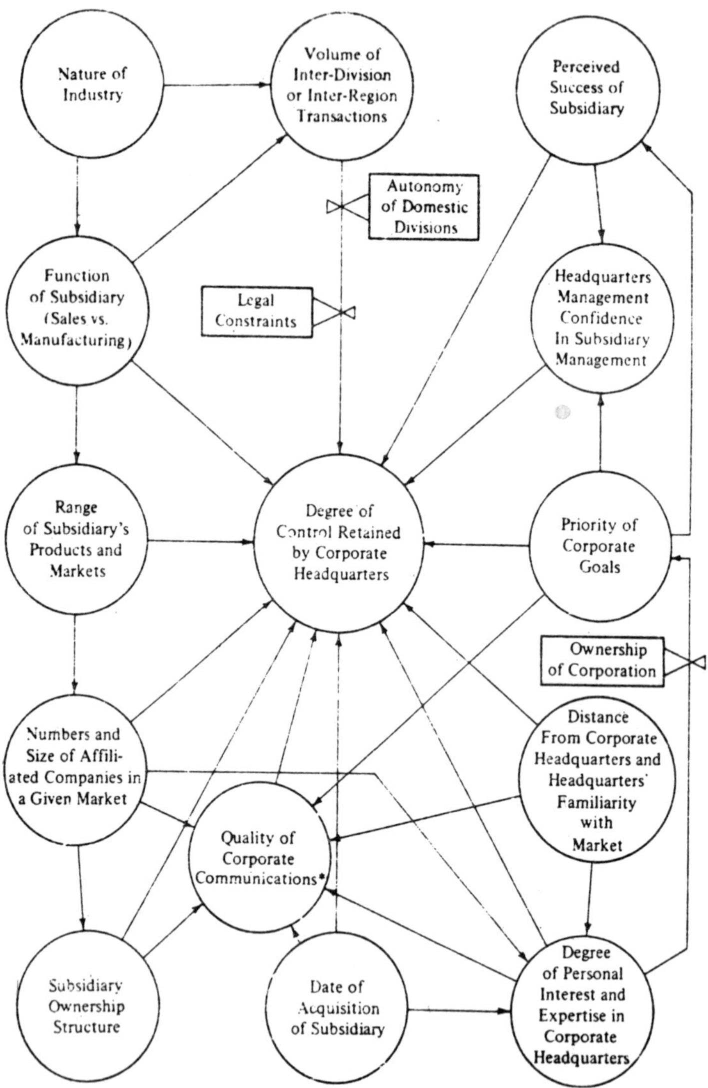

Fig. 2 Major factors relating to degree of control retained by corporate headquarters

example, in the marketing area, Aylmer found considerable dispersion. As can be seen, local management was primarily responsible for 86 percent of the advertising decisions. But product design was quite another matter.

Aylmer went on to develop data that strongly suggested that the most important firm characteristics influencing location of marketing authority were the relative importance of the firm's international operations and the relative importance of the affiliate's position within the firm. The higher the firm's international sales as a percentage of total sales, the greater was the tendency for marketing decisions to be centrally controlled. Also, the greater the relative importance of an affiliate in terms of percentage of total sales, the less likely was it that decisions were imposed by headquarters.

There would appear to be mounting evidence that money management tends to be highly centralized in many corporations operating internationally, possibly spurred by the floating of exchange rates among major trading currencies since 1973. As Prindl pointed out, the arguments for centralized control are strong:

1. Local executives can rarely know the liquidity position of the group.
2. They cannot analyze the exchange exposure of the group in either its component parts or as a consolidated entity.
3. The central financial office, no matter what shape it takes, draws on formation from a wide number of financial institutions and can formulate a broader decision on the probable nature of financial events and protection against them.

Prindl goes on to caution, "Centralized control must be weighed against the lack of whole-hearted support for rationalizing systems experienced by a number of companies when local management feels its sphere of influence is limited or its achievement down-graded." The solution, he suggests, is to make certain that local finance managers are judged within the constraints placed upon them, and that they know it. He concludes, "Most multinational corporations impose a direct and centralized control over their international affiliates."

The findings of a 1974 study of perceived changes in the degree of control exercised by one large U.S.-based corporations over their foreign subsidiaries, all of which had at least three overseas subsidiaries that contributed at least 20 percent of total sales, were surprising.

It should be noted that the labor negotiation function remained primarily in subsidiary hands and investment decisions in parent company hands.

Typically, control of certain legal, ownership, financial, and R&D strategies is retained at the corporate level regardless of type of firm. In the final analysis, corporate control over strategy should be maintained only in those functional areas in which a suboptimization problem is likely to arise as between the division and the entire corporate family, or as between subsidiary and division. Such problems may appear when important economies of scale arise in the joint utilization of scarce resources, including high-cost specialized personal. Even in the latter situation, however, specialized personnel at the corporate level may be used only in an advisory capacity to division or subsidiary managements in determining strategy.

Variations in corporate structure are outlined in figure. Bear in mind here that we are really concerned with the reality of the decision-making structure rather than any empty organizational or legal shell.

In types A,B, and C, the domestic divisions may be defined by geographical area, product, function, process, or customer. In type C, the international division is, by definition, regional. In type D the first layer of organization under corporate headquarters, whatever called, may likewise be defined by geographical area, product, function, process, or customer. Hence, D is a regionally organized multinational firm. Henceforth, let it be noted that in this test, the terms foreign-orientation, international, multinational, and transnational are not used interchangeably.

Also possible are Types E and F, firms, which, insofar as the flow of authority goes, look that same as Type D. Type E, the "transnational" firm, becomes such when its members develop loyalty to the firm of s sort that transcends national identity, thus eliminating covert or psychologically based national bias in decision making and making possible an optimum allocation of corporate resources insofar as the impact of national law on corporate decisions permits. Corporate headquarters itself becomes multinational in terms of personnel. Indeed, key decision-makers may, in fact, no longer reside in the parent country. A firm owned and managed multinationally becomes, almost by definition, transnational. Several international corporate mergers within Europe have given rise to true transnational firms. Temporary transnational ventures are likewise to be found in Europe, such as those related to Atlantic, Hawk, Main Battle Tank, Concorde, and Nadge projects. A major problem associated with this type of transnational venture lies in the fact of their temporary nature. Managers assigned to the ventures anticipate returning to their parent firms and, hence, are in a position of great role conflict.

A further word about the definition of the multinational corporation is in order. The multinational corporation (MNC), technically defined, is characterized by four factors:

1. Ownership and management of a parent corporation essentially by the nationals of one country.
2. An integrated international production system.
3. Equity-based control.
4. A legal domicile within the country with which the preponderance of parent company owners and managers identify.

If one changes any one of these four dimensions, a different type of enterprise emerges, from which one can expect different behavior.

For example, if one postulates ownership and management of the parent corporation by the nationals of more than one country to a significant degree, one has a *transnational corporation*. If the corporation is not managing an integrated international production system, then it is simply an *international holding company* of some sort, possibly based on financial linkages and some vaguely defined policy guidelines, characteristics of the international corporation. If its control is not equity based, but rather rests on contracts, we have an *international service company*, which can range all the way from the general trading companies of Japan, which are essentially selling marketing services, to the company marketing a specific service, such as engineering, construction, and the like. And if one changes the fourth part of the definition of the multinational either by domiciling the parent corporation in a country with which neither owners nor top managers identify or by permitting the parent corporation special legal status under international convention, one either has the *dedomiciled multinational* or, in the latter case, the *supranational corporation* of which we have only public and quasipublic examples. another, the Agro-Industrial Development Corporation, was urged for the Middle East at one time, but dropped.

One of the difficulties with so much research in the international business area, is that it has not seen the nature of the international enterprise itself as an important variable. For example, much data has been collected on "multinational corporations" which in fact includes information on many firms that are not multinational as defined above. Only rarely is such data classified by type of corporation. One might service data for corporations with or without international divisions, but it is exceedingly important to distinguish between those corporations that have had an international division in the past and dissolved it in favor of a true multinational structure and those firms which have never evolved far enough beyond export to have created an international division. And, in some instances an international division is retained *after* multinationalization, simply as a staff-support, planning, and/or integrative unit.

The taxonomy of international corporate form has been further compounded by the United Nations' insistence on using the term "transnational" to cover all firms operating internationally. Given the definitions used here and elsewhere in the more technical literature, the term "transnational" as used by the United Nations includes export-oriented, international, multinational, and transnational firms, plus international service companies, international holding companies, and dedomiciled multinationals. The point is that each type of corporation gives rise to different public policy issues. For example, of the multinational is in greatest conflict with host country governments, one might argue that the transnationals are likely to be in greatest conflict with *parent country* governments. It is important to make these definitional distinctions because it seems very likely that they impact on corporate behavior and, hence, on public policy issues. Curiously, there has been virtually no research as to how the internationalization of the firm, and subsequently its multinationalization and transnationalization, impact on the nature and quality of corporate decisions. However, national differences in corporate behavior may be aggressive.

Evolution of the firm

In speaking of the evolution of the firm in its international dimension, one must superimpose tow related but distinct processes. There is, first, the pattern of geographical dispersion of corporate resources and, second, the pattern of functional and organizational development as the perceived corporate market internationalizes.

Carlson observed:

> As long as the survival of a firm is not threatened, its primary objective is to grow. Its immediate goal is to increase its sales, with the qualification that it can at the same time reach a certain profit level, a certain level of financial stability, etc. If these conditions cannot be

> fulfilled in its present operations, it starts to search for new alternative activities. But since new alternatives generally seem more uncertain than old ones, we assume that this search will be directed to alternatives which are as similar as possible to those with which it is already familiar.

Carlson goes on to point out that the uncertainty the firm feels during such a search is due to four factors:

1. Lack of knowledge of the existence of possible new alternatives.
2. Lack of knowledge of the conditions, internal or external to the firm, which will determine the consequences of a new alternative.
3. Lack of knowledge of what consequences may be expressed in relevant terms of goal fulfillment.

It has been noted frequently that uncertainty increases with the time which elapses between decision and outcome and with the degree of unfamiliarity in respect to the place of that outcome, that is, its "degree of foreignness." Carlson adds the uncertainty associated with what he dubs "frontier problems," such as the variety of laws and regulations relating to the cross-border movement of goods, money, and people. Export experience reduces both elements of this uncertainty over time, and hence usually precedes any major commitment of corporate assets to the purchase of fixed assets abroad. In any event, the accumulation of the new information sufficient to reduce uncertainty bears a cost. The information must be collected, transmitted, and interpreted.

Carlson uses the notion of "cultural distance," which

he defines in terms of the difference between home country and foreign market in respect to level of development, education, business language, everyday language, cultural distance, and extent of the connection between the two countries. Various Swedish studies reported by Carlson, his own included, seem to establish hat buying preferences of Swedish firms correlate negatively with cultural distance, so likewise the degree of corporate commitment in exploiting foreign markets although once a firm has progressed to the point of establishing a sales *subsidiary* in a particular country, it seems to be more influenced by size of market than by cultural distance. Finally, another Swedish study reported by Carlson concluded that Swedish firms "start to establish subsidiaries in culturally nearby countries before they do so further away, but there seems to be a certain difference in the chronological order as between different periods, different branches of industry, and different sized firms. Firms that produced technology-intensive products seemed to be more influenced by cultural distance than other firms, and small firms were more influenced than large firms." These studies support the observation that historically U.S. firms very frequently moved assets first into Canada, then into the United Kingdom and other English-speaking countries, even before the firm became either multinational or international in structure and it was often true that these first investments came about as the result of some personal relationship or interest at the top, not as the result of a global scanning process.

If the evolution of administrative structure is viewed alongside growth of foreign sales of the firm, types A, B, C, and D tend to follow one another in time for a given firm.

In type A, each domestic division handles its own foreign sales, which arise initially in response to largely unsolicited orders from overseas. If the potential foreign market is indeed small, if divisions are organized on a product basis, and if divisions are relatively autonomous and large, type A may be optimal. One problem is that the foreign market potential from the point of view of each division may be seen as relatively small, in which event no one in the firm develops sufficient interest to examine the potential of various foreign markets and to combine corporate resources for full exploitation. Nor are experts employed who are capable of realizing such foreign-market potential, nor the specialists capable of facilitating product movement into such markets.

In part out of realization of this deficiency, the firm may move to type B, in which case authority for foreign market development is centralized in corporate headquarters within a foreign or export department. Strategy determination follows. The ease with which this move may be made is very largely a function of the perceived relative profitability of the foreign business by top corporate management. That is, if profits derived on foreign sales are greater than average, the attention of the chief executive is attracted. The expert or foreign department is likely to appear first as a staff office, but subsequently gains more and more line authority in respect to overseas activities, thereby causing friction with the operating divisions. Also, the foreign department may have difficulty in inducing the product divisions to fill export orders promptly or at all. Meanwhile, sooner or later top management will perceive that the optimum entry strategy in respect to one or more foreign markets is through licensing or direct investment, not exports. A decision-making processing that is not functionally biased requires individuals whose careers do not rest on a record of successful export and who have some knowledge of production as well as sales in the foreign context. These sources of fictions, plus the need for line control over foreign operations by qualified people, push a firm to introduce a type C structure, the characteristic hallmark of which is the international division.

Ideally an international division should be so organized and staffed as to facilitate a functionally and geographically bias-free search for the most profitable opportunities abroad. It should also have the capacity to recruit corporate resources to; take advantage of perceived opportunities, to start up operations overseas, and to control overseas operations. In each function, specialized skills are required in such areas as negotiation, law, finance, marketing, personnel, accounting, R&D, and line management with manufacturing competence. Note that virtually all the *technical* skills required for establishing and maintaining a manufacturing facility are embedded in the domestic divisions, and embodied in people with little or no foreign experience and typically with an exaggerated notion as to the superiority of their own nationality, national business system, and technical competency.

As the foreign part of a firm's business achieves a significant percentage of the total, certain frictions are likely to develop within the firm. The international division may find it difficult to attract competent operating personnel from the domestic manufacturing divisions, to induce corporate staff departments to develop the relevant expertness and interest, or to stimulate R&D in reference to product and processes so as to be more responsive to differing market environments. The domestic divisions may assign their least competent, most expendable personnel to overseas projects. If a division manager is being evaluated on his profit and loss, why should he do otherwise unless participation in the overseas project somehow contributes to division profit?

The last consideration has on occasion induced a system of interdepartmental administrative credit memos. The international division negotiates with a domestic division for certain technical assistance and personnel, say, for plant construction, start-up, and training of foreign personnel. For such assistance, the domestic division might be awarded a contract. But, over time, such a system can create an onerous and costly internal accounting problem, and profit expectations may not be realized. In any event, the R&D and staff problems remain, as well as those inherent in the ethnocentric attitude of many of the managers and technicians. The result is that there is a demonstrable tendency for an international division eventually to start building up its own staff. It can do so more easily, of course, if it is physically separated from corporate headquarters, which in fact is often the case for U.S. corporations headquartered outside of New York City in that international divisions are often located in the city.

The type C structure, thus, tends to create divided loyalties and to isolate virtually all interest and expertness in foreign operations within the international division. Even in the formation of the international division, those with special knowledge or interest in international business were probably pulled out of corporate headquarters and the operating divisions. The upshot is that overseas projects are likely not to be given the same attention as comparable domestic projects by the corporate staff or on the strategy decision-making level. And risk attached to overseas projects tends to be exaggerated. All of these problems are compounded if the international division is located physically apart from corporate headquarters. The influence of the internationally oriented managers on the rest of the firm may thus be reduced as their division becomes isolated and physically removed from corporate headquarters.

Characteristically, a type C firm initially tends to expand its overseas operations rapidly. If the international division is relatively isolated from corporate headquarters, and if it is perceived by top management as a distinct organization, a discontinuity in decision making may appear, which facilitates this rapid growth. A certain capital budget may be established for the division, which means that so long as it does not attempt to capture more corporate resources, decisions relative to overseas expansion can be made very largely on the division level. And for a time, there may be an understanding that the division earnings can be retained for investment. Given this new willingness to commit resources through a wider band of strategies to develop important overseas markets, the firm is very likely to enjoy a sudden spurt in overseas business. This pressure for expansion, plus division management's desire to prove itself may well lead to a willingness to enter into joint ventures and contractual arrangements. At this point, there is little awareness of the possible advantages to setting up integrated production and marketing systems regionally or globally. Indeed, the company has usually not developed foreign markets sufficiently at this point so as to make integration across borders an attractive proposition. Hence, there is little pressure for centralized control except over purely technical and financial matters.

However, as the system builds, as market penetration goes deeper, and as foreign environmental expertise builds up in division headquarters, control over production and marketing is very likely to become more centralized. A corollary is that an increasing number of U.S. nationals are dispatched abroad to manage foreign manufacturing and marketing subsidiaries. And an effort begins to buy up the local equity held in the corporation's far-flung enterprises, so that the newly centralized control can be exercised with less resistance. The advantages in exercising some flexibility in transfer pricing become apparent, which provides further reason to avoid joint venturing wherever possible. We now have what might be dubbed "the mature international corporation," one that is ripe for evolution into the multinational phase. But until that move is made, a distinction remains. Decisions relating to the allocation of corporate resources overseas continue to be made largely in the international division. If it wants to grow at a rate faster than retained earnings permit, the division faces a challenge from internal corporate politics. Its demand for a greater allocation of the corporate pie is likely to face the opposition of equally ambitious domestic division managers, who probably outscore the international division management in terms of numbers and seniority within the corporation.

In a study of 12 major Japanese companies, Kobayashi described Japanese corporate decision-making processes relative to the commitment of assets to overseas markets. Despite the previously-described unique features of Japanese management, Kobayashi's 12 corporations can be classified according to the scheme offered here. In fact, in his concluding remarks, he observes:

> Systems for decision-making in connection with overseas investments vary from one company to another, depending upon (1) the kind of industry or business in which one engages, (2) the size of the business activities, (3) the degree of commitment to overseas activities and also (4) the degree of diversification... lines. However, in my survey, I have found that among the companies...made a start...overseas activities earlier than others, there gradually emerge organizations which are almost identical, at least in form, to the Western vision of the International Division system.

But of possible significance, only one of the 12 had apparently moved beyond the international phase by melting the functions of the international division into the rest of the corporation, thereby transforming itself into a true multinational. Kobayashi also emphasized the "culture unfamiliarity and information gap" on the part of the managements he studied.

The international division is possibly optimum if (1) sales outside the United States remain a small part of the total corporate sales. (2) the firm has activities in a very limited number of countries, (3) there are few internationally experienced executives within the firm, (4) the firm has few product lines, or (5) the products are of such a nature that the environmental influences on sales and production strategy vary little if at all from one national market to another. The last is likely to be more true of capital-intensive, technologically complex products sold to a sophisticated market.

But if any of these conditions fails to be satisfied, pressures are very likely to develop within the firm pushing it toward the multinational form or type D structure. And, overtime, as foreign markets continue to grow, one or more of these conditions will, in most cases, fail to be satisfied. The level of foreign sales, which is roughly equal to those of one of the larger domestic divisions, may be the critical level psychologically in bringing about a change in corporate structure. It will then be perceived by top corporate management that the international division lacks the leverage with the corporation to sell overseas projects and to recruit adequate corporate resources to service the expanding foreign market opportunities.

As one U.S. executive observed:

> We abolished the international division because it was quickly apparent that it was a Parkinson's Law appendage which jealously guarded its authority and prerogative—thus very effectively shielding the international operations from all goods ideas in the domestic group.

Another U.S. executive made somewhat the same point when he said:

> While undue influence from the domestic organization is to be avoided, so should the international organization refrain from becoming too exclusive or remote and beyond the comprehension of the other management personnel. There is a considerable tendency on the part of international executives to guard closely the activities of their divisions or operations. In doing so, they divorce themselves

> from the rest of the organization. Cooperation between domestic and international divisions becomes more difficult and any desire on the part of domestic personnel to become more familiar with the international operations gradually dies.

Still another: "If we split the company strictly between foreign and domestic business, we would have ended up with two general staffs. And if people grew up in only one area of the company, we would have lost the advantage of being able to interchange them freely." The disappearance of the international division continues on the part of the more mature international firms. The Harvard study of 187 "multinational" corporations revealed that "57 of the 72 enterprises that adopted at some point in their development had given it up by 1968."

But not everyone agrees. Professor Schollhammer reports, on the basis of a study of 12 large chemical pharmaceutical companies, that he could find no evidence that the firms had changed their respective structures or intended to do so. He concluded, "The experience of the 12 companies refutes the idea that with an increasing magnitude of the international business activities a firm would shift its organization structure from a domestic orientation to an international division approach, and, finally, to a global approach." The problem may be that Schollhammer's time span was too short. Also, the experience of 12 forms in one industry hardly constitutes a general refutation. It may be, however, that there are at least two intervening variables of significance between a firm's perception that its market is internationalizing and its structural response, specifically, the levels of the technologies and cultures involved. If one is dealing with a relatively static technology in relatively advanced societies, the firm may drop the international division structure more slowly in favor of some form of global management than if it were involved with a more dynamic technology in less developed countries. In the latter case, an international division would probably be unable to compete effectively for corporate skills in exploiting the rapidly changing technology internationally, nor would it be able to exert sufficient pressure to effect environmentally inspired product and process changes.

In any event, the ease with which the transformation from international to multinational can be made obviously varies enormously, and is a relevant variable. Great size, a prior domestic *regional* organization, a strong corporate headquarters, and personal interest and expertness in key places obviously facilitate matters greatly.

In the case of the regionally-organized multinational, a useful bit of research would be the identification of the location of the regional headquarters of firms, the reasons for the choice, and the magnitude of the benefits flowing to the host country. One knows that Brussels is a common choice for the European headquarters of U.S.-based multinationals, in part because of the need to interface with the EEC bureaucracy. We also know that many U.S. multinationals have located their Latin American headquarters in Coral Gables, Florida, in part because of the ease of communicating with Central and South America from that point. also, one suspects that as a group of corporate regional headquarters becomes situated in a particular site, for whatever reason, others are attracted. And, of course, the greater the number, the more pressure can be exerted on telecommunications and airline companies to improve services. Elsewhere the pattern is not so recognizable. In Southeast Asia, a number of countries are competing for corporate regional headquarters by offering relief from certain taxes and work permit requirements for foreign personnel. The Philippines and Malaysia have offered special facilities. In France, there is a special official at the Finance Ministry charged with welcoming foreign headquarters. Materials promoting the selection of France as the site for European regional headquarters have been circulated, and residence permits for headquarters' employees have been expedited.

Business International has reported that some MNCs have recently moved their regional executives into corporate headquarters. The reasons given: need to improve communication between regional staff and upper corporate management at headquarters, the realization that technically intraregional communication is no better than between the United States and the region, and reduced cost. It was estimated that a company might realize a 30 to 50 percent saving by having regional executives in the United States. One cannot help but speculate that the physical presence of upward mobility of foreign managers into top corporate management, thereby facilitating the transformation into a transnational.

As was the case of the international corporation before it, the multinational corporation has built into it the seeds its own destruction. It is not in stable equilibrium either with itself or with the environment. Point one: although corporate personnel are given multinational responsibilities, characteristically many have had little international experience and no relevant technical-professional training. Point two: being members of a corporate headquarters peopled almost entirely with fellow nationals, the executives with new global responsibilities possess a set of values and a world perception that is very likely to bias their decision making. Although they may posses a *willingness* to allocate corporate resources optimally on a global basis, in fact, they are *psychologically* and *legally* incapable of doing so. Point three: given the nonavailability of headquarters personnel equipped to operate effectively overseas, and the lower cost of employing *local* national managers abroad rather than home country expatriates, plus the rapid rate of expansion often characteristic of the multinational stage, the firm employs largely local nationals to manage its new foreign facilities. It may also continue to enter into a number of joint ventures, which are often legally required in the LDCs. Hence, it may lack the capacity to maintain really effective central control. It depends upon how "mature" the international divisions had become prior to the transformation into a multinational.

Although perhaps initially inclined for these reasons to permit substantial autonomy to their associated foreign firms, the multinationals, as they mature and gain international experience at the center eventually begin to accelerate the centralization process. The benefits to be derived from integrating the worldwide movement of corporate resources become increasingly apparent as the contribution to corporate profits from overseas activity mounts and as the skill to effect such integration appears in corporate headquarters. They then begin to try to capture control at the center and to buy up whatever partially owned affiliates remain.

Louis Wells has demonstrated that a firms's propensity to enter joint ventures seems to lessen as its products become more mature, particularly if the firm pursues the strategy of devoting resources to marketing techniques to create product differentiation or a strategy of allocating resources to R&D in order to generate new products to serve *traditional* needs and customers. On the contrary, a firm seems to demonstrate a somewhat lower joint venture entry ratio if it pursues a strategy of allocating resources to R&D for generating products diversified as to function and customers or a strategy of retaining control over raw material sources. His research also suggests that relatively small firms and late entrants to foreign markets have a greater propensity to enter joint ventures than larger firms and earlier entrants. These findings tend to support the evolutionary model developed here.

In an event, the capture of control at corporate headquarters is very likely to generate powerful internal conflicts. On the one hand, we have competent and now experienced, local national managers moving upward toward their respective national subsidiary ceilings in terms of promotion. On the other hand is the fact of increasingly centralized control within the multinational corporate headquarters. The local manager may respond by pushing for greater autonomy of his own operation, which is often signaled by a breakdown in communication between subsidiary and headquarters, an exaggerated importance given to environmental factors in decision making, and continued inability of the firm to maintain effective control. Or, the local manager may leave the employ of the firm. Host governments tend to support the local manager's desire for greater autonomy, for the increased external control over the allocation of domestic resources sooner or later becomes politically unacceptable. The environmental factor thus, in fact, becomes blown up so likewise, the loss of key manpower.

The managers in Western Europe—often triggered off by the impact of the Americans—have been accompanied by an obsessive interest in managerial education, corporate reorganization, and the activities of management consultants. These efforts have often appeared faintly laughable, or even sinister to Europeans. But they have helped to make European-owned industry more competitive, and they have been reinforced by the extremely valuable training ground provided by the American-owned companies in Europe. There is a constant drain from these concerns of able men fretting at the strict controls under which they have to operate and the knowledge that, in most American-owned companies, they cannot rise above the management of the subsidiary of their own country. And no European company now feels secure without its quota of men trained by Ford or Proctor & Gamble.

Eventually, the multinational headquarters perceives the cost inherent in the communications breakdown, loss of control, mounting political pressures, and possible loss of key foreign managerial personnel. As it does so, nationality barriers are removed, and foreign nationals are likely to begin appearing in responsible managerial spots outside their respective national subsidiaries, first in regional headquarters if there are such, then in corporate headquarters itself. This is where the model begins to diverge from the Japanese, because it is almost inconceivable that non-Japanese managers could work effectively at high levels within the corporate headquarters of a Japanese corporation, particularly when one considers the system of permanent employment and relatively permanent work groups still characteristic of large Japanese corporations. How can the non-Japanese manager be thrust into such a situation horizontally and be expected to relate effectively? Commenting somewhat along the same line, Tecoz observed:

European corporations have long ago understood the importance and efficiency of having on their boards nationals of the countries where they export, or manufacture for that matter.

U.S. companies were completely closed to non-U.S. board members until some years ago, but they now have begun to open up.

But Japanese corporations seem to stay very reluctant in that evolution. Returning to our non-Japanese model, one should note that several forces combine over time to multinationalize the ownership of the multinational corporation. Among these for the U.S. based multinational are the attraction of swapping U.S parent company stock for foreign assets, the foreign sale of debentures convertible to parent company stock, and the listing of parent company stock on foreign stock exchangers. For the European-based multinationals, the relatively small size of the local capital market pushes in the direction of multinational ownership, including the appeal of cross-border mergers and/or repeated joint venturing among multinationals. In fact, as already noted, a number of European transnationals have appeared. In addition, there have been several thousand common undertakings by European firms of different nationalities, which, over time, look very much like transnational enterprises. One also suspects that repeated participation in transnational ventures of a temporary nature could lead to more permanent association.

Both in the more and less developed countries one

may be compelled to recognize host society demands-often translated into political pressures-for a share in the profit derived from its market. It is even conceivable that an LDC government, rather than compelling the spinoff of ownership in the local subsidiary, might opt to trade MNC access to local market and resources in return for parent company stock of equivalent value, plus some sort of representation at the top level of the corporation. Although not yet actually proposed, the idea has been discussed among some LDC decision-makers.

The degree to which ownership has been in fact multinationlized is another inadequately researched subject for which we have not empirically based trend line. The Harvard multinational corporate study found, "The stock ownership of U.S.-controlled multinational enterprises is overwhelmingly in the hands of U.S. nationals. Only a very few of the outstanding shares of the parent firm—something in the order of 2 or 3 percent—are owned by foreigners." Some have speculated, however, that the many billions of dollars in the hands of foreign central banks might constitute a pressure on these governments to induce American-owned subsidiaries to sell a substantial part of their common stock to host country residents. It was reported by early 1972 that one central bank had already committed $ 100 million for the purchase of U.S. common stocks. As of the end of 1975, foreigners owned $ 26.7 billion in U.S. corporate stocks and $9.8 billion in U.S corporate bonds. In any case, substantial local ownership of foreign subsidiaries may induce such a conflict of interest as to push the mature multinational firm to swap its own stock for the local equity in its associated overseas enterprises.

Many firms are undoubtedly now in this transitional state between the multinational firm and the truly transnational firm. The latter is simply a corporation that has lost its national identity except insofar as legal restraints may impact upon its decisions and operations. It is owned and managed by the nationals of more than one country. It is possibly true that in the long run a necessary, if not sufficient, condition for maximum corporate growth is multinational ownership and management at all levels. Thus, the transnational corporations may grow more rapidly than the multinational.

Likewise supporting this line of argument is the possibility that in the transnational case technology would move more easily there would be a reduced fear of losing national control. Also, the R&D effort of a truly transnational firm would possibly be less culturally biased there should be a greater readiness to address R&D directly to the problems suggested within specific markets.

Transnationals with annual gross sales of upward of $50 billion may soon not be uncommon. It has been predicted that there will be some 300 such corporations by 1985 controlling a very large part of the fixed industrial assets of the free world. But, in fact, will they? Their sheer size, and absence of all national loyalty inherent in their multinational ownership and management,may bring such corporations onto a collision course with the nation-state. Indeed, there is considerable evidence that even though governments may be promoting or permitting *national* mergers and industrial concentrations, increasingly they are resisting mergers and arrangements among the giant multinationals and transnationals. As noted elsewhere, it is U.S. antitrust policy to prevent mergers, wherever they take place or whatever the nationality of the merging companies, if the effect of the merger would be to reduce competition significantly within the United States or with the foreign trade of the United States. The European community seems to be setting precedent barring the further acquisition of important national companies by large multinationals or transnationals. The Japanese have been restrictive in this regard for some time, and one sees no reason that they should shift direction. But to achieve effective political control of such giant multinational and transnational firms requires new international institutions, particularly in regard to the *dedomiciled* multinationals and transnationals because of their greater growth potential and absence of national loyalty or bias. No national government, or even an international regional agency such as the EEC, can claim the right to determine the law under which a multinationally owned and multinationally managed corporation, with resources strewn around the world, should operate. This rationale will be particularly relevant to corporations operating beyond the reach of any national sovereignty—the deep ocean bed, arctic regions, space, and icebergs. In the final analysis what one faces is the management of global resources.

Therefore, the next stage in the evolutionary process may be the appearance of the supranational firm. Such entities must necessarily rest on special intergovernmental agreements or treaties, which in each case provide the legal basis for a governing body. One can expect two further near-team developments: (1) the emergence of a European corporation charted and controlled—if not taxed—under an EEC law and (2) the appearance of an international seabed authority which would charter, control, and possibly tax corporations operating on the bed of the deep sea. Various proposals have been made for a *general* international convention, under which some sort of commission would be created for the chartering, controlling, and taxing of corporations satisfying certain conditions in respect to multinationality of ownership and management, but this seems far off.

It would appear that during the past 20 years or so the real value of worldwide sales of the large corporations has been increasing about 10 percent a year, while the real GNP of the nation-states has been growing at the most by 5 percent. It has been pointed out that if one assumes a 20 percent growth rate for a firm with present sales of a billion dollars, and a 6 percent world growth rate, by the year 2035 the firm's sales would exceed the world's GNP. For the large firms, continued rapid growth is obviously a short-run phenomenon. And, once the limit has been reached, then it will not be the large firms that will be growing, but the smaller ones. It is entirely possible that many of the super-firms of the near future will break up because they will be unable to attract resources.

But in the meantime, the size of these multinationals and transnationals is likely to be viewed by nation-states as politically intolerable. The degree to which economic power may become concentrated in the hands of decision-makers virtually unreachable by any government could render it impossible for any single nation-states, or even regional groupings, to regulate these firms. The common interest of nation-states almost compels them to participate in an effort to harmonize national policy in regard to antitrust, taxation, corporate law, and restraint on resource allocation.

The common interest becomes irresistibly compelling if one adds the mounting pressure to internationalize political decision making as we approach the finite limits of our global environment. Obviously, the rate of resource usage, energy consumption, atmospheric and oceanic pollution can only be resolved on a global basis. Finally, there is no evidence leading one to believe that the giant multinational or transnational corporation will voluntarily incorporate any mechanism rendering it socially responsible other than through the market place, which even within the United States is perceived as inadequate in respect to the protection of consumer, investor, worker, and the general welfare. It would appear that either the nation-states in concert will dominate the giant multinationals and transnationals or the reverse will occur. Bear in mind that the former implies an international convention creating a body of basic law and a representative body with adequate resources to control these corporations. The international corporate law may specify, for example, that national shareholders will be represented in the corporate board by a government appointee approved by those shareholders. Given such a system of international law and control, the possibility of a truly supranational corporation appears.

If nations find it impossible to collaborate to this degree, they are very likely to act to restrain further transnational corporate growth, first by forbidding further mergers and acquisitions and, if this is seen as an inadequate impediment to further growth, then by expropriating local assets. Most vulnerable, of course, would be integrated plants in mature industries that serve primarily the local market and that belong to transnational corporations in which there is little or no local equity involvement.

Or, it may just be that the pattern apparently emerging in Japan and elsewhere for some of the reasons already suggested will prove so profitable that the large North American and Western European-based multinationals and transnationals will be induced to change their structure. What seems to be developing in Japan is the multinational *association*, more commonly known as the general trading company. At the other center is a Japanese-owned and managed corporation, which is linked internationally by a web of contractual relations with largely locally owned and managed associated firms. The center supplies capital-intensive, scarce resources, such as new technology, management and managerial training, international marketing services, purchase and sale contracts, debt capital, and possibly initial high-risk equity that is later withdrawn. The associated, eventually largely locally owned and managed, firms produce. Such an association becomes transnational if the central corporation is owned by the associated foreign firms.

There are many pressures combining to push multinationals to evolve more in the direction of the international association than into transnationals. *First,* many managements are learning-in part through experience in East-West trade, which is necessarily limited to contract in most cases—that the sale or lease of capital-intensive inputs can be very lucrative, more so than the return on direct investment. Not only may the rate of return on corporate assets committed be heightened, but the risk of costly adverse political acts may be significantly reduced. The corporation has few fixed assets in place subject to expropriation. In most cases, payment for services provided under contract parallels the delivery of those services. Hence, the corporation has greater flexibility it can walk away from an unpleasant situation more easily than if it had fixed assets in place for which it hoped to earn a return through dividends spread over several years. *Second,* experience shows that most host countries under balance of payments pressure are inclined to make foreign exchange available for the payment of fees, royalties, imported goods, and interest before permitting the remittance of earnings in the form of dividends. The host country can easily perceive the *quid pro quo* in the sale or lease of a particular item or service for a specified price. It can see the value of that for which payment is made. Not so in the case of a dividend, particularly if the investment has been in place for any period of time. Increasingly, the host country may see those remittances as representing "unearned" foreign profit derived from the local market, local labor, locally available technology, and local capital. Under exchange pressure, dividends are invariably the first to suffer. Third, the contract route also permits a systematic periodic renegotiation as the benefit-cost rations shift, which, for instance, would be signaled when another firm is prepared to provide comparable inputs at less cost. Increasingly are the LDCs unwilling to accept alien ownership of a local enterprise without a specific date for withdrawal of that ownership. Hence, even ownership is taking on the coloration of a contractual relationship. *Fourth,* in part for these reasons, plus the gathering worldwide movement toward public sector enterprises, profit-sharing enterprises, and management-sharing enterprises also suggest that this pattern may indeed be the wave of the future, that the multinational and transnational corporation as presently conceived will prove to be relatively short-lived transitional forms. The point is that the degree of international integration, hence centralized control, required for multinationals and transnationals may become unrealistic in view of mounting pressures for *local* control.

Briefly, management of an integrated international marketing system may prove to be the most profitable and least risky form of international business. In fact, there is some evidence that it is the most rapidly growing. Although figures in this area are slippery, it would appear that the average growth of the multinationals and transnationals in the 10 percent range, of the large general trading companies, 20 to 30 percent. A more refined monitoring of the rates of growth of various types of international business activity is needed as a guide to the future.

One is thus driven to the conclusion that either a mechanism is created for providing international political control over the giant transnational firms,which could constitute an important next step on the long road to effective world government, or the Japanese model of multinational associations is very likely to dominate. As these associations become transnational in nature, at which point the Japanese may find themselves at a disadvantage, the need for some form of international political control will again arise. such control is also dictated by the environmental problem and the global resource allocation process such implies. So, following either route, the pressure of world business is likely one day to force the nation-states into a posture of cooperation thus far unknown.

It can be seen that we have been discussing the locale and structural-psychological restraints on decision making. To summarize:

1. In type A firms, there is no particular interest or

expertness engaged in searching for and developing foreign markets. Decision making is prejudiced against any commitment to overseas activity and is entirely responsive to external pressures, not to an internally generated search process.

2. In type B firms, international interest and expertness are limited to a staff department and are restricted to searching for and developing export markers only, but decisions are made in the domestic divisions and domestically oriented staff departments, hence, such decisions are strongly biased nationally.

3. In type C firms, interest and expertness are in an international division, but with functional expertness remaining in the domestic divisions and domestically oriented staff departments. Decisions are less biased in terms of the type of foreign market entry strategy that will be considered, but are still heavily biased nationally. Initially, the capacity to exercise centralized control over foreign operations is weak and the pressure to grow rapidly high. Hence, a joint venturing and contracting strategy may be adopted. But in time, pressure toward increased control and centralization emerge and key positions overseas are filled with home country nationals

4. In type D firms, international interest and expertise are located throughout the firm, but top corporate managers are still home country nationals and initially lack international experience and expertness. There is, nonetheless, an effort to make decisions less nationally biased, but an inability to effect a true centralization of control persists in headquarters, particularly if local equity participation continues to be permitted. As the

firm grows locally, political p[pressures develop to compel greater local control and, hence, subsidiary autonomy. In the meantime, as the firm gathers more environmental expertness in headquarters and perceives more clearly the advantages of greater integration, it will attempt to reestablish central control over its foreign operations, including the buying-up of local equity. Conflict with host governments tends to increase.

5. In type E firms, which are owned and managed multinationally, decision making is centralized but free of national bias except as legally imposed. The firm loses loyalty to a single nation, thereby putting it on a collision course with its parent government.

6. In type F firms, management is free structurally, psychologically and legally to allocate resources on a global basis in conformance with corporate goals insofar as they do not conflict with the international political regime controlling the corporation.

The point is made that if a firm's foreign market is perceived as growing relative to the domestic, all of these types are unstable except the last. Pressures in the system either propel a firm to the next level or push it back. An alternative to the supranational corporation, if the legal basis fails to materialize, might be the multinational or transnational association. The center might or might not be owned and managed multinationally,. But if it is, thereby differentiated from a multinational association and becomes transnational.

It will be noted that Perlmutter's three-type classification system, with some modification, identifies the characteristic behavior of the international, multinational, and *transitional* multinational firm.. Its shortcoming is that it falls short of describing a dynamic system in that it does not specify the pressures pushing a firm from one orientation to another nor does it go far enough. It fails to specify the distinctive orientation of the truly transnational and supranational firms. Neither does it refer to the interrelationship between orientation and structure, nor to the interrelationship between these two aspects and the priority of control centers.

Internal structure

As already noted, whatever the type of corporation, a division, a "group", or a "headquarters" may be identified with a product-line, a function, a region, a process, or a class of customer. Coordination within a large organization may be necessary along more than one of these dimensions. For a firm expanding internationally a very real question is, which one of these linkage should be given priority and represent the primary chain-of-command line? Which are the staff lines? Or, different line authority may be delegated along different dimensions, which brings one to the subject of the matrix organisation.

In U.S.-based firms, one is more likely to find the product divisions in the vertical position; the functional, in the horizontal. The latter are most frequently called "coordinating committees" or "groups." European firms are more likely to give priority to the functional division or possibly to make both the product and functional divisions vertical. The foreign trade organizations of Soviet bloc countries are almost invariably organised on a product-line basis.

The three-dimensional matrix management can be diagramed most easily as in Figure 3. We assume the APF

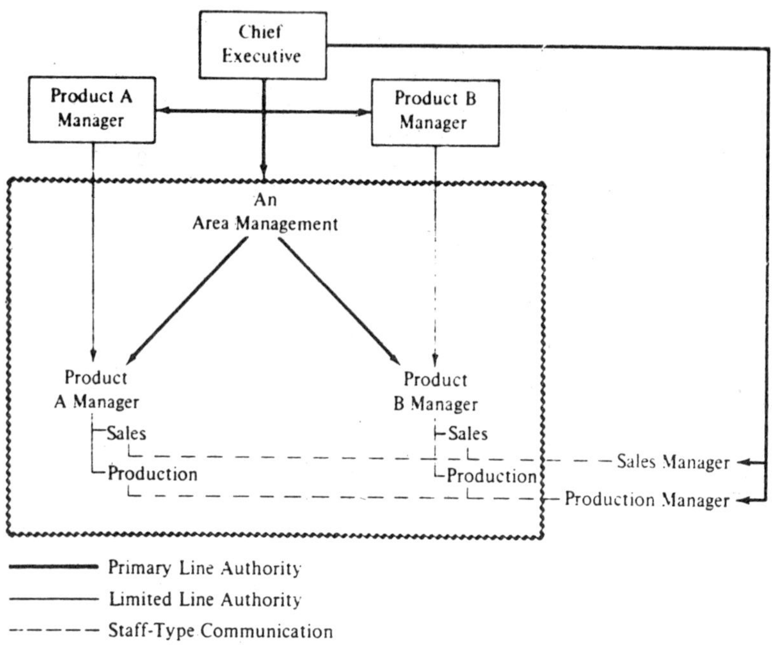

Fig. 3 A three-dimensional matrix management of the APF type

variety, which is possibly the most common for the big U.S.-based multinationals. The Harvard "multinational" corporation study revealed that of the 72 corporations without an international division, 24 percent were organized regionally, 41 percent by product division, and 35 percent had a mixed structure. This last category included three enterprises "organized on the principle that every operating unit would report both to a product division and to an area division simultaneously and 22 organized partially on a product division and partially on an area division breakdown.

The obvious next question is, under that circumstances should a firm with international operations opt for one form or another, say for a PAF, an APF, or an FAP? Which are apparently the most common? Key questions here have to do with specifying the most important similarities and dissimilarities. For example:

1. Is each differentiated region essentially homogeneous in respect to functions and products and significantly different from other regions along one or more important dimensions? If so, a regional structure is suggested.

Probable firm characteristics: Those with products or manufacturing processes significantly influenced by environmental factors that differ marketedly from one definable region to another. Tends to be true generally for low-technology, mature, consumer-oriented products not closely related to one another an in respect to which political pressure for local control is likely to develop. Another probable characteristic is a substantial economy of scale in production. Large-scale interregional sales or resource transfers are unlikely because of the environmental influence.

2. Does each differentiated *product line* possess essentially the same characteristics insofar as function and region are concerned but remain significantly different from other product lines? If so, the product division approach is suggested.

Probable firm characteristics: Those with products or manufacturing processes relatively little influenced by environmental factors or influenced by factors not differing *consistently* from one definable region to another. Tends to be true for firms with several relatively high technology, new capital intensive products that are not closely related.

3. Is each differentiated function essentially similar for different products and geographical areas? Is so, a functional structure is suggested.

   Probable firm characteristics: Those with a single or a few closely related products manufactured in the same plants, sold through the same channels to the same customers regardless of geographical area. Thus, environmental factors are minimal in respect to both product and manufacturing process, but may impact significantly on function.

In a study of European-based multinationals, Lorange concluded, "It seems as if the greater the diversity among the product lines and the greater the rate of change of products in the line, the greater the pressure towards a geographically dominated structure." He speculates that possibly such a structure is better able to cope with production scheduling problems and those associated with the frequent introduction of new products. In contrast, Stopford, in a study of 170 companies out of *Fortune's* list of 500, concluded that worldwide product divisions were characteristic of companies with a relatively high percentage of sales outside the major product line; area divisions, of companies with a relatively low percentage of sales outside the major product line.

From a number of observations, it is quite clear that some U.S.-based multinationals are now following the European model in that they "have abandoned the notion that concentration on one variable should dominate the organization." Characteristically, according to the Stopford and Wells study, U.S. firms opting for a true matrix type organization use product and geographical area. This is in contrast to the product and functional matrix structure characteristic of at least some European multinationals. Understandably, firms have been moving slowly in relinquishing the time honored notion of unity of command in favor of shared responsibility. But there are many pressures that may push a management in this direction. Some of the pressure sources are: (1) different product lines may share common facilities in smaller national markets, but not in others; (2) in different regions similar problems appear, which are related in that what happens in country A may serve as a model to country B; and (3) functions may vary widely from product to product in some countries, not at all in others. As a firm develops a full matrix management, the demands on the individual manager increase. He must now respond t different reporting requirements and act more as an integrator. Even greater training, maturity, and experience are possibly required.

Host-government pressures tend to push a corporation with multiple entities within a country to establish a national management for purposes of interfacing with the government. If such a headquarters is not in place, the government may face a number of relatively small enterprises; it has no ready way of communicating effectively with corporate headquarters. Recent research in Canada indicates that U.S. conglomerates with multiple and unrelated operations in Canada tend to be less sensitive to Canadian national interests. Figure 4 portrays a viable solution. In fact, it is now clear that at least some governments will hold all of the local subsidiaries of a single foreign parent collectively responsible for liabilities of any one of them.

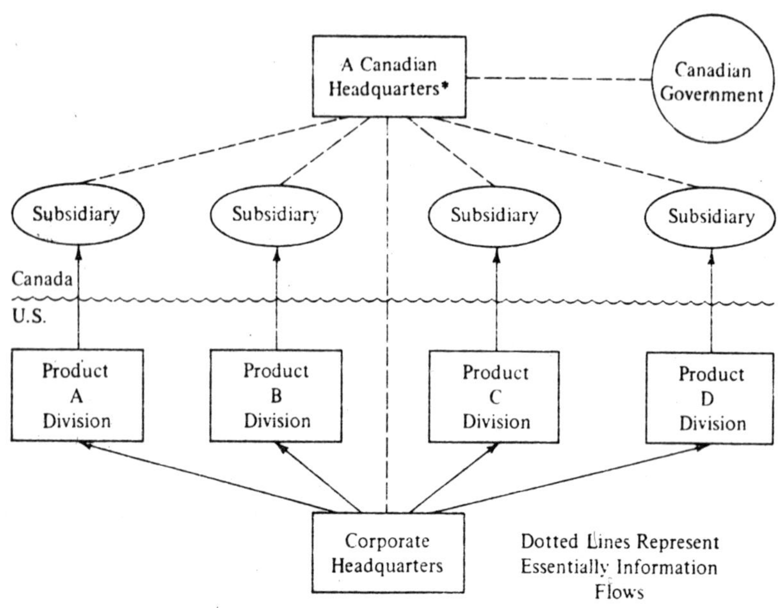

Fig. 4 The national headquarters concept

A similar situation arises whenever two or more countries enter into a continuing economic or political relationship such as a free trade area or common market. For a variety of reasons it may be highly desirable to have a regional headquarters to interface with the new regional institutions as lobbyist, negotiator, and a transmitter of information to corporate headquarters. It may also become virtually mandatory that the firm rationalize production and other functions on a regional basis to take advantage of special regional arrangements such as specialization agreements, complimentarily agreements, special financial institutions whose resources are available only to regionally oriented projects, and intraregional tariffs and other concessions.

It is all very well to speak of "decision-making authority," but in fact to what decisions does one refer? A comprehensive control strategy calls for distinguishing the level and the location on that level of each set of strategy alternatives discussed in the preceding chapters.

For example, at what level is policy in regard to management remuneration to be set and where on that level? If the firm were type A, and each division were free to select its own policy in this regard, the level of strategy decision would be the domestic division—but where in that division? If foreign operations were placed under an export or international department, the department director might, in fact, make the relevant decisions. Bear in mind that a the same time a corporate personnel officer may set down policy in regard to the remuneration of domestic management. Discordant policies between domestic and foreign and between divisions may thus emerge, which render the transfer of personnel from foreign to domestic assignment or interdivisional transfer of overseas personnel very difficult.

Ideally, strategy choices should be made for both the foreign and domestic markets at the same level by officers working in close cooperation. The relegation of policy decisions relating to foreign markets to domestic divisions is very likely to generate serious conflict in virtually very area, from substance of sales to choice of legal relationships. Indeed, it is precisely this conflict that generates pressure toward a type B structure once corporate management becomes aware of the conflict and of the importance of resolving it in order to effect an optimum allocation of corporate resources. An international staff department emerges, which eventually becomes an international division, due to previously discussed conflicts on the operating level.

In the truly internationally oriented firm, management tends to realize more clearly that strategy choices between the domestic and foreign markets are closely interrelated. The international division set-up, however, tends to isolate such choices. In a type D structure, each regional headquarters ideally possesses a staff competent to deal with strategy choices left open to it by corporate headquarters. For example, the latter may well set strategy in relation to source of product, intracompany competition, and intercompany competition, and leave other decisions in the sales strategy set to regional headquarters. In turn, the latter may leave choice of channels within a foreign market to the national operating subsidiaries or branches concerned. The type D structure probably facilitates this type of delegation, but the system is only feasible if the regional headquarters, one or more of which deal with the domestic market, handle a volume of business large enough to justify hiring comparable staff experts.

Corporate planning

But in all of these cases, optimum decision making is unlikely unless corporate goals have been spelled out and communicated, and a continuing planning process institutionalized so as to make the goals operational.

Corporate planning has been defined as follows:

> Corporate planning is the process of developing objectives for the corporation and its subparts as well as developing and evaluating alternative courses of action to reach these objectives:

doing this on this basis of a systematic evaluation of external threats and opportunities and internal audits of strengths and weaknesses.

In contrast, Steiner suggested a planning topology:

1. *Strategic planning*: Conducted by the highest levels of management and concerned with the development of fundamental goals and the major policies for deployment of corporate resources to meet those goals.
2. *Intermediate: or long-range planning*. Takes the overall strategies and defines action programs and steps for the accomplishment of the strategic objectives over a relevant time period.
3. *Technical planning*: The programming of activities through one or two year or shorter time period budgets.
4. *Planning studies*: Initiated at the request of top management to provide background for strategic and long-range planning.

On the basis of in-depth study of European and U.S. corporate strategic and long-range planning, the 1971 Schwendiman study reached several significant conclusions. Using Figure as the baseline, Schwendiman concluded that only about half of the companies investigated, both in Europe and the United States, even began to come close to the overall planning ideal suggested in that figure, Extension of planning to cover overseas activities, Schwendiman found, was relatively new. A weak point in all of the firms was environmental analysis.

> Headquarters' capability and proficiency was poor in analyzing political, economic, and social factors around the world. This arose, I suspect, because of a feeling that a continuing headquarters environmental assessment was really not needed with people "on the spot." But what if a venture is proposed for an area with no one "on the spot'? A common answer: an outside consultant or in-company task force was assigned to investigate the environment. However, these are "one-shot" approaches: follow-up is difficult. Even in companies with decentralized operations, top management should have some basis for evaluating proposals rather than relying completely on analysis from "on the spot company people" who may have prejudices or a distorted perspective.

Schwendiman also reported that many companies seemed to lack an in depth analysis of internal strengths and weaknesses as compared with their competitors. He suggests the possibility "that organizations as well as individuals tend to be 'satisficing' may explain the rather limited efforts at environmental and internal company assessment in the sample companies." Going on, he emphasized that formalized corporate planning is unlikely to be meaningful unless it has the enthusiastic participation of top management. Some of the most frequently mentioned international planning problems are (1) gaining top level support in articulating and communicating corporate goals, (2) lack of strategic integration of plans and operations, (3) gaining a personal commitment to planning at all management levels, and (4) the adequacy and economy of information flows—including that related to contingencies such as an inaccurate projection of sales or costs. It is obvious that commitment to long-run planning requires an incentive scheme built on something more than short-run performance.

One might suspect that the effectiveness of long-range planning in the Japanese firm would be significantly greater than in the characteristic European or U.S.-based firms. The permanent employment and lock-step promotion of managers in Japanese firms may make possible a longer-term evaluation before one is singled out for special reward. This changes the entire personal time-dimension of decision making. However, there is one bit of evidence suggesting that the Japanese are less satisfied with long-range planning than managers in other companies, including the United States.

Lorange writes, "Strategic planning in a multinational corporation has a two-fold task: to identify the strategic options most relevant to the corporation and to 'narrow down' these options into the one best plan." He goes on:

> The broad definition of the strategic planning tasks given above has several implications. In order to be able to identify the most relevant strategic options, the corporation needs to adapt continuously to the environment. Also, in order to narrow down the strategic options into the one best plan, the corporation must be able to integrate its many diverse activities.

He then proceeds to relate the nature and cost of the planning function to the structure of the multinational corporation. Admitting that other structures are possible, he chooses to deal with four, all being variations on what have been labeled here as product and regionally-organized multinationals. In fact, of course, very few multinationals, if any, would be organized exclusively by product or region. As Lorange points out:

Complete domination of corporate structure by one dimension can prove to be inefficient. For instance, there might be considerable duplication of effort in having the product divisions operate their own separate organizations in one country. When evolving from such a product structure, the matrix structure might be described as consisting of a leading product dimension and a grown area dimension.

Table 1

Summary of the Integration and Adaptation Planning Tasks of the Multinational Corporations in our Taxonomy

Taxonomy of corporations	Adaption	Integration
Worldwide product divisions	Along area dimension	Along product dimension
Product leading/area grown matrix	Primarily along area dimension; some along product dimension	Primarily along product dimension; some along area dimension
Area leading/product grown matrix	Primarily along product dimension; some along area dimension	Primarily along area dimension; some along product dimension
Geographical area divisions	Along product dimension	Along area dimension

Alternatively, when evolving out of an area-dominated structure, the matrix structure would have a leading area dimension and a grown product dimension.

Consequently, Lorange sees the structure of a multinational lying along a continuum from product-oriented on one extreme,e through product-leading/area-grown and area-leading/product-grown, to area-oriented on the other. he argues that the way in which the corporation is organized defines its integration and adaptation tasks, as in Table 1.

Following the Lorange argument further, the planning function is broken down into three phases:

1. Objective setting—Reexamine the fundamental assumptions for being in business; consider whether the relational for the firm's policies are still valid; in short, analyze where the firms stands relative to the environment
2. Planning—Follow up the major issues for adaption developed in phase one
3. Budgeting—Prepare more detailed budgets within the framework set out in the plans.

It is pointed out that integration plays a minor role in the objective setting phase, a somewhat more important role in the planning phase, and dominates in the budgeting phase. In that in each of the corporate types there will be different roles for the product and area dimensions with respect to performing the adaptive and integrative tasks, the relative importance of these tasks shifts as one goes forward with the planning function; that is, through the narrowing-down process. The implication of this is that "interaction among executives of the two dimensions of the matrix structure does not have to take place all through the narrowing-down process, but only during the middle stage; i.e., the planning stage," The consequence of this realization should be a considerable cost saving in the planning in that full-blown interaction between the dimensions at each stage of the process need not take place.

On the basis of a questionnaire sent to companies in six companies, which elicited pitfalls in long-range planning that companies around the world feel are the most important. Other conclusions from their study: (1) more companies are satisfied with their planning systems than are dissatisfied; (2) those companies with greater formality and greater documentation are the most satisfied; (3) divisionalized companies are more satisfied than those not organized into divisions; (4) companies with the longest experience with planning are the most satisfied. A few national characteristics were of some interest. The Japanese seemed to be somewhat less satisfied with the reported planning system and in all other aspects to be the reverse.

Unless consistent incentives are built into the system to participate and support planning activity, subsidiary managers, particularly in the international area, may feed in wholly inadequate or misleading data, and do so quite deliberately. In this manner they can shield themselves to a degree from overly centralized control and loss of subsidiary autonomy. For this reason, really effective international long-range planning may be limited to the transnational corporation.

If a normative rule can be laid down at all it is that control should be decentralized to the extent possible within the constraints of perceived managerial ability and the achievement of corporate goals. At the same time, it should be noted that national or even regional managers over time are likely to become emotionally attached to their respective areas. If so, reporting and decision making may become heavily biased, so much so that the firm will find it difficult to cut its losses and retire from a hopeless situation. At the same time, it is clear that centralized control cannot be effective in the absence of both the necessary functional competence and adequate understanding of the environment involved. The final word may be that of Gianluig Gabetti, president of Olivetti Underwood: "If a multinational firm is not centralized, at least for control and coordination, all the advantages of its worldwide association are lost."

Location of tactical decision-making authority

Operating of tactical decision-making authority may or may not be separated out from that authority making strategy choices. The larger the firm, the more compelling separation becomes, particularly in the international case. In the firm driving toward optimum penetration of foreign markets, the pressure for localizing tactical decision-making authority becomes almost compelling due to the myriad of cultural variables relevant to such decisions. It is one thing for an international division or regional or corporate headquarters to specify, for example, that the strategy in regard to choice of channels shall be overseas agencies. It is quite another to ascertain the identity of the agents to be used. A management remuneration policy is one thing: how much to pay Mr. X in Brazil is another. So it goes.

Experienced firms operating internationally tend to push all tactical decision-making authority down to the local level unless there is compelling reason for retaining it at divisional, regional, or even corporate level. Some compelling reasons are tax and antitrust considerations, a high degree of integration between different national enterprises, feedback effects, and political implications to which the parent government is sensitive. A word of caution should be entered here. It is not at all clear that the formulation of corporate goals should occur at one corporate level, long-range planning on another, strategy selection on another, and tactical decision-making on still another. Corporate headquarters is often in a position, by reason of greater breadth of information and a higher level of technical competence, to assist in tactical decision-making, just as local subsidiary managers may be helpful in strategy determination because of their greater environmental knowledge.

Methods of communicating decisions

Possible choices in this area are training indoctrination, a company journal, conferences, personal visits by decision-making personnel or their representatives, written SOPs, and budgets. Obviously, these choices are not mutually exclusive. To be considered in determining strategy in this regard are such factors as cost, the number of entities and people involved, and the extent to which decision-making authority is retained by higher headquarters.

Experienced managements offer a few guidelines:

1. All decisions made by a level higher than that implementing the decision, however the decision may be communicated initially, should be committed to writing. Given the pitfalls of inter-cultural communication, this rule is more important than in comparable domestic situations.

2. Visits by decision-making authorities or their representatives should be on a regular periodic basis, not occasioned exclusively by crisis situations.

3. Periodic conferences of key personnel of similar function from both domestic and foreign operations are of great utility in developing universally valid

strategies and in the delegation of tactical decision to lower levels.

4. Management training and development assumes greater importance for foreign operations because of the differences in cultural backgrounds, in the meaning of management, in the status of managers, and in sources of management recruitment as one moves from one national society to another. Such training facilities both the decentralization of decision-making authority and improvement in the quality and effectiveness of those decisions made at higher organizational levels.

5. Periodic rotation of overseas managers to regional or corporate headquarters may be one of the most effective ways of communicating overall corporate goals and the rationale for corporate strategy, including the degree of control retained at each level.

Means of reporting performance

Reports of performance should flow in a reverse pattern to decisions. The more decentralized the latter, the less the volume of the former. To require unnecessary reports is costly, particularly for those moving across language barriers, cultural frontiers, and great distances. Every report requirement should be carefully justified.

The range of possible reports is similar to that of a purely domestic operation, but certain difficulties arise peculiar to the foreign case. One of these is time lag, which may seriously reduce the value of a given report. For that reason the means of reporting may have to be changed. Essentially, there are six ways to communicate internationally other than by travel, all varying considerably in cost, namely, mail, telephone, cable, telex, leased channel, and computer conferencing. Which one is optimum in a specific situation depends on message frequency, average length, destination, urgency, and ease of personal communication. The various firms engaged in international communications supply analysts to assist individual firms making optimum choices.

It has been suggested that a number of firms become over-enthusiasitic about the advantage of telex and waste money by misusing it in sending short messages that could go more cheaply by telegram or cable. For a given location, one should obtain the minimum telex charges to each country, also the cable cost per word to the same destinations. If one then divides the minimum telex fee by the cable cost per word, the result is the break-even point between telex and cable costs, expressed in the number of words.

Another problem peculiar to foreign operations in establishing report strategy lies in securing report that contain information that may be properly evaluated; that is, compared with domestic and other national data. Some of the complicating factors are differential inflation rates, shifting exchange rates, imprecise statistical services, and different legal and accounting requirements.

Index